OECD Public Governance Reviews

OECD Integrity Review of Coahuila, Mexico

RESTORING TRUST THROUGH AN INTEGRITY SYSTEM

OECD

BETTER POLICIES FOR BETTER LIVES

Please cite this publication as:
OECD (2017), *OECD Integrity Review of Coahuila, Mexico: Restoring Trust Through an Integrity System*, OECD Public Governance Reviews, OECD Publishing, Paris.
http://dx.doi.org/10.1787/9789264283091-en

ISBN 978-92-64-28308-4 (print)
ISBN 978-92-64-28309-1 (PDF)
ISBN 978-92-64-28322-0 (epub)

Series: OECD Public Governance Reviews
ISSN 2219-0406 (print)
ISSN 2219-0414 (online)

Foreword

After developing one of the most advanced transparency frameworks among Mexican states, Coahuila now has an historic opportunity to move beyond transparency to set up a comprehensive and coherent integrity system. In July 2017, the Mexican state of Coahuila adopted a reform to create an Anti-corruption System, modelled on Mexico's National Anti-corruption System. The System will be crucial for providing a sustainable response to local risks of corruption and for driving the state's sustained economic growth towards inclusiveness and social cohesion.

Although the reform itself is a fundamental part of a new strategic approach to fighting corruption, the current implementation phase is just as important. Indeed, it poses a number of challenges common among states undergoing similar changes. To implement the reform, Coahuila needs to create new institutions and to amend or adopt secondary legislation. Most importantly, however, the implementation phase requires Coahuila to create a culture of integrity within the government, private sector, and in the whole-of-society, demonstrating to citizens the state's determination to tackle corruption in a decisive and comprehensive way.

*Trust in government is forged at the local and sub-national level in Mexico, including Coahuila and its municipalities. Local authorities have important responsibilities and provide a wide range of public services involving high exposure to the public such as the management of water, streetlights, waste, markets, and streets. Past scandals have fuelled disillusionment and loss of confidence among citizens in Coahuila; data from the National Institute of Statistics and Geography (*Instituto Nacional de Estadística y Geografía*) show that 44% and 38% of its population think corruption is common in the state government and in the municipalities, respectively. Through the implementation of the Local Anti-corruption System, Coahuila can restore trust in public institutions and therefore improve the willingness of citizens and businesses to endorse public policies and contribute to sustainable economic development and the rule of law.*

This Integrity Review analyses the integrity system of Coahuila and provides a series of recommendations based on international best practices according to the 2017 OECD Recommendation on Public Integrity. On the one hand, the Review acknowledges areas where significant steps have been taken in recent years. These steps have led to the creation of one of the most advanced transparency frameworks in the country, the establishment of standards of conduct for public officials, and a Conflict-of-Interest Manifest for state government suppliers. On the other hand, the Review identifies the key challenges Coahuila is facing in creating a comprehensive and effective integrity system. These challenges include establishing effective co-ordination with municipalities, building a culture of integrity, setting up a whistleblower protection framework, and implementing and supporting the internal control framework to better identify and mitigate corruption risks. Although each of these areas should be addressed differently, several important recurring themes emerge from the Review's recommendations. These include the need for more visible leadership to implement existing frameworks and closer engagement with civil society to further promote the public interest. Moreover, increased training, guidance and advice, as well as additional technical and financial resources are needed to sustain the effectiveness of the new local integrity system.

All around the world, local governments are increasingly expected to take part in national anti-corruption efforts. In doing so, they face limitations and challenges that require them to find effective and innovative solutions. Coahuila is the first sub-national entity to undergo an OECD Integrity Review. The following months and years will test whether Coahuila will assume the necessary leadership to face the challenges identified in the Integrity Review, but also to seize the opportunities presented by the implementation of a system involving all levels of government. While the solid transparency framework of Coahuila is a fundamental starting point for such an endeavour, the effectiveness and real impact of the new system will depend on its inclusiveness and the government's capacity to embed a culture of integrity among its officials.

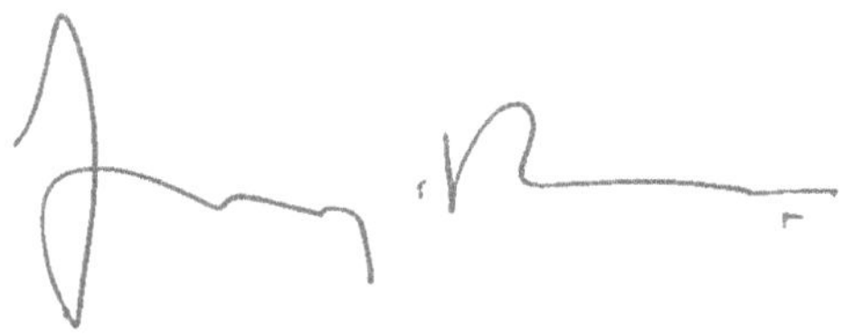

Luiz de Mello
Director a.i.
Public Governance Directorate, OECD

Acknowledgements

Under the direction and oversight of Rolf Alter, OECD Director for Public Governance, and János Bertók, Head of the Public Sector Integrity Division, this review was co-ordinated by Jacobo Pastor García Villarreal, Senior Policy Analyst, with the support of Julio Bacio Terracino, Deputy Head of the Public Sector Integrity Division. The authors of the chapters were Felicitas Neuhaus, Giulio Nessi, and Jennifer Moreau.

Valuable comments were received from Frédéric Boehm, Natalia Sandoval Peña, Jennifer Eddie, and Gavin Ugale. Editorial assistance was provided by Thibaut Gigou and Meral Gedik. Anaisa Goncalves, Pauline Alexandrov, Alpha Zambou, and Edwina Collins provided administrative assistance.

The OECD expresses its gratitude to the State Government of Coahuila for its fruitful co-operation and leadership. In particular, the OECD would like to thank Governor Rubén Moreira Valdez, Minister for Audit and Accountability Carlos Eduardo Cabello Gutiérrez, and former Minister for Audit and Accountability, Jorge Verástegui Saucedo, as well as the entire team and all the departments of the state government of Coahuila involved in this process. Ambassador Mónica Aspe and Maya Alejandra Camacho Dávalos, from the Permanent Delegation of Mexico to the OECD, were instrumental in supporting the OECD in this project.

This review is part of a series of governance reviews in OECD and G20 countries. It benefited from input provided by senior officials from Coahuila's Superior Audit Body, Coahuila's Institute for Freedom of Information (ICAI), state legislators, business chambers and civil society organisations, the state ministries for Audit and Accountability (SEFIR), Finance, Health and Social Development, among others, and the municipalities of Torreon and Ramos Arizpe, which participated in the debates in the state capital, Saltillo.

This report incorporates information shared during two OECD workshops on public ethics and management of conflicts of interest and on developing an integrity strategy, which took place on 7-8 December 2016 and 10 July 2017, respectively, in Saltillo. Special thanks to SEFIR and its officials for their support in organising and carrying out these workshops.

The OECD is also grateful to the lead reviewers who participated in the domestic debate: Christian Buske, Deputy Head, Department for Training and Education of the Government of Schleswig-Holstein, Germany, and Cristian Picón, Research Fellow, Universidad del Norte, Colombia.

The OECD Mexico Centre, under the leadership of Roberto Martinez, and the staff in charge of publications, notably Alejandro Camacho, were instrumental in co-ordinating the editorial process for the Spanish publication.

This document was approved by the OECD Working Party of Senior Public Integrity Officials (SPIO) on 7 April 2017 and declassified by the Public Governance Committee on 14 July 2017. It was prepared for publication by the OECD Secretariat.

Table of contents

Acronyms and Abbreviations ... 13

Executive summary ... 17

Chapter 1. **Toward a coherent and comprehensive integrity system in Coahuila** ... 19
- Introduction ... 20
- Strengthening institutional co-ordination for integrity ... 20
- Demonstrating political and management commitment to support the public integrity system ... 32
- Enhancing legitimacy through wide stakeholder participation in the system ... 35
- Proposals for Action ... 39
- References ... 40

Chapter 2. **Building a culture of integrity in the public sector in Coahuila** ... 43
- Introduction ... 44
- Building a legal and policy framework for public ethics and conflict of interest to ensure coherence throughout the administration ... 44
- Harmonising policies and practices ... 48
- Raising awareness and providing training ... 56
- Strengthening the asset disclosure system ... 65
- Ensuring effective monitoring and evaluation ... 71
- Proposals for Action ... 75
- References ... 77

Chapter 3. **Guaranteeting effective whistleblower protection in Coahuila** ... 79
- Introduction ... 80
- Guaranteeing strong protection for whistleblowers ... 82
- Ensuring effective review and investigation of reports ... 94
- Strengthening awareness ... 99
- Conducting evaluations and increasing the use of metrics ... 101
- Proposals for Action ... 102
- Notes ... 103
- References ... 104

Chapter 4. **Strengthening Coahuila's internal control and risk management framework** ... 105
- Introduction ... 106
- Demonstrating high-level commitment to integrity objectives and risk management ... 107

Overcoming implementation gaps for improved risk management 114
Strengthen the presence and impact of internal audit in Coahuila 123
Proposals for Action 127
References 128

Chapter 5. **Enhance transparency and participation for effective accountability in Coahuila** 131
Introduction 132
Leveraging information and data for more accountable institutions 132
Improving stakeholders' engagement to promote transparency and the public interest 140
Proposals for Action 147
References 148

Chapter 6. **Public procurement in Coahuila: ensuring integrity and value for money** 149
Introduction: Corruption risks in public procurement 150
Preserving public integrity through general standards of conduct and procurement-specific risk management tools 153
Promoting a culture of integrity among public procurement officials, potential suppliers, and civil society 162
Enhancing transparency and the disclosure of information around public procurement processes 168
Proposals for action 174
References 175
Annex 1. The integrity, transparency, and participation principles of the OECD recommendation of the council on public procurement (2015) 177

Chapter 7. **Plan of action for the implementation of the OECD recommendations** . . . 179
Toward a coherent and comprehensive integrity system 180
Building a culture of integrity in the public sector 182
Guaranteeing effective whistleblower protection 186
Strengthening the internal control and risk management framework 189
Enhance transparency and participation for effective accountability 190
Integrity in public procurement 191

Tables

1.1. Legal instruments to reform or adopt to implement the NACS in Coahuila 23
1.2. Constituent entities of the CLACS 23
1.3. Governance objectives and strategies of Coahuila's Development Plan (2011-17) 25
1.4. Administrative procedures perceived as most corrupt and corresponding level of administrative competence in Mexico 28
1.5. Agreements for vertical co-operation in Coahuila (as of July 2016) 30
1.6. The composition of the CAN (as of October 2016) 39
2.1. Key legislation regulating the standard of conduct for officials within the public administration of Coahuila 49

2.2. Types of verification checks on asset and interest declarations 68
4.1. The three lines of assurance model 115
5.1. Coahuila in National Transparency Rankings 134
5.2. Monitoring or social audit initiatives in Coahuila 142
6.1. Corruption risks associated with the different phases of the public procurement cycle 151
6.2. Leveraging internal control over the procurement cycle 161

Figures

1.1. Share of respondents who believe corruption is "very frequent" in Coahuila, according to institution/sector, 2015 27
1.2. Local anti-corruption systems address corruption where most prevalent, INEGI "corruption ratio" by level of government and region 28
1.3. Management Accountability Framework in Canada 35
1.4. The selection process of the Citizen Committee in the CLACS Law 37
2.1. Frequently-stated core public service values (2000 and 2009) 50
2.2. Statement of commitment to the Code of Ethics and Conduct for public servants in the executive branch of the state of Coahuila de Zaragoza 57
2.3. Publication of the Standards of Integrity and Conduct of New Zealand 59
3.1. Reasons for not reporting 81
3.2. Legal protections for whistleblowers in the public sector in OECD countries 81
3.3. Categories of wrongdoing constituting a protected disclosure in OECD countries 85
3.4. OECD countries providing protection from all discriminatory or retaliatory personnel actions 88
4.1. Coahuila's general standard for internal control 107
4.2. Risk management cycle according to ISO 31000: 2009 108
4.3. Coahuila's risk administration framework 109
4.4. Maturity levels of integrating internal control and risk management 114
5.1. OECD OURdata Index: Open, Useful, Reusable Government Data, 2014 135
5.2. Visits to Coahuila's online transparency portals 143
6.1. The 12 integrated principles of the OECD Recommendation on Public Procurement 152
6.2. Development of specific conflict-of-interest policy/rules for particular categories of public officials in the OECD countries 154

Boxes

1.1. Integrity and anti-corruption actors in Coahuila 21
1.2. Mexico's national anti-corruption reform 22
1.3. Regional Anti-corruption Commission in Piura (Peru) 26
1.4. SEFIR's integrity and anti-corruption-related tasks 33
1.5. Ensuring local integrity systems comply with national legislation 34
1.6. Government and non-government stakeholders in National Anti-corruption Commissions: Colombia and Peru 38
2.1. Germany's contact persons for corruption prevention 46

2.2. Canada: Senior officials for public service values and ethics and departmental officers for conflict-of-interest and post-employment measures 47
2.3. Revision of the Australian Public Service values 50
2.4. Code of Ethics for Public Officials at the Federal Level 52
2.5. Guiding public officials in facing ethical dilemmas in Australia 52
2.6. Consultation for an organisation-specific code of conduct in Brazil 55
2.7. Coahuila's Programme of Ethics and Values 58
2.8. Catalogues of questions and answers in Germany 60
2.9. Brazil's training programme on ethics 62
2.10. Dilemma training in the Flemish Government (Belgium) 62
2.11. Common financial and non-financial disclosures in OECD countries 65
2.12. Mandatory asset declaration for selected officials in Argentina 67
2.13. The High Authority for Transparency in Public Life of France 69
2.14. Monitoring the implementation of the Code of Ethics in Poland 72
2.15. What makes good performance indicators 74
3.1. Whistleblower protection in Alberta 83
3.2. A detailed definition of protected disclosures in the United Kingdom 86
3.3. Comprehensive protection in Korea 89
3.4. Section 425.1 of the Canadian Criminal Code prohibiting reprisals against whistleblowers 90
3.5. Sanctions for retaliation in Korea 92
3.6. Remedies for public sector whistleblowers in Canada 93
3.7. Options for making a protected disclosure of wrongdoing in Canada 96
3.8. Office of the Public Interest Commissioner in Alberta 97
3.9. External reporting channels in German states 98
3.10. Example of a statement to staff reassuring them to raise concerns 99
3.11. Change of cultural connotations of "whistleblower" and "whistleblowing": The case of the UK 100
3.12. The United States' approach to increasing awareness through the Whistleblower Protection Enhancement Act (WPEA) 101
4.1. Corruption risk management guidance in New South Wales (Australia) 110
4.2. Dedicated fraud and corruption risk management frameworks: the United States and Colombian examples 110
4.3. Key measures towards developing an environment non-conducive to corruption 113
4.4. United States Office of Management and Budget (OMB) Circular A-123: Management's responsibility for internal control 116
4.5. Leveraging internal control over the Deming's management cycle 116
4.6. Practical guidance for risk administration in Victoria (Australia) and Colombia 119
4.7. Leveraging data analytics for managing corruption risks 121
4.8. Data analytics and data sharing for managing fraud and corruption risks in the United Kingdom and United States 122
4.9. Offices of Internal Control (Órganos Interno de Control) at the federal level in Mexico 124
4.10. Fraud and Corruption - Internal Audit's Role 125

4.11. Professionalization and capacity-building of the internal audit service....... 126
5.1. The Mexican National Transparency System 133
5.2. G20 Anti-corruption open data principles 136
5.3. Montreal's "View on the Contracts" (Vue sur les contrats) platform (Canada) 137
5.4. Open data portals with visualisation tools in Italy......................... 138
5.5. The Transparency Portal of Spain 139
5.6. OECD Guiding Principles for Public Participation in Policy Making 140
5.7. Colombia's Crystal Urn (Urna de Cristal) 143
5.8. Public participation in draft regulations in Spain......................... 143
5.9. Citizen engagement mechanisms to improve transparency and open data portals 145
5.10. Local Transparency Indexes for Regions and Municipalities in Slovakia....... 146
6.1. The contribution of the 12 principles of the OECD Recommendation to the fight against corruption.. 152
6.2. Mexico's Ethics Code and Rules of Integrity: Provisions related to public procurement.. 155
6.3. Conflict-of-interest management during tender evaluation in Australia 157
6.4. Examples of red flags for corruption in procurement 161
6.5. Integrity training in Germany 165
6.6. Implementation of social witnesses at federal level (in Mexico) 168
6.7. The Federal e-procurement system CompraNet.......................... 173

Acronyms and Abbreviations

ACFE	Association of Certified Fraud Examiners
APS	Australian Public Service
ASEC	*Auditoría Superior del Estado de Coahuila de Zaragoza* Supreme Audit Institution of the State of Coahuila
CAN	*Comisión de Alto Nivel Anticorrupción* High-level Commission against Corruption (Peru)
CFE	*Comisión Federal de Electricidad* Federal Electricity Commission
CGAP	Certified Government Auditing Professional
CIA	Certified Internal Auditor
CIDE	*Centro de Investigación y Docencia Económicas* Centre for Economic Research and Teaching
CLACS	*Sistema Local Anticorrupción de Coahuila* Local Anti-corruption System of Coahuila
CNCLCC	*Comisión Nacional Ciudadana para la Lucha Contra la Corrupción* National Citizens Committee for the Fight against Corruption (Colombia)
CNM	*Comisión Nacional de Moralización* National Moralisation Commission (Colombia)
CONAGO	*Conferencia Nacional de Gobernadores* National Conference of Governors
COSO	Committee of Sponsoring Organisations of the Treadway Commission
CPCE-F	*Comisión Permanente de Contralores Estados-Federación* National Permanent Commission of State-Federation Controllers
CPCE-M	*Comisión Permanente de Contralores Estado- Municipios* Permanent Commission of State-Municipal Controllers
CRA	*Comisiones Regionales Anticorrupción* Regional Anti-corruption Commissions (Peru)
DNC	*Encuesta de Detección de Necesidades de Capacitación* Survey on the Identification of Training Needs
GAO	Government Accountability Office (United States)
HATVP	*Haute Autorité pour la Transparence de la Vie Publique* High Authority for Transparency in Public Life
HCS	Head of the Civil Service (Poland)
HRM	Human Resource Management

IARD Programme	Internal Auditor Recruitment and Development Programme (Canada)
ICAC	Independent Commission Against Corruption (New South Wales, Australia)
ICAI	*Instituto Coahuilense de Acceso a la Información Pública* Institute for Access to Public Information of Coahuila
IIA	Institute of Internal Auditors
IMCO	*Instituto Mexicano para la Competitividad* Mexican Institute for Competitiveness
INAI	*Instituto Nacional de Transparencia, Acceso a la Información y Protección de Datos Personales* National Institute for Transparency, Freedom of Information, and Personal Data Protection
INE	*Instituto Nacional Electoral* National Elections Institute
INEGI	*Instituto Nacional de Estadística y Geografía* National Institute of Statistics and Geography
LAACSEC	*Ley de Adquisiciones, Arrendamientos y Contratación de Servicios para el Estado de Coahuila de Zaragoza* Law on Acquisitions, Leasing, and Services for the State of Coahuila de Zaragoza
LACS	*Sistema Local Anticorrupción* Local Anti-corruption Systems
LAIP	*Ley de Acceso a la Información Pública y Protección de Datos Personales* Law on Access to Public Information and Protection of Personal Data
LFACP	*Ley Federal Anticorrupción en Contrataciones Públicas* Federal Anti-corruption Law on Public Procurement
LGRA	*Ley General de Responsabilidades Administrativas* General Law on Administrative Responsibilities
LOAP	*Ley Orgánica de la Administración Pública de Coahuila de Zaragoza* Public Administration Organic Law of the State of Coahuila de Zaragoza
LOPSEC	*Ley de Obra Pública y servicios relacionados con las mismas para el Estado de Coahuila de Zaragoza* Law on Public Works and Related Services for the State of Coahuila de Zaragoza
LRSPEMEC	*Ley de Responsabilidades de los Servidores Públicos Estatales y Municipales del Estado de Coahuila de Zaragoza* Law of Responsibilities of Public Servants at State and Municipal Level of the State of Coahuila de Zaragoza
MECI	*Modelo Estándar de Control Interno* Standard Internal Control Model
MENA	Middle East and North Africa

MIT	*Ministero delle Infrastrutture e dei Trasporti* Ministry of Infrastructure and Transportation (Italy)
NACS	*Sistema Nacional Anticorrupción* National Anti-corruption System
NGO	Non-Governmental Organisation
OCI	*Oficina de Control Interno* Internal Control Office
OSC	United States Office of Special Counsel
PEP	Politically Exposed Person
PGJE	*Procuraduría General de Justicia del Estado de Coahuila de Zaragoza* Attorney General's Office of the State of Coahuila de Zaragoza
PTAR	*Programa de Trabajo de Administración de Riesgos* Programme of Work for Risk Management
REPROCO	*Registro Estatal de Proveedores y Contratistas* State Registry of Contractors and Suppliers
SEFIN	*Secretaría de Finanzas* Ministry of Finance
SEFIR	*Secretaría de Fiscalización y Rendición de Cuentas* Ministry for Audit and Accountability
SFP	*Secretaría de la Función Pública* Ministry of Public Administration
SINTAD	*Sistema Integral de Adquisiciones* Comprehensive Procurement System
SITODEM	*Sistema de Información y Transparencia de Obras para el Desarrollo Metropolitano* Information and Transparency System on Public Works for Metropolitan Development
ST	*Secretaría de Transparencia* Transparency Secretariat (Colombia)
TBS	Treasury Board of Canada Secretariat
TIAPS	Training for Internal Auditors in the Public Sector (Canada)
TM	Transparencia Mexicana
UEEPCI	*Unidad Especializada en Ética y Prevención de Conflictos de Interés* Specialized Unit for Ethics and Prevention of Conflicts of Interest
UNCAC	United Nations Convention against Corruption
WPEA	Whistleblower Protection Enhancement Act (United States)

Executive summary

The northern Mexican state of Coahuila de Zaragoza is in the process of aligning its legislative framework with the national reforms that established the National Anti-corruption System (NACS). In particular, the constitutional reform establishing the NACS requires federal states to establish their own anti-corruption systems in accordance with the model defined for the federal level in July 2016. This process is not only a unique opportunity for Coahuila to upgrade its integrity system, but also to incorporate good international practices and respond to declining trust in government. This Review provides analysis and proposals to support Coahuila in seizing such an opportunity, based on the OECD Recommendation on Public Integrity as well as best practices.

In order to build a coherent and comprehensive public integrity system, the implementation of Coahuila's Local Anti-corruption System (CLACS) should rest on two critical elements: sustained leadership from the highest political and managerial levels and broad participation of stakeholders and institutions at the state and municipal levels of government. The heads of public institutions need to be fully aware of the implications of the CLACS and should take a leading role in implementing the system, defining clear responsibilities, and allocating the necessary resources. In line with the process followed to create the NACS, Coahuila should follow Open Parliament practices during the design and discussion of the remaining secondary legislation required to set up the local anti-corruption system. In doing so, leaders and institutions will be made accountable for the implementation of the reform. Using the NACS creation process as a guide, Coahuila will be on the right path to ensuring the highest degree of transparency and seeking the strong engagement of its civil society, business community, and municipalities. In fact, Coahuila's Ministry for Audit and Accountability (*Secretaría de Fiscalización y Rendición de Cuentas*, SEFIR) set up a working group with these stakeholders to allow participation and to facilitate buy-in for implementation.

Coahuila has created a Code of Ethics and Conduct applicable to all public servants of the state government and a specific Code of Conduct for SEFIR's officials. However, public servants still need to understand how to apply the principles and values of these codes in their daily work. By mainstreaming integrity throughout all institutions of the government of Coahuila and effectively communicating about shared principles and values, Coahuila could cultivate a culture of integrity. The government of Coahuila could set up Integrity Contact Points in every ministry and agency to ensure the implementation of integrity policies. Translating regulations into practical situations through manuals, training, and continuous guidance could help clarify what is expected from public officials. Furthermore, Coahuila needs to develop clear guidelines for public officials facing conflicts of interest and should complement the existing requirements for government suppliers to disclose such cases.

The current asset disclosure system could be strengthened by reviewing and auditing the disclosure forms in a systematic manner. For this purpose, SEFIR should pursue authorisation to cross-check information with other databases such as those of tax and banking authorities.

The design of the CLACS is an opportunity for Coahuila to go beyond the model of the NACS and pass dedicated whistleblower protection legislation. Such legislation would clearly define the nature of protected disclosures, call for sanctions on individuals who exercise reprisals against whistleblowers, shift the burden of proof to employers, allow redress for civil servants who experience reprisals, and facilitate anonymous reporting. By building an open organisational culture within the state institutions, trust in the reporting lines can be strengthened and potential whistleblowers will be encouraged to come forward.

Internal control is a critical element in safeguarding integrity and enabling effective accountability. Coahuila has developed a General Standard for Internal Control including a risk management framework to be applied in the state government. However, further efforts are needed to embed internal control activities into the strategic and operational activities of public sector institutions. Indeed, public officials from operational levels claim that a stronger tone emanating from the heads of public institutions would help establish internal control and risk management as a responsibility of every public official, not just top management. The use of data analytics and the creation of Internal Control Units in ministries where risks are most significant also have the potential to improve internal control activities in Coahuila.

Coahuila has developed one of the most advanced transparency frameworks in the country. According to rankings compiled by think-tanks and non-governmental organisations, its level of sophistication is a result of a strong legal framework, extensive disclosure of budget information, and the performance of the guaranteeing institution. For instance, the Mexican Institute for Competitiveness (*Instituto Mexicano para la Competitividad*, IMCO) measured compliance with budget transparency criteria at state level and, for the second year in a row, Coahuila was the only state where all municipalities complied. The state government has also developed a strategy on open data after a broad public consultation process involving all state regions. Public entities in Coahuila could improve data socialisation and develop online visualisation tools to make transparency an effective mechanism to promote accountability. Furthermore, Coahuila could further promote public engagement and oversight by using existing tools more effectively and developing new innovative ones.

The state government has also taken steps to ensure integrity and value for money in public procurement, which is particularly vulnerable to integrity violations due to its high complexity, close interaction between the public and private sectors, and the large volume of transactions processed. It has developed a Code of Conduct and a Conflict-of-Interest Manifest for suppliers. Nevertheless, it still lacks a specific code of ethics for procurement officials. The state government has improved transparency in public procurement by reducing direct awards thresholds and the live transmission of tender events. Coahuila could maximise transparency by developing a unique online portal for public procurement and an e-procurement system. Additional reforms could include developing co-operation agreements and integrity pacts with the private sector, and improving engagement with civil society through mechanisms such as the social witness programme.

OECD Integrity Review of Coahuila, Mexico
Restoring trust through an integrity system

Chapter 1

Toward a coherent and comprehensive integrity system in Coahuila

This chapter examines the institutional arrangements for integrity in Coahuila and assesses whether they enable the functioning of a coherent and comprehensive integrity system in line with the principles of the OECD Recommendation on Public Integrity. First, it analyses the implications of the National Anti-corruption System and the reforms needed for the Local Anti-corruption System of Coahuila to embrace a whole-of-government approach and ensure effective vertical and horizontal mechanisms. Second, this chapter discusses the impact of politicians' and managers' commitment to enhancing public integrity and minimising corruption risks, and describes why their role is fundamental in ensuring effective implementation. Lastly, this chapter addresses the added value of building an inclusive public sector integrity system where civil society plays a central role and which involves different stakeholders from the whole-of-society.

Introduction

The experience of OECD and non-OECD countries shows that an effective, comprehensive, and coherent public integrity system is fundamental in enhancing public sector integrity and in preventing and curbing corruption. Managing integrity is not the responsibility of one single institution but rather a common endeavour of all public entities as well as of civil society, the private sector, and citizens. The present chapter examines the arrangements and mechanisms governing the public integrity system of Coahuila. It focuses on the relevant principles set forth in the OECD *Recommendation on Public Integrity* (OECD Recommendation) (OECD, 2017), which calls upon states to build a coherent and comprehensive public integrity system.

Considering that the promotion of integrity involves many different actors, states have to ensure clear institutional responsibilities at the relevant levels of government and establish mechanisms for horizontal and vertical co-operation to avoid fragmentation, overlap, and gaps between the elements of the system. Furthermore, country practices and experiences show that politicians and managers at the highest levels should display and demonstrate commitment, ensuring that the public integrity system is integrated into the wider public management and governance framework. For this purpose, they should ensure that appropriate legislative and institutional frameworks are in place to enable public organisations to take responsibility. They also must ensure that appropriate mandates and capacities are secured so that organisations may fulfil their responsibilities. Third, it is recognised that enhancing public integrity most effectively involves a whole-of-society approach, with participation by the private sector, civil society, and individuals. Accordingly, the OECD Recommendation stresses the importance of engaging with relevant stakeholders when governments elaborate, update, or implement their public integrity strategy as a way to enhance the integrity system for the public sector.

Taking stock of these latter elements needed to sustain an effective integrity system, the present chapter addresses issues concerning co-ordination, commitment, as well as participation of non-governmental organisations, taking into particular consideration the recent developments introduced by the National Anti-corruption System (NACS) in Mexico, which led to the creation of Coahuila's Local Anti-corruption System (CLACS) in July 2017. However, the following analysis goes beyond the implementation of the CLACS and provides recommendations which aim to support Coahuila in creating a coherent and comprehensive integrity system through a whole-of-government and whole-of-society approach.

Strengthening institutional co-ordination for integrity

Although the CLACS is a valuable framework for co-ordinating relevant institutions, the system should ensure that integrity policies are mainstreamed through the whole-of-government and that they are linked with state-wide strategies.

Preventing, investigating, and sanctioning corruption as well as enhancing integrity are complex tasks that involve several institutions across the executive, legislative, and judicial powers. Managing public integrity is therefore a whole-of-government responsibility involving many organisations within the public sector, where duplication and overlap often take place. The latter risks threaten the effectiveness of integrity systems and may lead to impunity. As such, clear, comprehensive, and effective arrangements must be made in order to ensure an effective integrity system.

As in most governments, there are various public institutions in Coahuila that are directly involved in either corruption prevention or detection, or both, including the Ministry for Audit and Accountability (*Secretaría de Fiscalización y Rendición de Cuentas*, or SEFIR), the Supreme Audit Institution of the State of Coahuila (*Auditoría Superior del Estado de Coahuila*, or ASEC), the Superior Court of Justice (*Tribunal Superior de Justicia*), and Coahuila's Institute for Access to Public Information (*Instituto Coahuilense de Acceso a la Información Pública*, or ICAI) (Box 1.1).

Box 1.1. **Integrity and anti-corruption actors in Coahuila**

Within the government of Coahuila, the Ministry for Audit and Accountability (*Secretaría de Fiscalización y Rendición de Cuentas*, or SEFIR) is given a number of corruption prevention responsibilities pursuant to the Organic Law of the Public Administration (*Ley Orgánica de la Administración Pública de Coahuila de Zaragoza*). These include competences on government and public procurement audit, efficiency of public administration, innovation, human resources, and transparency.

External audit is carried out by the Supreme Audit Institution of the State of Coahuila (*Auditoría Superior del Estado de Coahuila*, or ASEC), which is accountable to Coahuila's Congress and is responsible for auditing public accounts of the three state powers, municipalities, and public autonomous entities. The ASEC is also responsible to determine damages to the public accounts and assets of the state government and directly establish indemnities and economic sanctions.

The state judiciary is headed by a Superior Court of Justice (*Tribunal Superior de Justicia*). Judges of the Superior Court of Justice are appointed by the head of the Executive Power (Governor) with the approval of the state legislature. The superior court judges, in turn, appoint all lower state court judges. Criminal investigations are carried out by the Attorney General (*Procurador General de Justicia*), who is nominated by the Governor after ratification by the legislative power.

Coahuila's Institute for Access to Public Information (*Instituto Coahuilense de Acceso a la Información Pública*, or ICAI) is a state autonomous entity provided for in Article 7 of Coahuila's Constitution (*Constitución Política del Estado de Coahuila de Zaragoza*) in charge of guaranteeing the fundamental right of all citizens to share, investigate, and request public information. Its members are appointed by Coahuila's Congress through a large majority vote (at least two-thirds of the assembly) in line with Coahuila's Access to Information Law (*Ley de Acceso a la Información Pública*).

Source: Constitution of Coahuila (*Constitución Política del Estado de Coahuila de Zaragoza*), Public Administration Organic Law of Coahuila (*Ley Orgánica de la Administración Pública del Estado de Coahuila de Zaragoza*), Access to Information Law of Coahuila (*Ley de Acceso a la Información Pública*). All legal instruments in force in Coahuila, including the latter ones, are available at: *http://congresocoahuila.gob.mx/portal/?page_id=538*.

Following a May 2015 constitutional reform, Mexico initiated an ambitious national anti-corruption reform. This reform led to the creation of the NACS, whose primary objective is to be the co-ordination mechanism of all the institutions in charge of preventing, detecting, and sanctioning corruption across all levels of government (Box 1.2). The constitutional reform stipulates that such a system must be replicated in all Mexican states. Each state must establish its own Local Anti-corruption System in accordance with the model established at the federal level. The system must aim at co-ordinating state-level institutions and should facilitate vertical co-ordination with federal and municipal authorities.

Box 1.2. **Mexico's national anti-corruption reform**

On 27 May 2015, Mexico's Federal Official Gazette published the Decree by which several provisions of the Constitution were amended, added, or repealed (specifically, Articles 22, 28, 41, 73, 74, 76, 79, 104, 108, 109, 113, 114, 116, and 122). This reform first enshrined the National Anti-corruption System into law and set in motion the debates around and eventually passing of secondary legislation necessary for bringing the System to life. Just over a year later, on 18 July 2016, these secondary laws were promulgated by Decree (*Decreto por el que se expide la Ley General del Sistema Nacional Anticorrupción; la Ley General de Responsabilidades Administrativas, y la Ley Orgánica del Tribunal Federal de Justicia Administrativa*) and included:

- **The General Law of the National Anti-corruption System** (*Ley General del Sistema Nacional Anticorrupción*): the cornerstone piece of legislation that establishes the institutional and governance arrangements for the NACS and outlines its objectives and required activities. Because this law has status as a general law, it requires federal states to establish their own systems along similar lines. The law also requires specific information to be published and made available to the public on a newly-created digital platform (*Plataforma Digital Nacional del Sistema Nacional Anticorrupción*).
- **The Organic Law of the Federal Tribunal of Administrative Justice** (*Ley Orgánica del Tribunal Federal de Justicia Administrativa*): the federal tribunal was made autonomous under the constitutional reform of 2015, and this new law established the organisation of its courts, including regional courts. The law also sets out rules for the selection and removal of magistrates.
- **The General Law of Administrative Responsibilities** (*Ley General de Responsabilidades Administrativas*): this is a new law that replaced the previous Federal Law of Administrative Responsibilities expired in July 2017. It lays out the duties and responsibilities of public officials (including for the disclosure of private interest) and sets out administrative disciplinary procedures for misconduct, differentiating between less serious and serious offences, the latter of which may now fall under the jurisdiction of the Federal Tribunal of Administrative Justice. Notably, this law also expands liability for alleged integrity breaches to natural and legal persons.

Source: OECD (2017c), *OECD Integrity Review of Mexico: Taking a Stronger Stance Against Corruption*, OECD Publishing, Paris. *http://dx.doi.org/10.1787/9789264273207-en*.

The implementation of Mexico's National Anti-corruption Reform (Box 1.2) in Coahuila's legal system is imposed by the Mexican Constitution (Article 113), and it has emerged as an invaluable opportunity to strengthen Coahuila's existing institutional arrangements towards the creation of a coherent and comprehensive integrity system. In July 2017, Coahuila adopted the first set of legal reforms, namely the Constitutional Reform establishing the CLACS and the Law on the Local Anti-corruption System of Coahuila (*Ley del Sistema Anticorrupción del Estado de Coahuila de Zaragoza*, or CLACS Law). However, further instruments and amendments are needed to integrate and complete its Local Anti-corruption System (Table 1.1).

The CLACS can nevertheless be assessed in the current report. This is because its framework was defined by the Constitutional reform and the CLACS Law, and also because it replicates the governance structure established at the federal level in the General Law of the National Anti-corruption System. Furthermore, it was created according to the model laws designed by the federal Ministry of Public Function (*Secretaría de la Función Pública*, or SFP) in October 2016 to support federal states in advancing the implementation of the

Constitutional Anti-corruption reform at subnational level. In particular, Table 1.2 describes the bodies and institutions that form the CLACS.

Table 1.1. Legal instruments to reform or adopt to implement the NACS in Coahuila

Legal instruments to adopt	Legal instruments to reform
Local Anti-corruption System Law (*Ley del Sistema Estatal Anticorrupción*)*	Constitution of Coahuila (*Constitución Política del Estado de Coahuila de Zaragoza*)*
Administrative Justice Tribunal Law (*Ley del Tribunal de Justicia Administrativa*)	Public Administration Organic Law of Coahuila (*Ley Orgánica de la Administración Pública del Estado de Coahuila de Zaragoza*)
Whistleblower Protection Law (*Ley de Protección a Denunciantes de Actos de Corrupción*)	Accountability and Audit Law of Coahuila (*Ley de Rendición de Cuentas y Fiscalización Superior del Estado de Coahuila de Zaragoza*)
	Criminal Code of Coahuila (*Código Penal del Estado de Coahuila de Zaragoza*)
	Attorney General's Office Organic Law of Coahuila (*Ley Orgánica de la Procuraduría General de Justicia del Estado de Coahuila de Zaragoza*)
	Municipal Code of Coahuila (*Código Municipal del Estado de Coahuila de Zaragoza*)
	Responsibilities Law of State and Municipal public officials of Coahuila (*Ley de Responsabilidades de los Servidores Públicos Estatales y Municipales del Estado de Coahuila de Zaragoza*)

*Approved by the State Legislature in July 2017.

Source: Sistema Nacional Anticorrupción y su Impacto en el Estado de Coahuila, website of ASEC (Auditoría Superior del Estado de Coahuila), *www.asecoahuila.gob.mx/revista-digital-equilibrio-coahuila-diciembre-2016/*.

Table 1.2. Constituent entities of the CLACS

Entities	Members	Main tasks
Co-ordination Committee	President: President of Citizen Participation Committee Members: SEFIR's Minister, Superior Auditor of ASEC, President of ICAI, Specialised Anti-corruption Prosecutor [to be created in Coahuila], President of Coahuila's Administrative Justice Tribunal [to be created in Coahuila] and representative from Coahuila's Superior Court of Justice	Establishes basis and principles for effective co-ordination among members, including municipalities. It also defines the state integrity policy and stablishes the State Information System.
Executive Secretariat to Co-ordination Committee, which includes	Technical body of the system led by the President of the Citizens' Committee and comprised of the members of the Co-ordination Committee	Provides technical support and task-related input to the Co-ordination Committee
Technical Secretary	Elected by the Governing Board members of the Executive Secretariat among people with same profile of members from the Citizen Participation Committee	Manages the Executive Secretariat and serves as intermediary among the Co-ordination Committee, the members of the CLACS, and the Citizen Participation Committee
Executive Commission to the Co-ordination Committee	Technical Secretary and Citizen Participation Committee (with exception of this Committee's President)	Provides technical support and proposals for the design and implementation of Co-ordination Committee activities and responsibilities including annual reports and co-ordination with federal and other state-level anti-corruption systems
Citizen Participation Committee	Five reputable representatives from civil society who made outstanding contributions to transparency, accountability, or to the fight against corruption, chosen by a selection committee of nine experts who are chosen in turn by the Congress of Coahuila for a period of five years.	Channels inputs from civil society into the work of the CLACS and oversees progress and results
Coahuila Auditing System [to be created]	ASEC, SEFIR, internal and external auditing entities, and units of municipalities	Establishes actions and co-ordination mechanisms among members to support exchange of information, ideas, and experiences to improve the development of the audit of public resources
Municipalities	Representatives from municipalities	No formal role or task is given to municipalities.

Source: Constitution of Coahuila (*Constitución Política del Estado de Coahuila de Zaragoza*), Law on the Local Anti-corruption System of Coahuila (*Ley del Sistema Anticorrupción del Estado de Coahuila de Zaragoza*). All legal instruments in force in Coahuila, including the latter ones, are available at: *http://congresocoahuila.gob.mx/portal/?page_id=538*. The model laws developed by the federal Ministry of Public Function (Local Anti-corruption System Model Laws) are available at *www.gob.mx/sfp/documentos/leyes-modelo-para-las-entidades-federativas*.

The institutional arrangements of the CLACS help ensure that the three main functions of a coherent integrity system (prevention, detection, enforcement) are present along with additional oversight mechanisms by civil society and the Judicial Power for the functioning and legality of the system as a whole. This is reflected in the composition of the Co-ordination Committee, which is presided by the President of the Citizen Participation Committee and is made up of the heads of SEFIR, ASEC, ICAI, the Specialised Anti-corruption Prosecutor (yet to be created in Coahuila), a representative from Coahuila's Judicial Power, and the President of the Coahuila's Administrative Justice Tribunal (yet to be created).

The CLACS represents a significant step in ensuring a co-ordinated integrity system in Coahuila in that it brings together key players capable of co-operating in the implementation process. It will therefore allow for a better alignment of policies and approaches. Moreover, the inclusion of ASEC and ICAI representatives support synergies with complementary agendas for stronger accountability and transparency policies by aligning to two other co-ordination systems. These systems will also be set up in Coahuila. The first is Coahuila's Auditing System, which will formally be part of the CLACS and will be led by the ASEC and SEFIR. The second is Coahuila's Transparency System, which will be headed by ICAI. Likewise, the inclusion of the Tribunal and Specialised Anti-corruption Prosecutor allows for better co-ordination on investigating and prosecuting integrity breaches and ensures that new laws will be enforced and procedures applied consistently.

Preventing, detecting, and enforcing corruption is a cross-cutting responsibility of public institutions. In spite of the developments made in setting the premises for a more co-ordinated system, there are additional areas of the public sector that could contribute to integrity policies and which are not formally included in the existing institutional arrangements. These include, for instance, the Ministry of Government (*Secretaría de Gobierno*) which has key responsibilities with respect to co-ordination and collaboration between the government and municipalities. A further actor in the executive power not currently represented in the system is the Technical and Planning Ministry (*Secretaría Técnica y de Planeación*), which plays an important role in monitoring compliance with the developments in the implementation of the State Development Plan (*Plan Estatal de Desarrollo*) and therefore in linking sectorial policy objectives with broader development objectives. The Ministry of Education (*Secretaría de Educación*) could also have a stronger role in incorporating awareness-raising on corruption in education policy by adapting curricula requirements. Finally, entities responsible for law-making and legal coherence, such as Coahuila's Congress and the Governor's Legal Affairs Office (*Consejería Jurídica*), are also currently absent from the Co-ordination Committee.

Neither the NACS or the CLACS Law include these actors in the Co-ordination Committee. It is true that their full participation may not be desirable because it could hinder the agility and effectiveness of the Committee. However, mechanisms should be introduced to allow continuous consultation and co-ordination with all relevant actors of Coahuila's public sector, for instance by formalising their involvement through agreements providing for their participation (at least) when discussing and elaborating the state's anti-corruption policy, which is part of the Co-ordination Committee tasks.

In addition, in order for the work of the CLACS to further embrace a whole-of-government approach, it is necessary that all its plans, programmes, and measures link with state-wide strategies such as Coahuila's State Development Plan (*Plan Estatal de Desarrollo*), which currently sets a number of strategic objectives on several topics which are relevant to public sector integrity (government and procurement audits, innovation, human resources, transparency, and public resources management) and is complemented with an online system following up on developments and indicators (Table 1.3). However, the current plan (2011-17) does not explicitly mention key concepts and issues such as ethics, conflict of interest, and integrity. The next plans should deal more specifically with corruption and make specific links with the CLACS's policies and action plans.

Table 1.3. **Governance objectives and strategies of Coahuila's Development Plan (2011-17)**

Planning and assessing public management
Carry out the management of the government of Coahuila based on short- and long-term programmes aligned to the Development Plan and which contain the following elements: objectives, means to address them, and mechanisms to assess results.

Efficient and orderly administration
Improve the quality of the state public administration processes and of services offered to citizens.

Responsible management of public finances
Support a responsible and orderly policy in the management of public finances.

Government innovation
Establish a permanent innovation policy and continuous improvement of the state administration processes.

Transparent Government
Make Coahuila a leader entity in transparency and accountability.

Professional and committed human resources
Shape an administration made of trained and honest public officials committed to government projects.

Source: Government of Coahuila (2015), Coahuila's State Development Plan 2011-17 (2015 update), *http://coahuila.gob.mx/archivos/pdf/Publicaciones/PED-Actualizado-211216-webaccesible.pdf*.

Other key state-wide strategies which should be closely linked with the CLACS are:

- Coahuila's Programme for Administrative Modernisation, Audit, and Accountability (*Programa Estatal de Modernización Administrativa, Fiscalización y Rendición de Cuentas*), which defines the pillars of state action in the realms of audit, efficiency, and innovation.
- Coahuila's Special Programme for Transparency (*Plan Especial de Transparencia*), which defines strategic objectives to manage public resources responsibly and to establish a transparent government.
- Coahuila's Open Government Action Plan (*Plan de acción Gobierno Abierto Coahuila*), which is a co-ordinated effort of the government, ICAI, and civil society and forms the basis for designing and advancing initiatives on transparency, citizen participation, and technology.

Nominating a contact point within each of the CLACS constituent institutions could strengthen the co-ordination with its governing bodies and favour the implementation of its activities throughout the government.

The functioning of the CLACS does not only rely on the formal adoption of new bodies, but also on the responsiveness of its participants to contribute and facilitate implementation of the activities which will be decided by its governing bodies. This issue is in part addressed by Article 31 of the CLACS Law, which gives the Executive Commission the responsibility to monitor constituent institutions and develop non-binding recommendations in light of the results that emerge in the annual report. The Executive Commission will also produce a follow-up report to monitor the extent to which these recommendations have been addressed. Since "gathering credible and relevant data on the level of implementation, performance and overall effectiveness of the public integrity system" is a key element in building a strategic approach for the public sector, according to the OECD *Recommendation on Public Integrity*, Coahuila could further favour the implementation of the activities and decisions taken by the CLACS by clearly delineating each institution's participation in the system and role in implementing its decisions. For this purpose, the CLACS could require that each participating institution nominate a contact point responsible for co-ordinating the work with the different bodies of the system and ensure implementation of relevant decisions. For this purpose, Coahuila could consider the practice used in the Regional Anti-corruption Commission of Piura (Peru), where all public entities have to establish an Anti-corruption Unit or Office in charge of complying with the objectives, plans, and activities set by the Commission (Box 1.3).

Box 1.3. **Regional Anti-corruption Commission in Piura (Peru)**

Regional anti-corruption commissions (CRAs) were established in Peru through Law no. 29976, which also created the High-level Anti-corruption Commission (*Comisión Alto-nivel de Anti-corrupción*, or the CAN), the national body promoting horizontal co-ordination and guaranteeing the coherence of the anti-corruption policy framework in Peru.

Amongst the tasks of the CRAs is the elaboration of an anti-corruption plan. Such a plan has the potential to reflect the specific issues and challenges of each region. However, until now, only six regions have developed a plan (San Martín, Pasco, Amazonas, Cusco, Piura, and Huancavelica), and it is unclear to what extent these plans have been effectively implemented.

Piura's regional anti-corruption commission was created though Regional Ordinance no. 263 of 2013, which brings together representatives from the executive and the judicial powers as well as from municipalities, the private sector, and professional associations. Piura's commission is supported by an executive committee responsible for implementing the policies identified by the commission. Co-ordination between the commission and the executive committee is carried out by the commission's technical secretariat. Finally, the system is governed by anti-corruption units within each public entity, which – among other tasks – are in charge of implementing the policies approved by the commission, providing support in ensuring compliance with the Code of Ethics for the public service, co-ordinating the elaboration and approval of the Anti-corruption Plans of the entity, preparing a report of anti-corruption activities, and presenting this report during public hearings.

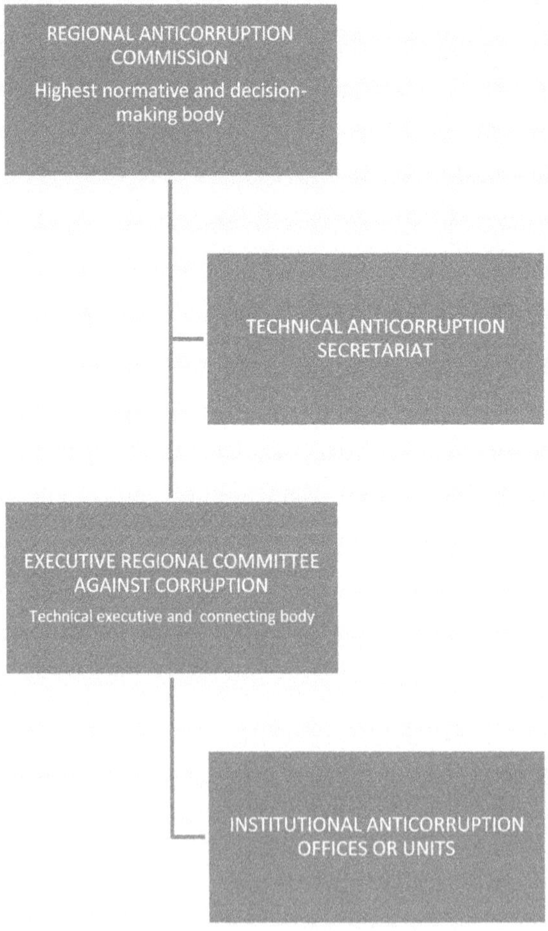

Source: OECD (2017b), *OECD Integrity Review of Peru: Enhancing Public Sector Integrity for Inclusive Growth*, OECD Publishing, Paris. *http://dx.doi.org/10.1787/9789264271029-en*, and Powerpoint presentation prepared by Piura's Regional Anti-corruption Commission. *http://anticorrupcion.regionpiura.gob.pe/detalle.php?idpag=3&pagina=uni_lucha&verper=0&tit=2.*

The participation of municipalities in the CLACS provides for mechanisms to improve vertical co-ordination of integrity policies in the State of Coahuila. However, municipalities should be fully involved during the implementation of the system. Coahuila could create an ad-hoc working group in charge of elaborating co-ordination mechanisms and providing continuous support to build coherent municipal anti-corruption systems.

Corruption of all types is a concern at all levels of government in Mexico, but particularly at state and municipal levels, where 52% and 45% of citizens, respectively, report that corruption is "very frequent". Similar figures emerge from specific data on Coahuila, where the state governments and municipalities rank third and fifth amongst the institutions perceived as most corrupt, and where 44% and 38% of the population, respectively, think corruption is very frequent in these institutions (Figure 1.1).

Figure 1.1. **Share of respondents who believe corruption is "very frequent" in Coahuila, according to institution/sector, 2015**

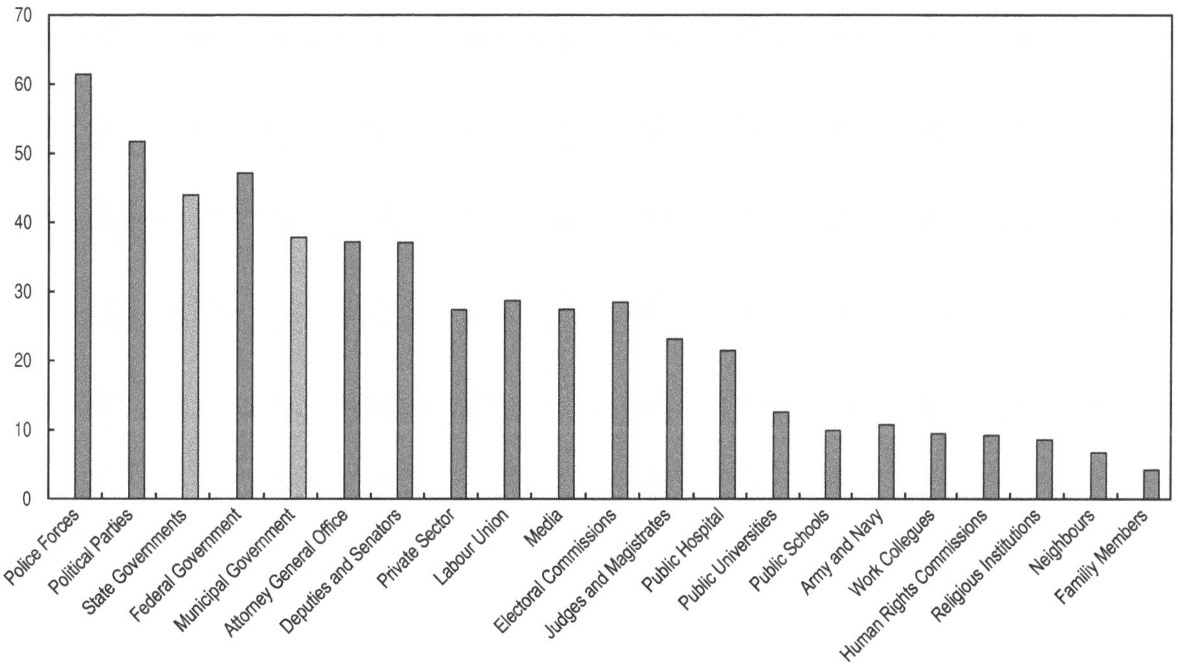

Source: INEGI (2015), *Encuesta Nacional de Calidad e Impacto Gubernamental 2015, www.beta.inegi.org.mx/proyectos/enchogares/regulares/encig/2015/.*

The fact that corruption is a multi-level issue is confirmed by the fact that nine of the ten procedures perceived as most corrupt in Mexico concern competences spread across levels of government or within municipalities (Table 1.4). Indeed, opportunities for certain types of corruption can be more likely at subnational levels than on the national level. This may be due to the fewer capacity-building and training programmes organised at the local level, but also to the more frequent interaction between local authorities and citizens/firms. The latter type of interaction creates opportunities to test the integrity of officials working in subnational levels of government. Article 115 of the Mexican Constitution and Article 102 of Coahuila's Municipal Code (*Código Municipal para el Estado de Coahuila de Zaragoza*) provide proof of the wide-ranging responsibilites of municipalities, including a number of services involving high exposure to the public such as the management of water, streetlight, waste, markets, cemeteries, streets, and police.

Table 1.4. **Administrative procedures perceived as most corrupt and corresponding level of administrative competence in Mexico**

Administrative procedure	Corruption perception (%)	Level of government responsibility
Administrative offence (*Faltas administrativas*)	37	Multi-level
Traffic violation (*Infracción por incidente de tránsito*)	35	Multi-level
Parking violations (*Infracciones al estacionarse*)	28	Municipal
Land use permits (*Permiso de uso de suelo*)	19	Municipal
Request for cleaning service (*Solicitud de servicio de limpia*)	18	Municipal
Proof of car polluting substances (*Verificación vehicular de contaminantes*)	16	State
Request for water pipeline (*Solicitud de una pipa de agua*)	12	Multi-level
Procedures in the Office of the Attorney (*Trámites ante el ministerio público*)	11	Multi-level
Permit for street-selling (*Permisos para vender en vía pública*)	8	Municipal
Border procedures (*Trámites de aduana*)	5	Federal

Source: IMCO with data from ENCIG 2014. Adapted from *http://imco.org.mx/indices/documentos/2015_IHE_Presentacion.pdf*.

Corruption at the subnational level in Mexico, including in northeast Mexico, where Coahuila is located, is also attested by data from a biennial survey conducted by Mexico's National Statistics Office (INEGI) on citizens' experiences with public sector corruption in a standardised sample of government-provided services. The survey calculates a "corruption incidence" ratio by dividing the total number of citizens who interacted with public authorities in the request or receipt of a service by the number of acts of corruption reported in interactions with public authorities. The ratio is a proxy for the extent to which certain interactions have been subject to corruption. It is not an exact figure of experienced corruption. Insofar as the provision of public services is concerned, and as Figure 1.2 shows, state and municipal governments showed greater incidences of experienced corruption compared to the federal level (OECD, 2017c).

Figure 1.2. **Local anti-corruption systems address corruption where most prevalent, INEGI "corruption ratio" by level of government and region**

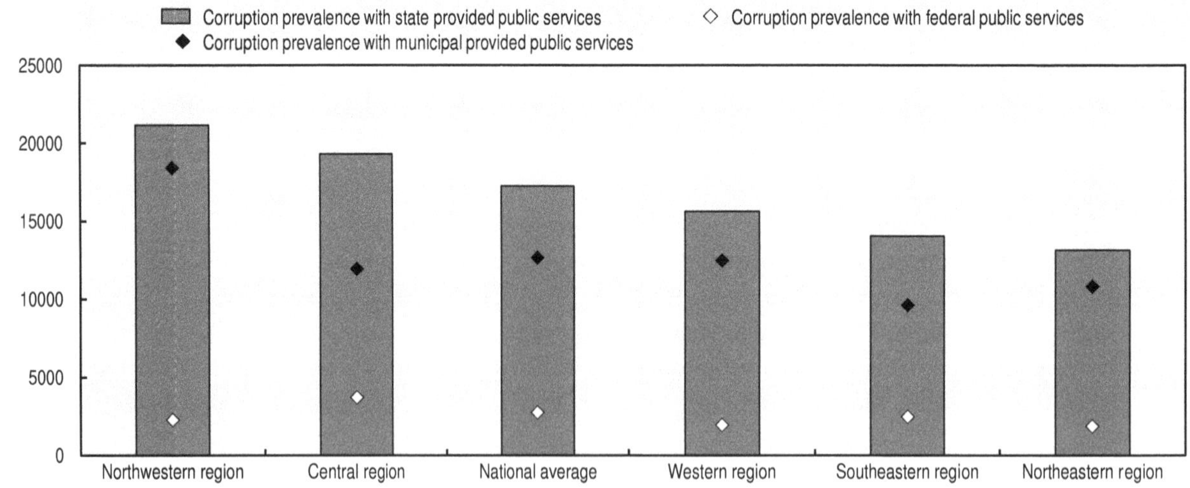

Source: INEGI. *Encuesta Nacional de Calidad e Impacto Gubernamental*, 2015. *http://www.beta.inegi.org.mx/proyectos/enchogares/regulares/encig/2015/*.

Note: The central region comprises Ciudad de México, Guerrero, Hidalgo, Estado de México, Morelos, Puebla, and Tlaxcala; the western region comprises Aguascalientes, Colima, Guanajuato, Jalisco, Michoacán de Ocampo, Nayarit, Querétaro, and Zacatecas; the southeastern region comprises Campeche, Chiapas, Oaxaca, Quintana Roo, Tabasco, Veracruz de Ignacio de la Llave, and Yucatán; the northwestern region comprises Baja California, Baja California Sur, Chihuahua, Sinaloa, and Sonora; and the northeastern region comprises Coahuila de Zaragoza, Durango, Nuevo León, San Luis Potosí, and Tamaulipas.

The worrisome levels of corruption at the subnational level call for increased efforts to strengthen co-operation among levels of government in Mexico. This is also the primary objective of the NACS, whose constitutional mandate is to be the co-ordination mechanism of all the institutions in charge of preventing, detecting, and sanctioning corruption at all levels of government (Article 113 of the Constitution and Article 1 of the NACS Law). Accordingly, the Local Anti-corruption Systems – including the CLACS – are formally part of the national system, and NACS Co-ordination Committee must establish co-ordination mechanisms and be able to invite their representatives to national system meetings. In particular, the framework of the CLACS mirrors the one established at the national level and co-ordination between all state entities is identified as their main objective (Article 1 of the CLACS Law). Furthermore, municipalities are addressed directly by the CLACS in Article 7 of the CLACS Law, and Article 9 stipulates that co-ordination mechanisms are to be established by the Co-ordination Committee.

Given that the NACS is currently in the process of implementation in Coahuila, vertical co-ordination on integrity-related matters between Coahuila and relevant federal and municipal-level institutions currently rests on ad-hoc agreements (*convenios*), which in some cases are part of specific initiatives such as the National Permanent Commission of State-Federation Comptrollers (*Comisión Permanente de Contralores Estados-Federación*, or CPCE-F), the Permanent Commission of State-Municipal Controllers (*Comisión Permanente de Contralores Estado- Municipios*, or CPCE-M), and the National Conference of Governors (*Conferencia Nacional de Gobernadores*, CONAGO) (Table 1.5).

The implementation of the CLACS will introduce institutional mechanisms to strengthen co-ordination with municipalities and therefore to avoid fragmentation, overlap, and gaps between the national and subnational integrity systems, in line with the OECD Recommendation. However, municipalities interviewed during the fact-finding mission in July 2016 lamented that the NACS is a "top-down" exercise and they had not yet been consulted on its implementation in Coahuila. Furthermore, although municipalities are formally part of the LACS, the governance envisaged by the CLACS Law does not provide for any specific role or responsibilities within the governing bodies of the System, such as a co-ordination committee, executive secretariat, or citizen participation committee (Table 1.2).

In order to ensure a whole-of-government approach and strengthen co-ordination with all levels of government, municipalities should actively contribute to the work of the CLACS. To this end, they should not only be regularly involved in discussions about the implementation of the system, following the example of the workshop organised by SEFIR with the comptrollers and legal officers of municipalities of Coahuila on 24 February 2017, but they should also contribute substantially to it. In the manner of the NACS Law's provision for co-ordination with Federal States, the CLACS Co-ordination Committee is likewise empowered to convene municipalities in order to carry out its work (Article 13). However, to improve co-ordination at a more technical level, a working group within the Executive Secretariat, including representatives from municipalities, could be created and could meet periodically to encourage communication and information exchange among municipalities. Another task of such a working group could be to design tools and instruments to establish co-operation with municipalities, the latter being one of the system's main objectives.

In carrying out its work, the CLACS Co-ordination Committee should take in particular consideration the specificities of Coahuila's 38 municipalities, which are spread out over a territory of 151 595 km^2, making it the third-largest state in Mexico. As the fact-finding mission revealed, each municipality has unique needs and capacities. Rodrigo, Allio, and Andres-Amo (2009) note that "[e]xpanding a framework for high-quality regulation at all levels of government can only be achieved if countries take into consideration the diversity of local needs and the particularities of lower levels of government." As a consequence, in order to deal with subnational government particularities, the CLACS Co-ordination Committee could periodically gather in different municipalities across the State in order to address local needs, but also to involve their authorities and citizens in the functioning of the system. Furthermore, at an early stage of its work, the Co-ordination Committee could carry out a preliminary assessment of existing anti-corruption policies and structures among municipalities: this would not only help to develop effective mechanisms for their involvement and co-operation, but it would also allow the CLACS to address gaps in information, capacity, funding, and policy. It would also be an opportunity to address the duplication of rules, overlapping, and low-quality regulations, which are common challenges in multi-level regulatory governance relations (Charbit and Michalun, 2009).

Table 1.5. **Agreements for vertical co-operation in Coahuila (as of July 2016)**

Co-ordination tool	Thematic Area	Challenges
Agreements between Coahuila and SFP: • Agreement for the strengthening of the state control and evaluation system, as well as for collaboration on transparency and the fight against corruption (*Acuerdo de Coordinación que celebran la Secretaría de la Función Pública y el Estado de Coahuila de Zaragoza, cuyo objeto es la realización de un programa de coordinación especial denominado Fortalecimiento del Sistema Estatal de Control y Evaluación de la Gestión Pública, y Colaboración en Materia de Transparencia y Combate a la Corrupción*). • Agreement with 32 state entities for the implementation of the "one-stop contact point" strategic project (*Convenio realizado con las 32 Entidades Federativas para implementar el proyecto estratégico de la Ventanilla Única Nacional de Trámites y Servicios por parte de la Unidad de Gobierno Digital, para la consulta e impresión de actas de nacimiento del Registro del Estado Civil de las personas en línea desde cualquier lugar*).	Support on ethics, public sector integrity policies, and public procurement tools	No binding mechanisms for compliance, voluntary, no monitoring or evaluation
Agreements with Municipalities • Co-ordination agreement between SEFIR and municipalities to strengthen the state control and evaluation system (*Carta compromiso que celebran la Secretaría de Fiscalización y Rendición de Cuentas y los Municipios del Estado que tiene como propósito la realización de un programa de coordinación con la finalidad de fortalecer el Sistema Estatal de Control y Evaluación de la Gestión Pública*).	Internal control and audit	No binding mechanisms for compliance, voluntary, no monitoring or evaluation
Multi-level agreements: • Agreement establishing the mandatory use of electronic means to submit the asset declarations by state and municipal officials (*Acuerdo que determina como obligatorio el uso de medios electrónicos de comunicación para la presentación de las Declaraciones de Situación Patrimonial de los Servidores Públicos Estatales y Municipales*).	Asset declarations	No binding mechanisms for compliance, voluntary, no monitoring or evaluation
Permanent Commission of State and Federal Controllers (CPCE-F), including: • Working plan of the Permanent Commission of State and Federal Controllers to improve the public management and public administration systems (*Programa de trabajo derivado de la Comisión Permanente de Contralores Estado-Federación promoverán en sus respectivos ámbitos de competencia, la modernización de los esquemas, instrumentos, mecanismos de control, verificación y evaluación de la Gestión Pública y el desarrollo de la Administración Pública*).	Internal control and audit	Member of National Auditing System, voluntary compliance
National Conference of Governors (CONAGO), including: • Framework agreement between SFP and CONAGO to co-ordinate actions on ethics, transparency, and the fight against corruption (*Convenio marco de colaboración para la coordinación de acciones específicas en materia de ética, transparencia y combate a la corrupción, que celebran por una parte, la Secretaría de la Función pública y por la otra, la Conferencia Nacional de Gobernadores*).	Several matters, including ethics, transparency, and anti-corruption issues	Political institutions of governors and mayors. Does not provide enough technical assistance to support implementation.

Source: Powerpoint presentation by SEFIR during OECD visit in Coahuila, 4 July 2016.

Lastly, links should also be established between the work of the CLACS and existing co-ordination agreements with municipalities (Table 1.5), whose effects in the harmonisation of integrity policy is currently limited because of the lack of commitment and follow-up activities by its members. For this reason, the CLACS should leverage such instruments by strengthening and institutionalising some of them, such as the CPCE-M, which currently consists in the signing of a *Carta Compromiso* between SEFIR and municipalities, as well as by providing the technical support to improve their effectiveness.

The success of the institutional arrangements provided for by the CLACS will also depend on adequate planning and allocation of resources.

Sufficient financial resources are needed to set up and implement reforms such as the one establishing the CLACS. The CLACS does not only provide for new activities and co-ordination mechanisms, but it also relies on the creation of new institutions and tools which require investment from the part of Coahuila. Adequate financing is essential to achieve the system's goals and ensures it can function without undue influence.

While it is true that many of the CLACS activities will be divided across institutional mandates and resourced by existing organisations, and that synergies and efficiencies will be generated through greater co-operation, there are nonetheless also additional costs associated with the reform. These include:

- New institutions, such as the State Tribunal for Administrative Justice (*Tribunal Estatal de Justicia Administrativa*) and Specialised Anti-corruption Prosecutor (*Fiscalía Especializada de Combate a la Corrupción*)
- New horizontal activities, such the State Digital Platform (*Plataforma Digital Estatal*)
- Scaling up of staff and activities within pre-existing institutions
- Strengthening co-ordination mechanisms, especially with municipalities

According to the CLACS Law, the Executive Secretary will rely on assets from the government, yearly resources from the state budget, and goods transferred at any other title (Article 26). On the other hand, it is unclear how the fee for participants in the Citizen Participation Committee (*contratos de prestación de servicios por honorarios*) as well as the activities of the Co-ordination Committee will be budgeted. As of March 2017, there is no evidence that the government of Coahuila has allocated any budget for it. Budgetary planning for the CLACS thus remains very uncertain. Similarly, no budgetary increases for future CLACS member institutions have been decided as yet. This raises concerns over the timing of the implementation and the success of the reform in Coahuila. For this reason, Coahuila should consider starting planning and discussing the budget implications of the CLACS as other States and the federal level have done. This is the case, for instance, of Mexico City, whose Inter-institutional Preparatory Council for the Implementation of the Anti-corruption System (*Consejo Interinstitucional Preparatorio para la Implementación del Sistema Anticorrupción - Coipisa*) in July 2016 reported an overall cost of MXN 131 million (around EUR 5.6 million) for the year 2017 (Proceso, 2016). A similar exercise was carried out at the national level, where the Finance Research Centre of the Chamber of Deputies estimated that the national framework of the NACS (i.e. not including individual LACS programs) would cost around MXN 1.5 billion (around EUR 65 million) (*Cámara de Diputados*, 2016).

In addition to financial resources, human resources are important. This is particularly relevant for the Executive Secretariat, which should be equipped with adequate and talented human resources with expertise on a wide range of subjects in line with its diverse responsibilities (legal research and investigation, IT, public management, accounting, finance, sectoral knowledge, adequate support staff, etc.). The Technical Secretariat may therefore consider specifically monitoring the quality and quantity of human resources for anti-corruption efforts across government as part of its annual report, so as to be able to identify this as a bottleneck and make relevant recommendations. The Co-ordination Committee should also consider human resources as a central component of its action plan. Capacity-building initiatives, merit-based recruitment and hiring practices, and performance assessments are indeed the norm across the public sector.

Demonstrating political and management commitment to support the public integrity system

The implementation of the CLACS rests on the commitment at the highest political level to face the technical challenges involved, address political resistance, and favour an inclusive transition into the new system.

Political leaders are responsible for maintaining a high standard of propriety in the discharge of their official duties. Their commitment is demonstrated by their conduct and action at the political level, which includes: creating legislative and institutional arrangements that reinforce ethical behaviour and establishing sanctions against wrongdoing; providing adequate support and resources for ethics-related activities throughout government and avoiding the exploitation of ethics rules and laws for political purposes (OECD, 2009).

The implementation of Mexico's National Anti-corruption reform (Box 1.2) in Coahuila's state legal system is an invaluable opportunity to demonstrate the highest commitment of Coahuila's political leadership and senior public officials to enhance integrity and reduce corruption. Furthermore, it would allow Coahuila to align to the OECD *Recommendation on Public Integrity*, which recommends that states ensure "that the appropriate legislative and institutional frameworks are in place to enable public-sector organisations to take responsibility for effectively managing the integrity of their activities, as well as that of the public officials who carry out those activities" (OECD, 2017).

In Coahuila, the lack of awareness of representatives from most institutions about the implications of the NACS reform seems to reflect senior managers' insufficient commitment to establishing appropriate institutional frameworks for integrity. Most representatives from institutions interviewed during the fact-finding mission of July 2016 were not aware of any step taken to prepare the implementation of the reform, nor of the effects and consequences such reform would generate in terms of responsibilities and co-ordination. However, a working group consisting of SEFIR, the Governor's legal office and the state congress was set up in August 2016 to assess state legislation and elaborate the legal changes required by the Constitutional Reform. These included the amendment of Coahuila's Constitution and the CLACS Law, both approved by Coahuila's Legislature in July 2017.

Nevertheless, as of July 2017 there are still secondary regulations of the CLACS pending discussion and approval (Table 1.1). This unfinished state of the system shows the extent to which it is difficult to implement a complex legislative and political process. Coahuila's highest political institutions and representatives from the legislative, executive, and judicial powers of the state should discuss the laws to be introduced or amended and, at the same time, should come up with a sustainable action plan with fixed timelines, objectives, and resources in order to make progress on implementing the reform. Such a process could be facilitated by the package of model laws which was released by the federal Ministry of Public

Function (*Secretaría de la Función Pública*, SFP) in October 2016 to support states in advancing the implementation of the NACS at subnational level. Furthermore, Coahuila could consider the working method followed by other states in Mexico, such as Mexico City, which set a clear roadmap for implementing the NACS reform.

In Mexico City, the preparation of the roadmap for the NACS implementation was led by the Office of the Comptroller General (*Contraloría General de la Ciudad de México*). In Coahuila, the Ministry for Audit and Accountability (*Secretaría de Fiscalización y Rendición de Cuentas* or SEFIR), which has important responsibilities in promoting integrity within the government of Coahuila (Box 1.4), should take the lead in this transitional phase and ensure the full engagement and commitment of all relevant ministries and municipalities. In this way, Coahuila could be brought in line with the Constitutional reform.

Box 1.4. **SEFIR's integrity and anti-corruption-related tasks**

Within the government of Coahuila, SEFIR is given the mission to run the public administration with legality, transparency, and effectiveness. For this purpose it is given a number of responsibilities pursuant to the Public Administration Organic Law (*Ley Orgánica de la Administración Pública de Coahuila de Zaragoza*, LOAP) which gives SEFIR competence on government and public procurement audit; efficiency of public administration; innovation; human resources and transparency. In particular, SEFIR is in charge of:

- Controlling and monitoring public expenses
- Monitoring compliance with rules regulating instruments and procedures on control, transparency, and assessment of public administration
- Checking compliance of departments and entities with legal provisions on budget planning and accounting, human resources, and procurement
- Issuing the general rules to carry out audits, inspections, and evaluation of departments and entities
- Nominate, co-ordinate, and advise heads of internal control entities (*órganos de control interno*, or OCI) of departments and the Attorney General Office
- Providing administrative rules and guidelines to ensure compliance on procurement matters
- Keeping a register of contractors
- Dealing with complaints from private citizens in relation to tenders or contracts
- Collecting and registering the public officials' assets declarations, as well as verifying their content through relevant investigations
- Initiating and investigating administrative responsibilities of public officials, applying sanctions and eventually, forwarding the complaints to the prosecutor's office
- Formulating policies in relation to efficiency, transparency, accounting, and access to information
- Ensuring consistency among departments' internal regulations and manuals
- Simplifying administration and promoting e-government tools

Source: Public Administration Organic Law (*Ley Orgánica de la Administración Pública de Coahuila de Zaragoza*, LOAP).

The secondary legislation defining NACS framework at the federal level, intended to be replicated by subnational entities, also gives state legislators key responsibilities to implement and put the system in motion. On the one hand, Coahuila's congress should avoid legislative bills that are not harmonised with the federal laws and that are weaker in nature, thus shielding the corresponding executive power from sanctions. Indeed, other Mexican states have had to deal with this problem (Box 1.5).

Box 1.5. **Ensuring local integrity systems comply with national legislation**

In the spring of 2016, the then-outgoing Governors of Veracruz, Chihuahua, and Quintana Roo introduced bills to establish their respective states' anti-corruption systems, including the offices of the Anti-corruption Prosecutor and judges for the administrative tribunals.

These bills were criticised by opposition parties and other organisations as containing provisions to shield them from future prosecution for corruption. Following the passing of these bills, the incoming governor-elect of Quintana Roo filed a constitutional challenge against all three of the proposed bills. His challenge argued that the bills were not consistent with the principles of Mexico's proposed National Anti-corruption System.

In September 2016, the Supreme Court of Justice (*Suprema Corte de Justicia de la Nación*, SCJN) declared the respective anti-corruption laws of the states of Chihuahua and Veracruz unconstitutional, on the grounds that the regulations for the local anti-corruption systems had been issued and approved before the federal laws of the National Anti-corruption System had been adopted.

The SCJN also declared that while the laws passed by the states of Chihuahua and Veracruz for the Anti-Corruption Prosecutors were unconstitutional, they could not remove nor invalidate the appointed prosecutors from their posts. Nevertheless, by virtue of these laws being unconstitutional, all acts derived from that law (such as their appointment) are void.

Source: OECD (2017c), *OECD Integrity Review of Mexico: Taking a Stronger Stance Against Corruption*, OECD Publishing, Paris. *http://dx.doi.org/10.1787/9789264273207-en.*

On the other hand, Article 18 of the CLACS Law establishes that the Congress of Coahuila has the responsibilities to select nine members of the Selection Committee. This committee will ultimately choose the Citizen Participation Committee after collecting proposals from the corresponding state's academic and research institutions, as well as from civil society organisations. Without key members of the Co-ordination Committee in place, the CLACS cannot start properly working and therefore its implementation may be delayed. Strong political leadership on the part of Coahuila's legislative power to fill these positions is thus required; at the same time, the need to advance this process should not undermine the open and merit-based character of the appointment process, the nominations of which should not be politicised in order not to undermine the legitimacy and effectiveness of the CLACS.

Considering the key role of senior and middle managers in implementing the CLACS, mechanisms should be introduced to define clear responsibilities and hold them accountable throughout the reform process.

The success of the CLACS reform implementation depends on the highest political will to set the necessary legal and institutional framework, but also on managerial commitment to implement obligations at the organisational level and, more generally, to advance the integrity agenda. Managerial commitment emerged as a weak point in key areas such as ethics and internal control.

The implementation of the CLACS reform package implies numerous reforms to organisational integrity policies and tools such as manuals and guidelines. In other words, managerial commitment will be crucial for the implementation of the system at the organisational level. As a consequence, Coahuila should introduce mechanisms to link specific responsibilities to each management level by integrating assessment results in a broader performance framework to favour accountability for implementing the necessary reforms. As Coahuila is working to implement integrity systems, a parallel effort to improve performance and managerial assessment, in general, would help create a work environment that encourages ethical behaviour (OECD, 2005). In this context, Coahuila could consider the experience of the Treasury Board of Canada Secretariat (TBS) Management Accountability Framework, which provides a model for widening the framework of performance assessments beyond managerial results to include public sector values, people management, and management of policy and programmes (Figure 1.3).

Figure 1.3. **Management Accountability Framework in Canada**

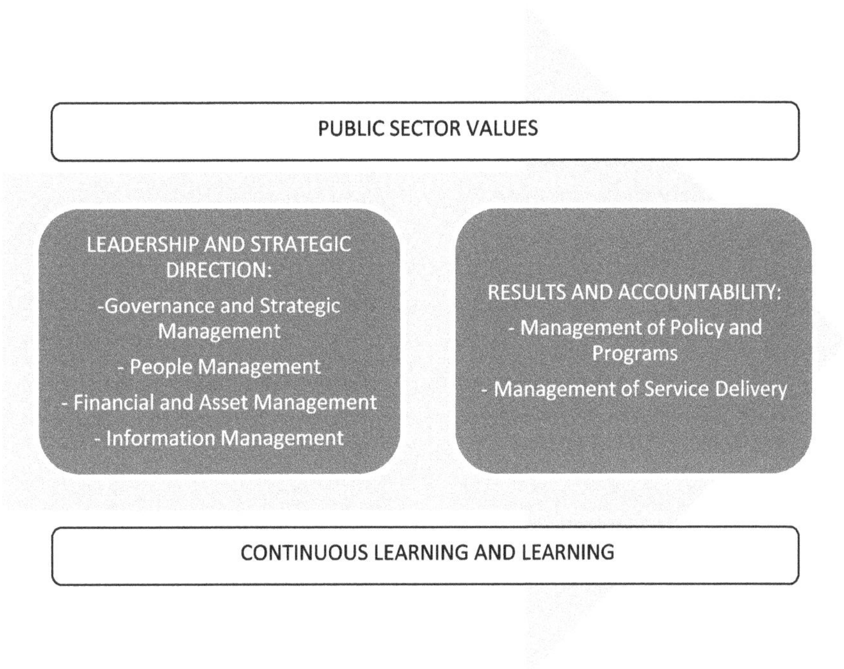

Source: Government of Canada, *Management Accountability Framework, www.canada.ca/en/treasury-board-secretariat/services/management-accountability-framework.html.*

This is nevertheless complicated by the fact that in Coahuila, as in Mexico more generally, there is a high turnover rate and many senior officials are not included under the General Employment Framework of the civil service. As a result, these positions are not subject to the same standards of performance assessment and evaluation, and accountability for objectives is made less clear. Indeed, the government of Coahuila has not developed a professional and formal civil service.

Enhancing legitimacy through wide stakeholder participation in the system

Coahuila has to ensure that the appointment and renewal procedures for members of the Citizen Committee are carried out in an open and transparent way.

The reform that gave birth to the National Anti-corruption System placed great emphasis on the role of civil society as one of the most fundamental actors in defining policies and overseeing the work of the system as a whole. This is reflected in the governance set by the CLACS, which identifies the Citizen Participation Committee as a pillar and gives it the Presidency of both the Co-ordination Committee and the Executive Secretariat. Among its tasks, the Citizen Participation Committee is called to propose co-ordination mechanisms and non-binding recommendations, build a network of civil society organisations and experts, channel the inputs of civil society and academic institutions into the system, and implement its own annual work programme. This annual work programme may include research, investigations, and projects for improving the digital platform or citizen reporting of corruption.

The institutional framework envisaged by the NACS and CLACS Law is in line with the OECD Recommendation on Public Integrity, which stresses the importance of working together with the whole of society to build effective public integrity systems, and which calls upon states to engage relevant stakeholders in the development, regular update, and implementation of the public integrity system. Similarly, it goes along the lines of the United Nations Convention Against Corruption (UNCAC), encouraging states to "promote the participation of society and reflect the principles of the rule of law, proper management of public affairs and public property, integrity, transparency, and accountability" (Article 5(1)). However, as stressed by Fundar, a leading research and investigation centre in Mexico, one of the main challenges in the implementation of the Local Anti-corruption System is the configuration of the Citizen Participation Committee. This committee should develop mechanisms that allow citizens to truly take part in local systems (Animal Político, 2017a).

In order for civil society to be a leading body of the CLACS, the first priority for Coahuila is to ensure that the appointment procedure is carried out through open and transparent means enabling the participation of independent and reputable experts representing various components of civil society. This will not only enable the effective contribution of civil society, but it will also help to strengthen the overall legitimacy of the system.

According to the procedure laid down by the CLACS Law, the selection of the Citizen Participation Committee will be conducted by members of civil society and research institutions, who are in turn elected by the State Congress. In particular, the latter will set up a Selection Commission consisting of nine experts, five of whom will come from research and academic institutions, and four who will be part of civil society organisations specialised on integrity, audit, and anti-corruption issues (Figure 1.4).

Considering the pivotal role of state-level congresses in initiating and leading the selection process for the Citizen Participation Committee, Coahuila's Congress should make sure that all steps to create the Selection Committee are subject to the highest standards of transparency and guarantee the fairness and inclusiveness of the process. In this sense, both Coahuila's Congress and the Selection Committee could consider providing additional information concerning the justification for the final decision – including explicit reference to the experience and knowledge of the selected members – as well as some financial information concerning the selected candidates. This information could include their assets and activities, and a signed declaration disclosing any conflict of interest which could affect their work.

With regards to the selection process of the Citizen Committee – but also to the legislative work concerning all the instruments and amendments which will need to be adopted to implement the CLACS (Table 1.1) – Coahuila should also consider following the highest standards of parliamentary openness set in the Declaration on Parliamentary Openness (Opening Parliament, 2012), a document supported by more than 140 organisations from over 75 countries and which identifies 44 principles on openness, transparency, and accessibility of parliaments grouped in the following areas:

- Promoting a culture of openness
- Making parliamentary information transparent
- Easing access to parliamentary information
- Enabling electronic communication of parliamentary information

Figure 1.4. **The selection process of the Citizen Committee in the CLACS Law**

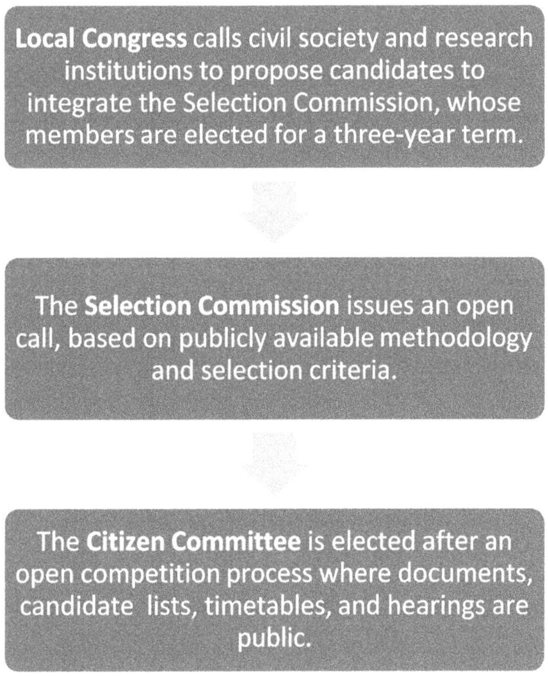

Source: OECD elaboration from CLACS Law.

A broader participation of stakeholders into the local anti-corruption system of Coahuila can help to build a more inclusive and responsive public sector integrity system.

The involvement of civil society in the National and Local Anti-corruption Systems in Mexico is a key factor in the success of a whole-of-society approach to public integrity. However, stakeholder participation into the system currently seems narrow in scope, because the Citizen Participation Committee will consist of citizens who made outstanding contributions to transparency, accountability, or the fight against corruption (Article 16 of CLACS Law and Table 1.2). Similarly, Local Congresses nominate the Selection Commission, calling upon civil society and research institutions to propose candidates (Article 18 of CLACS Law and Figure 1.5). This was confirmed by the election, in January 2017, of the first Citizen Participation Committee of the National Anti-corruption System. Indeed, most of its members belong to academia or to civil society organisations (Animal Político, 2017b), or have previously held positions in autonomous bodies such as the National Elections Institute (*Instituto Nacional Electoral*, INE) and the National Institute for Transparency, Freedom of Information, and Personal Data Protection (*Instituto Nacional de Transparencia, Acceso a la Información y Protección de Datos Personales*, INAI).

The activities of the public sector require interactions with a wide range of stakeholders. Corruption often takes place when public officials interact with the private sector. Interviews with private sector representatives during the fact-finding mission of July 2016 provided valuable input and ideas which could help to improve the integrity system of Coahuila; similarly, their involvement in the CLACS could contribute to a relevant and effective integrity system for the public sector. At the same time, bringing diverse stakeholders would guarantee further checks and balances among different actors and increase expectations that they will adhere to the standards and policies developed by the system. Third, a continuous dialogue and co-operation with state-wide or sectorial business associations could induce the development of their own integrity standards and initiatives, such as in Colombia, where the National Citizens Committee for the Fight against Corruption (*Comisión Nacional Ciudadana para la Lucha Contra la Corrupción*, CNCLCC) leverages such partnerships to promote, among other things, codes of conduct for the private sector. Coahuila could introduce mechanisms to ensure a multi-stakeholder participation scheme which includes private sector but also other non-governmental organisations such as trade unions and media. Countries such as Colombia and Peru have used such schemes (Box 1.6). With specific reference to the CLACS, its members could leverage the possibility provided for by Article 28 of the CLACS Law and regularly invite organisations not included in the Citizens Committee to the Co-ordination Committee through the Executive Secretary. In order to build continuous co-operation with these organisations, the mutual commitment could be formalised in agreements and monitored within the yearly reports of the Co-ordination Commission.

Box 1.6. **Government and non-government stakeholders in National Anti-corruption Commissions: Colombia and Peru**

Colombia

The Anti-corruption Statute established the National Moralisation Commission (*Comisión Nacional de Moralización*, CNM), a high-level mechanism to co-ordinate strategies to prevent and fight corruption. The CNM is a multipartite body including the President of the Republic, the Inspector General, the Prosecutor General, the Comptroller General, the Auditor General, the head of Congress, and the President of the Supreme Court. The National Committee for Moralisation is responsible for information and data exchange among the bodies mentioned above in order to fight corruption; it also establishes mandatory indicators to assess transparency in public administration; it adopts an annual strategy to promote ethical conduct in public administration, including workshops, seminars, and pedagogic events on topics such as ethics and public morality, as well as public officials duties and responsibilities.

The same Anti-corruption Statute of 2011 created the National Citizens Committee for the Fight against Corruption (*Comisión Nacional Ciudadana para la Lucha Contra la Corrupción*, CNCLCC), which engages Colombian citizens in assessing and improving policies to promote ethical conduct and curb corruption in both the public and private sectors. This Committee comprises representatives of a wide array of sectors such as business associations, NGOs dedicated to the fight against corruption, universities, media, social audit representatives, the National Planning Council, trade unions, and the Colombian Confederation of Freedom of Religion, Awareness and Worship. CNCLCC issues a yearly report on anti-corruption policy evaluation and promotes codes of conduct for the private sector, particularly in the realm of conflict-of-interest prevention. It closely monitors the measures taken in the Anti-corruption Statute to improve public management as well as public procurement, the anti-paperwork policy, the democratisation of public administration, access to public information and citizen services, and it also promotes the active participation of social media in reporting corruption.

Box 1.6. **Government and non-government stakeholders in National Anti-corruption Commissions: Colombia and Peru** *(cont.)*

Peru

Peru's High-level Anti-corruption Commission (*Comisión Alto-nivel de Anti-corrupción*, or CAN) was established by Law no. 29976 and its regulation in decree no. 089-2013-PCM, which also outlines the CAN's mandate and responsibilities. The CAN's main activities are articulating efforts, co-ordinating actions of multiple agencies, and proposing short, medium, and long-term policies directed at preventing and curbing corruption in the country.

Like in Colombia, the CAN involves public and private institutions and civil society and co-ordinates anti-corruption efforts and actions. Non-governmental actors include representatives of private business entities, labour unions, universities, media, and religious institutions. Bringing diverse stakeholders regularly around the table aims at encouraging horizontal co-ordination and guaranteeing the coherence of the anti-corruption policy framework. At the same time, it contributes to protecting the CAN from undue influence by narrow interests.

Table 1.6. **The composition of the CAN (as of October 2016)**

Members with vote (10)	Members with voice but without vote (11)
• President of Congress (*Congreso de la República*) • President of the Judiciary (*Poder Judicial*) • President of the Cabinet Office (*Presidencia del Consejo de Ministros*, PCM) • Minister of Justice and Human Rights (*Ministerio de Justicia y Derechos Humanos*) • President of the Constitutional Court (*Tribunal Constitucional*) • President of the National Council of the Judiciary (*Consejo Nacional de la Magistratura*) • Attorney General (*Fiscalía de la Nación*) • President of the National Assembly of Regional Governments (*Asamblea Nacional de Gobiernos Regionales*) • President of the Association of Municipalities (*Asociación de Municipalidades*) • Executive Secretariat of the National Agreement (*Acuerdo Nacional*)	• Comptroller General (*Contraloría General de la República*, CGR) • Ombudsman (*Defensoría del Pueblo*) • Executive Director of the Supervisory Body of Public Contracting (*Organismo Supervisor de las Contrataciones del Estado*, OSCE) • President of the National Assembly of Deans (*Asamblea Nacional de Rectores*) • President of the National Council for Public Ethics (*Consejo Nacional para la Ética Pública, Proética*) • President of the National Confederation of Private Business Entities (*Confederación Nacional de Instituciones Empresariales Privadas*) • Representative of the labour unions of Peru • Representative from the Catholic church • Representative from the Evangelic church • Executive Director of the Peruvian Press Council (*Consejo Prensa Peruana*) • General Co-ordinator of the CAN (*Coordinador General de la CAN*)

Source: OECD (2017d), *Integrity Review of Colombia*, OECD Publishing, Paris; OECD (2017c), *OECD Integrity Review of Mexico: Taking a Stronger Stance Against Corruption*, OECD Publishing, Paris. *http://dx.doi.org/10.1787/9789264273207-en.*

Proposals for Action

The implementation of the national anti-corruption system in Coahuila is a crucial step in building a coherent and comprehensive integrity system. To face the challenges involved in the process and leverage the possibilities offered by the new framework established by the reform, the OECD recommends that Coahuila considers taking the following actions:

Strengthening institutional co-ordination for integrity

- Although the CLACS is a valuable framework for co-ordinating relevant institutions, the system should ensure that integrity policies are mainstreamed through the whole-of-government and that they are linked with state-wide strategies.
- Nominating a contact point within each of the CLACS constituent institutions could strengthen the co-ordination with its governing bodies and favour the implementation of its activities throughout the government.

- The participation of municipalities in the CLACS provides for mechanisms to improve vertical co-ordination of integrity policies in the state of Coahuila. However, municipalities should be fully involved during the implementation of the system. Coahuila could create an ad-hoc working group in charge of elaborating co-ordination mechanisms and providing continuous support to build coherent municipal anti-corruption systems.
- The success of the institutional arrangements provided for by the CLACS will also depend on adequate planning and allocation of resources.

Demonstrating political and management commitment to support the public integrity system

- The implementation of the CLACS rests on the commitment at the highest political level to face the technical challenges involved, address political resistance, and favour an inclusive transition into the new system.
- Considering the key role of senior and middle managers in implementing the CLACS, mechanisms should be introduced to define clear responsibilities and hold them accountable throughout the reform process.

Enhancing legitimacy through wide stakeholder participation in the system

- Coahuila has to ensure that the appointment and renewal procedures for members of the Citizen Committee are carried out in an open and transparent way.
- A broader participation of stakeholders into the local anti-corruption system of Coahuila can help to build a more inclusive and responsive public sector integrity system.

References

Animal Político (2017a), "¿Opacidad en los sistemas locales anticorrupción?", *www.animalpolitico.com/blogueros-res-publica/2017/01/13/alto-la-opacidad-los-sistemas-locales-anticorrupcion/*.

Animal Político (2017b), "Dar resultados y ganar legitimidad, retos del nuevo Comité Ciudadano del Sistema Anticorrupción," *www.animalpolitico.com/2017/01/retos-comite-ciudadano-anticorrupcion/*.

Camera de Diputados (2016), Comisión de Transparencia analiza requerimientos presupuestales para el Sistema Nacional Anticorrupción - Boletín N°. 2305, *www5.diputados.gob.mx/index.php/esl/Comunicacion/Boletines/2016/Octubre/12/2305-Comision-de-Transparencia-analiza-requerimientos-presupuestales-para-el-Sistema-Nacional-Anticorrupcion*.

Charbit, C. and M. Michalun (2009), "Mind the Gaps: Managing Mutual Dependence in Relations among Levels of Government", *OECD Working Papers on Public Governance*, No. 14, OECD Publishing, Paris. *http://dx.doi.org/10.1787/221253707200*

Government of Coahuila (2015), Coahuila's State Development Plan 2011-17 (2015 update), *http://coahuila.gob.mx/archivos/pdf/Publicaciones/PED-Actualizado-211216-webaccesible.pdf*.

OECD (2009), "Towards a Sound Integrity Framework: Instruments, Processes, Structures and Conditions for Implementation", Global Forum on Public Governance, 4-5 May, Public Governance and Territorial Development Directorate, Public Governance Committee, GOV/PGC/GF(2009)1.

OECD (2017a), *Recommendation of the Council on Public Integrity*, Paris, *http://www.oecd.org/gov/ethics/Recommendation-Public-Integrity.pdf*

OECD (2017b), *OECD Integrity Review of Peru: Enhancing Public Sector Integrity for Inclusive Growth*, OECD Publishing, Paris. *http://dx.doi.org/10.1787/9789264271029-en*

OECD (2017c), *OECD Integrity Review of Mexico: Taking a Stronger Stance Against Corruption*, OECD Publishing, Paris. *http://dx.doi.org/10.1787/9789264273207-en*

OECD (2017d), *OECD Integrity Review of Colombia: Investing in Integrity for Peace and Prosperity*, OECD Publishing, Paris. *http://dx.doi.org/10.1787/9789264278325-en*

OECD (2005), *Public Sector Integrity: A Framework for Assessment*, OECD Publishing, Paris. *http://dx.doi.org/10.1787/9789264010604-en*

Opening Parliament (2012), Declaration on Parliamentary Openness, *www.openingparliament.org/declaration.*

Proceso (2016), Sistema Anticorrupción en la CDMX costaría al menos 131 mdp, *www.proceso.com.mx/447513/sistema-anticorrupcion-en-la-capital-costaria-al-menos-131-mdp.*

Rodrigo, D., L. Allio and P. Andres-Amo (2009), "Multi-Level Regulatory Governance: Policies, Institutions and Tools for Regulatory Quality and Policy Coherence", *OECD Working Papers on Public Governance*, No. 13, OECD Publishing, Paris, *http://dx.doi.org/10.1787/224074617147*

OECD Integrity Review of Coahuila, Mexico
Restoring trust through an integrity system

Chapter 2

Building a culture of integrity in the public sector in Coahuila

This chapter discusses ways to strengthen public ethics and the identification and management of conflict-of-interest situations in Coahuila through improvements in the institutional design, guidance, and control. First, the chapter discusses the legal and policy framework for public ethics and conflict-of-interest management. Second, it analyses potential reforms that would harmonise policies and practices, streamline public ethics in the whole-of-government, and raise awareness among public servants. Third, it assesses the effectiveness of the asset disclosure system of Coahuila in its attempts to prevent corruption. Finally, it provides guidance on evaluation and monitoring mechanisms.

additional positions or directorships, and dealing with operating assets (OECD, 2013). In Australia, concrete guidance is given to public officials on how to think through an ethical dilemma situation (Box 2.5).

Box 2.4. **Code of Ethics for Public Officials at the Federal Level**

The new Code of Ethics involves both general principles and values and a set of desired and undesired behaviours. The general Code of Ethics comprises a set of constitutional principles (legality, honesty, loyalty, impartiality, efficiency) as well as additional values (public interest, respect, respect for human rights, equality and non-discrimination, gender equality, culture and environment, integrity, co-operation, leadership, transparency, accountability) that every public servant should follow. These principles and values largely overlap with those established in the Code of Conduct of Coahuila. Coahuila's Code, however, does not include the values of public interest, general respect, respect for human rights, equality and non-discrimination, gender equality, or co-operation.

On the other hand, a set of specific desired and undesired conducts is articulated in the Rules of Integrity, which complement the new Code of Ethics and which are divided in 12 specific domains:

1. Public behaviour
2. Public information
3. Public contracting, licensing, permits, authorisations, and concessions
4. Governmental programmes
5. Public procedures and services
6. Human resources
7. Administration of public properties
8. Evaluation processes
9. Internal control
10. Administrative procedures
11. Permanent performance with integrity
12. Co-operation with integrity

Source: OECD (2017b), *OECD Integrity Review of Mexico: Taking a Stronger Stance Against Corruption*, OECD Publishing, Paris. *http://dx.doi.org/10.1787/9789264273207-en.*

Box 2.5. **Guiding public officials in facing ethical dilemmas in Australia**

The Australian Government developed and implemented strategies to enhance ethics and accountability in the Australian Public Service (APS), such as the Lobbyists Code of Conduct, the register of "third parties", the Ministerial Advisers' Code and work on whistleblowing and freedom of information.

To support the implementation of the ethics and integrity regime, the Australian Public Service Commission enhanced its guidance on APS Values and Code of Conduct issues. This includes integrating ethics training into learning and development activities at all levels.

Box 2.5. **Guiding public officials in facing ethical dilemmas in Australia** *(cont.)*

To help public servants in their decision-making process when facing ethical dilemmas and choices, the Australian Public Service Commission developed a decision making model. The model follows the acronym ***REFLECT***:

1. **RE**cognise a potential issue or problem

   Public officials should ask themselves:

   - Do I have a gut feeling that something is not right or that this is a risky situation?
   - Is this a right vs. right or a right vs. wrong issue?
   - Can I recognize the situation as one that involves tensions between APS Values or the APS and my personal values?
2. Find relevant information
   - What were the trigger and circumstances?
   - Identify the relevant legislation, guidance, policies (APS-wide and agency-specific).
   - Identify the rights and responsibilities of relevant stakeholders.
   - Identify any precedent decisions.
3. Linger at the "fork in the road"
   - Talk it through, use intuition (emotional intelligence and rational processes), analysis, listen, and reflect.
4. Evaluate the options
   - Discard unrealistic options.
   - Apply the accountability test: public scrutiny, independent review.
   - Be able to explain your reasons/decision.
5. Come to a decision
   - Come to a decision, act on it, and make a record if necessary.
6. Take time to reflect
   - How did it turn out for all concerned?
   - Learn from your decision.
   - If you had to do it all over again, would you do it differently?

Source: Office of the Merit Protection Commissioner, "Ethical Decision Making" (2009), *www.apsc.gov.au/publications-and-media/current-publications/values-and-conduct*.

The Ethics Unit within SEFIR needs to ensure that such manuals are revised and updated regularly in order to be a useful resource for public officials. Furthermore, in co-ordination with the Integrity Contact Points (or persons), the Ethics Unit would be responsible for the distribution of the manuals throughout the entire administration, including municipalities, regulatory bodies, and state-owned enterprises.

A common overarching integrity management framework provides the opportunity to elaborate codes of conduct on the organisational level in a participative way and to implement them more effectively.

As a consequence of the code's concision, on several issues the adopted language omits important details (for example, regarding cases when an employee thinks that he or she has received an illegal instruction from a superior). The code needs to be relevant for different public officials who exercise different functions with varied levels of responsibility and vulnerability to corruption. It therefore needs to be concise and general. However, this concision is a common caveat of codes designed to address the whole of the public sector.

Just as different organisations face different contexts and kinds of work, they may also be faced with a variety of ethical dilemmas and specific conflict-of-interest situations. For instance, the challenges might differ significantly between the Ministry of Finance, the Ministry of Health, and the different supervisory and regulatory bodies. In particular, the OECD experience on conflict-of-interest management shows that public officials should be provided with real-world examples and discussions on how specific conflict situations have been handled. Organisational Codes of Conduct provide an opportunity to include relevant and concrete examples from the organisation's day-to-day business to which the employees can easily relate.

The organisational codes should be created using consensus and ownership, and should provide relevant and clear guidance to all public servants. Consulting and involving employees in the elaboration of the code of conduct through focus group discussion, surveys, or interviews can help build consensus on the shared values and principles of behaviour and can increase staff members' feelings of ownership and compliance with the code.

In addition, the experience of OECD countries demonstrates that consulting or actively involving external stakeholders – such as providers or users of the public services – in the process of drafting code may help to build a common understanding of public service values and expected standards of public employee conduct. External stakeholder involvement could thereby improve the quality of the code so that it meets both public employees' and citizens' expectations, and could thus communicate the values of the public organisation to its stakeholders.

Apart from SEFIR, no other entity has developed a separate, specific code of conduct. SEFIR's code responds to its specificities and provides guidance with respect to expected behaviour. By adopting their own codes of conduct, government entities can respond to specificities of functions that are considered particularly at risk. However, it may be challenging to maintain consistency among a large number of codes within the public administration.

The process over the coming months of elaborating an overarching integrated public integrity management framework opens the opportunity for drafting specific codes of conduct and ethics within the entities in alignment with the principles set by the Code of Conduct and Ethics at the state level. Therefore, SEFIR could consider stipulating that entities have to develop their own codes of conduct based on the existing state Code of Conduct and Ethics. SEFIR should provide clear methodological guidance to assist the entities in developing their own codes, while ensuring that they align with the overarching principles. Such methodological guidance should reduce as much as possible the scope for developing the code as a "check-the-box" exercise, and should include details on how to manage the construction, communication, implementation, and periodic revision of the codes in a participative way.

Coahuila can benefit from the experience at the federal level, where SFP has written a guidance note on how to elaborate a code of conduct. Similarly, in Brazil, the consultation process undertaken for the Comptroller General of the Union's code of conduct raised issues that served as input for the government-wide integrity framework (Box 2.6).

Another key aspect during the drafting process is to ensure that the codes of conduct are drafted in a way that clearly specifies their link to the Law on Responsibilities and possible sanctions for breaches of the provisions. Public officials must be aware of the responsibilities that come along with the Code of Conduct. Sanctions related to the codes should be reported to the Ethics Unit of SEFIR to be analysed, publicised, and to ensure that sanctions are adequate and consistent throughout ministries and entities. Effective control and visible sanctions are crucial in generating credibility. An overview of what characterises successful codes in the private sector, for instance, concludes that blatant impunity of violations of codes can generate cynicism and may lead to a culture of corruption in an organisation (Stevens, 2008).

Box 2.6. **Consultation for an organisation-specific code of conduct in Brazil**

The Professional Code of Conduct for Public Servants of the Office of the Comptroller General of the Union was developed with input from public officials from the Office of the Comptroller General of the Union during a consultation period of one calendar month, between 1 and 30 June 2009. Following inclusion of the recommendations, the Office of the Comptroller General of the Union Ethics Committee issued the code.

In developing the code, a number of recurring comments were submitted. They included:

- the need to clarify the concepts of moral and ethical values: it was felt that the related concepts were too broad in definition and required greater clarification
- the need for a sample list of conflict-of-interest situations to support public officials in their work
- the need to clarify provisions barring officials from administering seminars, courses, and other activities, whether remunerated or not, without the authorisation of the competent official

A number of concerns were also raised concerning procedures for reporting suspected misconduct and the involvement of officials from the Office of the Comptroller General of the Union in external activities. Some officials inquired whether reports of misconduct could be filed without identifying other officials and whether the reporting official's identity would be protected. Concern was also raised over the provision requiring all officials from the Office of the Comptroller General of the Union to be accompanied by another Office of the Comptroller General of the Union official when attending professional gatherings, meetings, or events held by individuals, organisations or associations with an interest in the progress and results of the work of the Office of the Comptroller General of the Union. This concern derived from the difficulty in complying with the requirement given the time constraints on officials and the significant demands of their jobs.

Source: OECD (2012), *Integrity Review of Brazil: Managing Risks for a Cleaner Public Service*, OECD Publishing, Paris, *http://dx.doi.org/10.1787/9789264119321-en.*

SEFIR could develop specific guidelines for at-risk categories of public officials such as senior civil servants, auditors, tax officials, political advisors, and procurement officials.

The role of ensuring clear guidance also encompasses taking into consideration the specific risks associated with the administrative functions and sectors that are most exposed to corruption (see also Chapter 4 on internal control and risk management). While the individual public official is ultimately responsible for recognising the situations in which conflicts may arise, most OECD countries have tried to define those areas that are most at risk and have attempted to provide guidance to prevent and resolve conflict-of-interest situations. Indeed, some public officials operate in sensitive areas with a higher risk for conflict of interest, such as justice, and tax administrations and officials working at the political/administrative interface. Special standards are needed for these sectors. For example, although the areas of activity

While the responsibility to disseminate and promote the code of conduct and ethics lies with each ministry and government entity, the Deputy ministry of Government Auditing and Administrative Development (*Subsecretaría de Auditoría Gubernamental y Desarrollo Administrativo)* within SEFIR has developed the Programme of Ethics and Values. This Programme comprises several initiative aimed at raising awareness not just among the public administration, but also among citizens (Box 2.7):

- Posters displaying values hung up in each ministry and government entity
- Dissemination through the internal network: in SEFIR, for example, a "value of the month" is displayed on employee's computer screens

Awareness-raising aimed at citizens consists of:

- Buttons with the slogan "With ethics and values, better public officials" (*Con Ética y Valores, Funcionarios Mejores)* for officials interacting directly with the public
- Banners with the values and principles as established in the code of conduct and ethics: these are hung up in visible places in each ministry and government entity
- Leaflets with specific information about the values and responsibilities of public officials

Box 2.7. **Coahuila's Programme of Ethics and Values**

The purpose of the State Public Values and Ethics program is to generate and promote a culture of principles and values that will strengthen the way public servants work in the public administration. The Code of Ethics and Conduct of the Public Servants was published in the Official Newspaper of the State in 2013. In addition, the strategy of "wanting, knowing, acting" (*querer, saber y actuar*) was established:

- "wanting": a continuous process of awareness-raising as well as dissemination through the promotion and distribution of banners, buttons, and triptychs
- "knowing" : continuous training on values and ethics
- "acting": revision of the applicable regulations and the implementation of a letter of commitment

Source: Information provided by the government of Coahuila.

However, there is little evidence that generic communication campaigns promote a culture of integrity and raise awareness of the importance of abiding by public service values and ethics in managing conflict-of-interest situations. While the current initiatives are an important first step, Coahuila could strengthen these efforts by making them more targeted. For examples, both the posters and the "value of the month" campaign are limited to the values in the Code of Conduct and Ethics. These initiatives do not provide information on any practical situations. If concrete examples were provided about what a particular value might mean, public officials would be encouraged to think about the value and internalise it. For example, the poster of the Standards of Integrity and Conduct of New Zealand (Figure 2.3), which is displayed to public officials and citizens in public institutions, gives concrete examples about what each value means.

Figure 2.3. **Publication of the Standards of Integrity and Conduct of New Zealand**

STATE SERVICES COMMISSION
Te Kōmihana O Ngā Tari Kāwanatanga

STANDARDS OF
INTEGRITY & CONDUCT

A code of conduct issued by the State Services Commissioner under the State Sector Act 1988, section 57

WE MUST BE FAIR, IMPARTIAL, RESPONSIBLE & TRUSTWORTHY

The State Services is made up of many organisations with powers to carry out the work of New Zealand's democratically elected governments.

Whether we work in a department or in a Crown entity, we must act with a spirit of service to the community and meet the same high standards of integrity and conduct in everything we do.

We must comply with the standards of integrity and conduct set out in this code. As part of complying with this code, our organisations must maintain policies and procedures that are consistent with it.

For further information see www.ssc.govt.nz/code

FAIR

We must:

- treat everyone fairly and with respect
- be professional and responsive
- work to make government services accessible and effective
- strive to make a difference to the well-being of New Zealand and all its people.

IMPARTIAL

We must:

- maintain the political neutrality required to enable us to work with current and future governments
- carry out the functions of our organisation, unaffected by our personal beliefs
- support our organisation to provide robust and unbiased advice
- respect the authority of the government of the day.

RESPONSIBLE

We must:

- act lawfully and objectively
- use our organisation's resources carefully and only for intended purposes
- treat information with care and use it only for proper purposes
- work to improve the performance and efficiency of our organisation.

TRUSTWORTHY

We must:

- be honest
- work to the best of our abilities
- ensure our actions are not affected by our personal interests or relationships
- never misuse our position for personal gain
- decline gifts or benefits that place us under any obligation or perceived influence
- avoid any activities, work or non-work, that may harm the reputation of our organisation or of the State Services.

newzealand.govt.nz

Published June 2007 ISBN: 978-0-478-30309-4

Source: State Service Commission (2007), *Standards of Integrity and Conduct*, available from *www.ssc.govt.nz/sites/all/files/Code-of-conduct-StateServices.pdf*, used under *https://creativecommons.org/licenses/by/3.0/nz/*

Well-formulated advice in the form of questions and answers is also useful and employed in, for example, Germany (Box 2.8).

Box 2.8. **Catalogues of questions and answers in Germany**

An example of a technologically basic but useful tool is the publication "Answers to frequently asked questions about accepting gifts, hospitality or other benefits" published by the Federal Ministry of Interior of Germany. This catalogue of questions and answers was not drafted exclusively by a controlling agency, but by a group of chief compliance officers from large and medium enterprises, federal ministries, and associations. As a result, it reflects not only a top-down imposed interpretation of rules but also a shared understanding between public and private parties. The publication covers:

- **Basic information**: Are federal administration employees allowed to accept gifts? What is meant by gifts, hospitality, and other benefits?
- **Dealing with gifts**: Is approval always required for accepting a gift, even promotional items? What should I do if I am not sure whether it is legal to give or accept a gift?
- **Gifts in kind**: Am I allowed to give a book or professional journal related to the employee's field of expertise?
- **Invitations, hospitality:** Is it possible to invite employees to a buffet meal or snack during or after a specialist event? Is it possible to invite spouses or life partners to events?
- **Paying for travel expenses**: Is it possible for a third party to pay an employee's travel expenses? What should a federal employee do if offered a ride in a taxi or rental car by a business partner?
- **Delegation travel**: What should one be aware of regarding delegation or factory visits? What should be noted when requesting reimbursement for travel expenses for a delegation or factory visit?
- **Private use of discounts**: When can the private use of discounts be approved? When is the private use of discounts prohibited?

Altogether, 52 questions are answered in a concise, easily accessible manner. An index of key terms with up-to-date hyperlinks facilitates the search.

Source: Federal Ministry of the Interior, "Private Sector/Federal Administration Anti-Corruption Initiative – Answers to frequently asked questions about accepting gifts, hospitality, or other benefits", *www.jaunde.diplo.de/contentblob/3809240/Daten/2296502/FragenkatalogKorruption.pdf.*, OECD (2016).

Furthermore, it seems that the current efforts are concentrated within SEFIR and rarely reach the other entities or municipalities. The creation of the Integrity Contact Points (or persons) in the entities and co-ordination with the UEEPCI in SEFIR will help to reach a wider audience. The UEEPCI could encourage the Integrity Contact Points (or persons) to develop specific awareness campaigns for their entities. Coahuila may also wish to issue a cross-departmental awareness campaign akin to that of the UK, where the Civil Service Commission, working in conjunction with the Cabinet Office and a group of Permanent Secretaries, produced a best practice checklist of actions for departments to uphold and promote the Code.

Under the lead of the Ethics Unit in SEFIR, a public integrity training programme could be developed based on the results of the survey on training needs (*Encuesta de Detección de Necesidades de Capacitación*) applied in 2014. A public ethics and conflict-of-interest training when joining the public service could be made mandatory for all public officials, and specific tailored trainings could be provided on an annual basis.

Training on ethics and conflict-of-interest management for public officials is one of the necessary instruments for building integrity in the public sector and ensuring high-quality public governance. Since staff may change over time, institutions must be committed to providing continuous training on applying public ethics and identifying and reacting to conflict-of-interest situations. The *United Nations Convention against Corruption* (UNCAC) requires that the state parties "promote education and training programmes to enable [public officials] to meet the requirements for the correct, honourable and proper performance of public functions and that provide them with specialised and appropriate training to enhance their awareness of the risks of corruption inherent in the performance of their functions" (UNCAC, Article 7 [d]). Similarly, the OECD *Recommendation on Public Integrity* (2017a) recommends offering induction and on-the-job integrity training to raise awareness and equip public officials with the necessary skills to apply public integrity values and standards.

As such, at least one public agency must be responsible for the overall framework for training on conflict-of-interest management and ethics, for central planning, co-ordination, and evaluation of results. In fact, most OECD countries' training modules are developed by a single central entity that also offers guidance on how public employees should apply their codes of conduct, particularly in sensitive situations. For example, in Turkey, the Council of Ethics for Public Officials is the leading institution in the provision of ethics training.

In Coahuila, SEFIR is responsible for the overall framework of training on conflict-of-interest management and co-ordination among the public entities. The state programme of administrative modernisation, audit, and accountability 2011-17 (*Programa Estatal de Modernización Administrativa, Fiscalización y Rendición de Cuentas*) foresees the development of a training programme to promote the professional development of public servants based on a 2014 survey aiming at detecting needs (*Encuesta de Detección de Necesidades de Capacitación*). SEFIR has established a state training programme including a mandatory course on values and ethics of public officials. In 2016, a total of 141 public officials received training on ethics and values, and 68 public officials received a training course on the reform of the conflict of interest policies. To systematise these efforts, the Anti-corruption System, the UEEPCI in co-ordination with central Human Resources Office in the Ministry of Finance, and the Institute for Training could develop a detailed training programme aimed at building the capacities of all public officials in the area of public integrity similar to the training programme on ethics in Brazil (Box 2.9). This could be part of the State Capacity Programme and should take into account the diagnostic resulting from the needs detection survey.

An induction training on public ethics and conflict of interest should be made mandatory. Such induction trainings are a valuable opportunity to set the tone with respect to integrity from the beginning of the working relationship. They provide an opportunity to explain principles, values, and the rules related to public ethics and conflict of interest. The most basic and generic parts of such a training could be implemented through e-learning modules, while a more targeted training aimed at recognising and managing conflicts of interest and resolving ethical dilemmas specific to situations commonly encountered in their area of work could be in-person training (Box 2.10).

Box 2.9. **Brazil's training programme on ethics**

In 2010, the Public Ethics Commission and the Office of the Comptroller General of the Union developed a management training and development course to support public officials on standards of conduct. The 40-hour course is organised in five modules, and its contents are based on Public Ethics Commission resolutions and other guidance materials. Satisfactory completion of this course has been proposed as a criterion for career progression. The modules offered in the course cover the following topics:

- Principles of ethics: key concepts, prevailing values and standards, their inter-relation and functions
- Principles of policy and public service: key concepts of public life and fundamental values of the Brazilian federal public administration
- Ethics management in the federal public administration: norms applicable to the federal public administration and governmental actors with responsibility for encouraging public ethics
- Ethics management in the federal public administration: exploring the code of professional ethics for the federal public administration
- Addressing ethical dilemmas: identifying dilemmas, ethical guidance and filing complaints, attributes and routines to reinforce ethics in the federal public administration

Sources: OECD (2012), *OECD Integrity Review of Brazil: Managing Risks for a Cleaner Public Service*, OECD Public Governance Reviews, OECD Publishing, Paris, p. 251, *http://dx.doi.org/10.1787/9789264119321-en*; OECD (2014), "Renforcer l'Intégrité en Tunisie : L'Élaboration de Normes pour les Agents Publics et le Renforcement du Système de Déclaration de Patrimoine", OECD, Paris, *www.oecd.org/mena/governance/Renforcer-* Intégrité-Tunisie-Élaboration-Normes-Agents-Publics.pdf.

Box 2.10. **Dilemma training in the Flemish Government (Belgium)**

In the Dilemma training offered by the Agency for Government Employees, public officials are given practical situations in which they face a difficult ethical choice. The facilitator encourages discussion among the participants about how the situation could be resolved to explore the different choices. As such, it is the debate, and not the solution, which is most important. Over the course of the debate, participants will learn to identify different, potentially conflicting values.

In most trainings, the facilitator uses a card system. He explains the rules and participants receive four "option cards" printed with the numbers 1, 2, 3, and 4. A stack of "dilemma cards" is placed on the table. The "dilemma cards" describe situations and propose four options for resolving them. In each round, one of the participants reads out the dilemma and options. Each participant indicates their choice by holding up the "option card" with the corresponding number and explains the choice. Following this, participants discuss the choices. The facilitator remains neutral, encourages the debate, and suggests alternative options on how to look at the dilemma (e.g. sequence of events, boundaries for unacceptable behaviour).

One example of a dilemma situation is as follows:

I am a policy officer. The minister needs a briefing within the next hour. I have been working on this matter for the last two weeks and should already be finished. However, the information is not complete. I am still waiting for a contribution from another department to verify the data. My boss asks me to submit the briefing urgently because the chief of cabinet has called. What should I do?

Box 2.10. **Dilemma training in the Flemish Government (Belgium)** *(cont.)*

1. I send the briefing and do not mention the missing information.
2. I send the briefing, but mention that no decisions should be made based on it.
3. I do not send the briefing. If anyone asks about it, I will blame the other department.
4. I do not send the briefing. I provide an excuse for its tardiness and promise that I will send it tomorrow.

Other dilemma situations could cover the themes such as conflicts of interest, ethics, loyalty, and leadership. The trainings and situations used can be targeted to specific groups or entities. For example:

You are working in Internal Control and are asked to be a guest lecturer in a training programme organised by the employers of a sector that is within your realm of responsibility. You will be well paid, make some meaningful contacts, and learn from the experience.

Source: Website of the Flemish Government, Omgaan met integriteitsdilemma's, available from *https://overheid.vlaanderen.be/omgaan-met-integriteitsdilemmas* (in Dutch).

Beyond the induction training, efforts should be undertaken to provide continuous training for high-level public officials. For example, in Catalonia, training participants have to develop their own integrity action plan. In this plan, each participant identifies integrity risks and challenges in their individual workplaces. During the follow-up trainings, participants discuss the implementation of their personal plan. They also discuss barriers that have been identified in implementing the actions proposed in their individual action plan, and provide support and share ideas about solutions.

Another tool would be to offer annual courses for public officials in which they can gain new integrity skills. Senior public officials in management positions or HR officers in each public entity could attend these courses. They could also be trained in disseminating conflict-of-interest policies in the organisation. Indeed, given the importance of high positions with leadership functions in promoting and ensuring a high level of integrity, many OECD countries rely on senior civil servants both in terms of individual development and in terms of special management rules, processes, and systems to provide guidance. Such guidances comes in the form of advice and counsel to lower-ranking public servants about how to resolve dilemmas at work and potential conflicts of interest. Senior civil servants embody and transmit core public service values, set the example in terms of performance and probity, and communicate the importance of these elements as a means of safeguarding public sector integrity.

Training and education may range from value-oriented to rules-based and dilemma type programmes in order to help public officials fully grasp the entire code of ethics. Senior management could attend each training programme in order to better lead by example and to offer constant guidance to staff on how to apply the code on a day-to-day basis. The training programme should also take into account the specificities of high-risk areas such as those encountered by auditors or public procurement officials (for further information see Chapter 6).

In addition, anticipating the new integrity framework that will be implemented through the local anti- corruption system, specific courses could be developed to present the recent and new provisions and tools. This could be done via an e-learning course that would be more accessible to public officials, given that physical attendance would not be required.

The impact of the existing Network of Trainers (Red Estatal de Instructores) could be amplified by formalising the network and building a pool of trainers in each ministry. As a form of recognition for their efforts, trainers could receive a formal qualification and/or remuneration.

With guidance from the UEEPCI, Coahuila could promote organisation-specific induction trainings related to the codes of conduct of the different entities. Such organisation-specific trainings could build upon more generic guidance and tools while making these more context-specific by introducing examples and cases related to the sector and the specific public services provided by the entity.

A Network of Trainers (*Red Estatal de Instructores*) has been created in which instructors are selected from each ministry to deliver specific trainings. This is a very positive step which could be strengthened. The network could be leveraged to implement tailored training programmes for entities and public officials in positions that represent a high risk of corruption. These specific trainings should be part of the induction trainings for new employees and the specific training throughout public servants' career. In this way, the network could be similar to an initiative in Estonia where the Ministry of Finance co-ordinates a horizontal "Central Training Programme" and is responsible for commissioning various training programmes such as the induction programme and the general programmes on civil service and public ethics.

In interviews with stakeholders, it was confirmed that due to the existing state of the network, the Network of Trainers would not be able to fulfil this function. The training activities provided are not formally recognised, and trainers need to give the courses in their spare time. As such, Coahuila could consider providing formal public integrity trainer certification courses to interested public servants. These certification courses could be held by the UEEPCI in collaboration with human resources departments. If each trainer were certified, the quality of the courses could therefore be improved. Furthermore, the additional certification could be an incentive for potential candidates. Once certified, trainers could be granted an allocated time per year during which they could hold training courses in their entities. Coahuila could consider giving the trainers a small remuneration or recognition for their efforts. Managers could encourage certain public servants to participate in the certification course if they perceive them to be good potential trainers.

The future Ethics Unit in SEFIR and Integrity Contact Points (or persons) in the entities could also consider raising awareness of the conceptual overlap of managing a conflict-of-interest situation on an ad-hoc basis and the annual asset declaration.

Interviews revealed some confusion amongst public officials concerning asset declarations and conflict-of-interest management. Clarifying the conceptual overlap between the procedures for ad hoc disclosure of actual conflict-of-interest situations under the policy guidance of the Ethics Unit in SEFIR and the annual declaration of assets is important. It needs to be clearly communicated that submitting the declaration does not relieve the public official from proactively declaring any potential or actual conflict-of-interest on an ad-hoc basis to their superiors or the Integrity Contact Points (or persons). These efforts could be embedded in the existing awareness internal and external campaign on the disclosure system (web portal, social media, emails, newsletter, video tutorials, and thematic chats).

Strengthening the asset disclosure system

Adapting state regulations to the General Law on Administrative Responsibilities will entail modifications of the current asset disclosure system and will require all public officials to submit an asset declaration. Narrowing down the circle of public officials required to submit an asset declaration to those in senior positions and those representing a high corruption risk would ensure that no culture of distrust is created and improve the system's cost-effectiveness.

The General Law on Administrative Responsibilities (LGRA) contains provisions related to the disclosure of both financial and non-financial interests. It requires that all public officials submit three types of disclosure forms: tax, assets, and interests (OECD, 2017b). Assuming that the asset disclosure system will adopt the same level of details as the federal level, the type of information requested from public officials in Coahuila, along with the subsequent levels of transparency, is generally in line with the information request in other OECD countries. For comparison purposes, Box 2.11 provides a summary of common information requirements in OECD member and partner countries.

Box 2.11. **Common financial and non-financial disclosures in OECD countries**

Generally, the following types of information are required to be disclosed in OECD member and partner countries. These can include financial and non-financial interests:

Financial interests

Reporting of financial interests facilitates the monitoring of wealth accumulation over time and the detection of illicit enrichment. Financial information can also help to identify conflict of interest situations.

- **Income**: Officials in OECD countries are commonly asked to report income amounts as well as the source and type (i.e. salaries, fees, interest, dividends, revenue from sale or lease of property, inheritance, hospitalities, travel paid, etc.). The exact requirements of income reporting may vary and moreover public officials may only be required to report income above a certain threshold. The rationale for disclosing income is to indicate potential sources of undue influence (i.e. such as from outside employment) as well as to monitor over time increases in income that could stem from illicit enrichment. In countries where public officials' salaries are low, this is of particular concern.
- **Gifts**: Gifts can be considered a type of income or asset, however, since they are generally minor in value, countries generally only require reporting gifts above a certain threshold, although there are exceptions.
- **Assets**: A wide variety of assets are subject to declaration across OECD countries including savings, shareholdings and other securities, property, real estate, savings, vehicles/vessels, valuable antiques and art. Reporting of assets permits for comparison with income data in order to assess whether changes in wealth are due to declared legitimate income. However, accurately reporting on the value of assets can be a challenge in some circumstances and difficult to validate. Furthermore, some countries make the distinction between owned assets and those in use (i.e. such as a house or lodging that has been loaned but is not owned).
- **Other financial interests**: In addition to income, gifts and assets, other financial interests to declare often include debts, loans, guarantees, insurances, agreements which may result in future income, and pension schemes. When such interests amount to significant values, they can potentially lead to conflict-of-interest situations.

Box 2.11. **Common financial and non-financial disclosures in OECD countries** *(cont.)*

Non-financial interests

While monitoring non-financial interests may not contribute to monitoring for illicit enrichment, they can nonetheless also lead to conflict-of-interest situations. As such, many countries request disclosure of:

- **Previous employment**: Relationships or information acquired from past employment could unduly influence public officials' duties in their current post. For instance, if the officials' past firm applied to a public procurement tender where the public official had a say in the process, his or her past position could be considered a conflict of interest.
- **Current non-remunerated positions**: Board or foundation membership or active membership in political party activities could similarly affect public officials' duties. Even voluntary work could be considered to influence duties in certain situations.

Source: OECD (2011), *Asset Declarations for Public Officials: A Tool to Prevent Corruption*, OECD Publishing, Paris. *http://dx.doi.org/10.1787/9789264095281-en*.

The current scope of coverage and transparency is considerably lower. The scope of coverage will increase to all levels of government and to public officials in all three branches of government. The coverage will also increase by requiring information of officials' immediate family members. In addition, the extent of transparency will increase. Publication is currently voluntary and remains at the discretion of the public official (OECD, 2017b).

These changes can strengthen public trust in government by clearly showing its commitment to transparency and by offering a tool with which to enable social accountability, given that citizens could analyse public officials' decisions in the light of the declared assets and relations (OECD, 2017b). Indeed there has been some recent empirical cross-country evidence showing that the expansion of financial disclosure systems positively and significantly affect a country's capacity to control for corruption in the years following the expansion (Vargas et al., 2016).

However, it could be argued that the reporting requirements should take into account varying levels of public officials and should adopt a risk-based approach. The first argument in favour of these two evolutions is that elected officials are expected to be more transparent so that citizens may make informed choices when voting in elections. Furthermore, once elected, such information may be necessary to assess any interests which may influence parliamentarians' arguments or voting decisions in Congress. It could also be argued that, given their decision-making powers, elected officials and senior civil servants are more influential and are at greater risk for capture or corruption. In addition, a blanket requirement for all public officials can have potentially detrimental effects on the morale of some public servants. For instance, some officials could interpret this requirement as creating an organisational culture whereby public servants are presumed to be corrupt. As such, the law may inadvertently increase the incentive for omissions and false information, and may reduce the attractiveness of working in the public sector, making it more difficult for government to recruit or retain top talent (OECD, 2017b).

Furthermore, despite the use of an electronic platform, the universal requirement to file an asset and interest declaration may overburden the bodies responsible for receiving and screening the disclosures, detecting irregularities, and fulfilling other activities related to their mandate if such tasks are not accompanied by appropriate human and financial resources.

To ensure an effective process, Coahuila could consider narrowing down the size of the disclosure population by applying common criteria used in other countries to determine who should declare (see Box 2.12 on the mandatory asset declaration for selected officials in Argentina), such as:

- branch of government
- hierarchy (for example, all officials at the director level and above)
- position (minister, deputy minister, director,etc.)
- function (administrative decision making, granting contracts, public procurement, tax inspection, etc.)
- risk of corruption: identifying filers based upon their role and the risk they could become involved in corrupt activity (building licenses, infrastructure contracts, customs, etc.) (World Bank, 2017)
- categorisation as a Politically Exposed Person (PEP) according to the Financial Action Task Force on Money Laundering

Box 2.12. **Mandatory asset declaration for selected officials in Argentina**

The government agency in charge of managing the Argentinian Assets Declaration System is the Anti-corruption Office under the Ministry of Justice and Human Rights, in co-ordination with the Federal Administration of Public Revenues Agency. The asset disclosure system in Argentina does not require all public officials to declare their assets. Individuals who are obligated to present their asset declarations are:

- hierarchical level: from the President to the officials with a position of National Director or equivalent
- nature of their function: those who, beyond the rank, are public officials or employees members of procurement commissions or are responsible for granting administrative authorisations for the exercise of any activity or controlling their operation. Also, those who control public revenues should present their asset declaration.
- candidates to national elective positions

These public officials have to present their declarations in three situations: 1) within 30 days of having started their public functions, 2) annually, and 3) after leaving the position. By June 2016, there were 48 494 obligations to present Asset Declarations.

Source: Government of Argentina, Presentar Declaración Jurada para funcionarios públicos, *www.argentina.gob.ar/presentardeclaracionjurada* (in Spanish).

The disclosure could be mandatory for those officials in high positions, those in functions with high risks of corruption, for instance based on the risk assessments carried out by public entities (Chapter 4), and those classified as PEP.

To effectively detect illicit enrichment, a systematic verification and audit process should be established. The electronic submission system could be leveraged by integrating the automatic verification of submission and automatic detection of "red flags".

It is essential to establish a system of oversight to provide monitoring and enforcement. Indeed, the effectiveness of the disclosure regime depends on the system's ability to detect

Box 2.13. **The High Authority for Transparency in Public Life of France** *(cont.)*

Verification and audit process

For members of the government and parliamentarians

For all other declarants

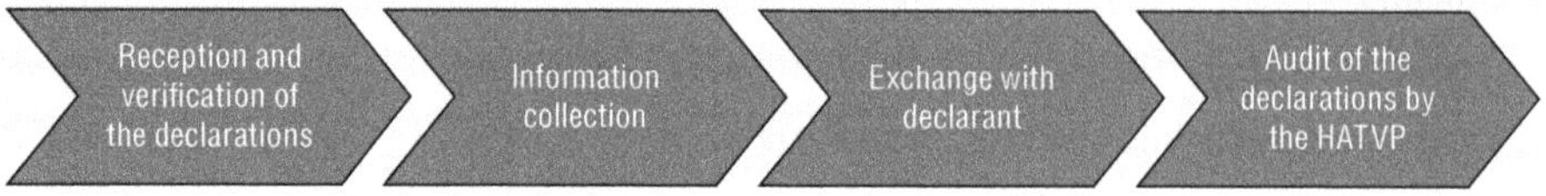

Source: Based on information provided by the French *Haute Autorité pour la Transparence de la Vie Publique*, HATVP.

- ***Simple verifications on a risk-based basis.*** Many simple verifications may also be programmed automatically, though at a later stage may require the intervention of a qualified investigator/auditor. As such, a lower number of declarations may be submitted to simple verification checks and a risk-based approach could be considered. The Co-ordination Committee should therefore conduct a risk assessment which could consider the following:
  - *Definition of high-risk positions*: public procurement officials, tax officials, officials in charge of granting or extending licences, permits, authorisations, concessions, and financial authorities can be considered at greater risk for conflict of interest. As mentioned earlier, senior civil servants and elected officials could also be at high risk. The Co-ordination Committee may wish to establish a defined list of high-risk positons for internal control bodies.
  - *Analysis of complaints from citizens and other officials*: both the Co-ordination Committee and internal control bodies may wish to assess and study complaints received in order to identify departments, sectors, regions, and officials at high risk that could warrant verification checks.
  - *Risks identified from the declarations themselves*: the Co-ordination Committee may wish to establish automatic verification checks for declarations which present certain trends such as late submissions, increases in wealth, major outside interests, inconsistencies between declarations, etc. ICT systems can be programmed to automatically detect "red flags" such as these and can be pre-programmed by internal control bodies.

Full-fledged audits should also be conducted on risk-based basis following simple or basic verifications.

Coahuila could co-ordinate with other State Comptrollers' Offices through the National Permanent Commission of State-Federation Comptrollers (Comisión Permanente de Contralores Estados-Federación, CPCE-F) and the National Conference of Governors (Conferencia Nacional de Gobernadores, CONAGO) to establish agreements with other agencies to cross-check databases.

Ensuring an effective verification and audit process depends on the availability of information from other sources, such as property registry, vehicle registry, company registry, financial intelligence units, and the tax administration. For example, information from financial institutions can help verify whether bank accounts have been truthfully disclosed (Rossi et al., 2017). Currently, SEFIR (or any other state comptroller) does not have the legal right to obtain information from financial institutions and tax administrations during the verification process. However, internal control bodies may need access to payroll information, as well as information from financial/banking institutions and tax authorities to verify the declared information. Therefore, Coahuila could consider the value of interagency co-operation to strengthen the verification process. For example, in France, the High Authority for Transparency in Public Life (*Haute Autorité pour la Transparence de la Vie Publique*, HATVP) can ask financial authorities to analyse an asset declaration. The tax administration must thereupon provide the necessary information for the HATVP to verify the asset declaration in question (Box 22). In the case of Coahuila, it will be critical to establish information-sharing agreements with entities both within and outside of government. In Coahuila, Memoranda of Understanding among the State Comptrollers' Offices and agencies, such as financial and banking institutions and tax authorities, could be established through the National Permanent Commission of State-Federation Comptrollers (*Comisión Permanente de Contralores Estados-Federación*, CPCE-F) and the National Conference of Governors (*Conferencia Nacional de Gobernadores*, CONAGO), in order to clarify the process of requesting and accessing information and for ensuring that information can be cross-checked.

Ensuring effective monitoring and evaluation

By designing tools and processes, including surveys, reviews of the guidance provided on the code, and statistical data on the disciplinary sanctions, effective monitoring and evaluation could be facilitated.

To determine whether the public integrity framework promotes the high standards of conduct within the public service that will ultimately lead to the creation of a culture of integrity, its implementation should be monitored. If it does not promote high standards, further guidelines may be drawn up to clarify the values and standards of conduct that the code lays down.

Active monitoring can entail specific initiatives to (OECD, 2011b):

- count and analyse violations of the Code (e.g. analysis of disciplinary actions) and trends thereof
- measure the awareness of civil servants (e.g. with the help of opinion surveys, including after training events)
- measure the opinion of clients of civil servants – usually also with the help of opinion surveys

In Coahuila, Article 37 of the Organic Law of the Public Administration of the State of Coahuila de Zaragoza stipulates that SEFIR is responsible for the evaluation of the public administration. SEFIR carries out a perception survey among the public evaluating each value established in the Code of Ethics and Conduct. The survey is conducted in those entities that have the most interaction with citizens. In 2015, 2 602 citizens responded to the survey of which 2 183 were exit surveys in public service offices and 419 were general public surveys. Overall, respondents answered positively, highlighting public officials' commitment to the values of respect, honesty, impartiality, loyalty to the institution, honour, and transparency.

Box 2.14. **Monitoring the implementation of the Code of Ethics in Poland**

A survey known as the monitoring of "Ordinance no. 70 of the Prime Minister dated 6 October 2011 on the guidelines for compliance with the rules of the civil service and on the principles of the civil service code of ethics" was commissioned by the Head of the Civil Service (HCS) in 2014. The HCS is the central government administration body in charge of civil service issues under the Chancellery of the Prime Minister.

The survey was given to three groups of respondents:

1. Members of the civil service corps

In this case the survey pertained, on the one hand, to the degree of implementation of the ordinance in their respective offices and, on the other hand, to their subjective assessment of the functioning and effectiveness of the ordinance. The members of the civil service corps were asked to complete a survey containing 16 questions (most framed as closed questions, with a few allowing for comments). The questions pertained to the following issues, among others:

- knowledge of the principles enumerated in the Ordinance
- impact of the entry into force of the Ordinance on changes in the civil service
- the need/advisability of expanding the list through the addition of new rules
- comprehensibility/clarity of the guidelines and principles laid down in the Ordinance
- the usefulness of the Ordinance for the purposes of solving professional dilemmas

In addition, the correct understanding of the principle of "selflessness" and "dignified conduct" as well as the need to provide training in the field of compliance were also assessed. The surveys were available on the website of the civil service department. The respondents were asked to respond and submit the survey electronically to a dedicated e-mail address.

2. Director Generals, directors of treasury offices, and directors of tax audit offices

In this case the survey was intended to verify the scope and manner of implementation of tasks which they were under duty to perform according to the provisions of the ordinance, including, for example:

- the manner in which compliance with the rules in the given office is ensured
- information on whether the applicable principles were complied with when adopting decisions authorising members of the civil service corps to undertake additional employment or authorising a civil service employee occupying a higher position within the civil service to undertake income-generating activities
- the manner in which the principles in question are taken into account in the human resources management programmes being developed
- the manner in which the relevant principles were taken into account in the course of determination of the scope of the preparatory service stage

3. Independent experts – public administration theorists and practitioners

In this case the survey was intended to obtain an additional, independent specialist evaluation of the functioning of ethical regulations within the civil service, to obtain suggestions on the ethical principles applicable to civil service, and to identify the aspects of the management process which may need to be supplemented or updated, clarified, or emphasised to a greater extent or even corrected or elaborated upon.

The response rate differed across the three groups. The HCS received 1 291 surveys completed by members of the civil service corps (the number of surveys completed represents approximately 1% of all civil service corps members), 107 surveys dedicated to the directors (that is, 100% of all directors generals, directors of treasury offices, and directors of tax audit offices (98 in total). Other surveys, filled in on a voluntary basis by the head of the tax offices, and seven replies from independent experts, or approximately 13% of all experts invited to the study, were also received. Given that this survey was the first such an exercise conducted on a large scale, information gathered could be used in further developing the integrity policy in the Polish civil service system.

Source: Adopted from the presentation by the Polish Chancellery of the Prime Minister at the OECD workshop in Bratislava in 2015.

Additionally, internal control units carry out a survey measuring the organisational climate. Each survey is designed by the entities themselves and information is not compared across entities. The survey contains questions related to ethics and the Code of Conduct. Measuring how familiar the public officials are with the Code of Ethics and Conduct in the Public Administration can suggest the degree of implementation of the code and internalisation of values in particular public office. For example, Poland monitors the implementation of the Code of Ethics through an employee survey (Box 2.14). While Coahuila conducts a survey on public ethics, the points outlined by the Polish example suggests a more expansive survey on public ethics implementation and efficiency across the public administration. In addition, SEFIR could elaborate a single survey for all entities which would allow for ranking entities and could create an incentive for improvement.

While perception surveys can indicate how well the values and principles are established within the public sector, they provide subjective evidence and are not necessarily based on direct experiences. Individuals are susceptible to conform to a majority opinion which may – or may not – be based on objective evidence or direct experiences and may be positively or negatively influenced by recent news. Also, surveying citizens does not depict adequately how familiar public officials are with the code of ethics and conduct and whether it promotes high standards within the public service.

In addition, Coahuila has not developed any evaluation of the effectiveness of its awareness-raising activities or training measures to promote ethical behaviour. To strengthen the integrity system and adopt appropriate measures, Coahuila could consider assessing the current situation through evaluations on which basis improvements could be made. Specifically, Coahuila could consider:

- monitoring the implementation of the Code of Ethics and Conduct through diagnostic tools such as surveys within the public administration and statistical data (see Box 2.14)
- assessing public officials' knowledge of the Code of Ethics and Conduct to determine the effectiveness of training and awareness-raising measures and to determine if further guidance is necessary
- consulting public officials on the provisions of the Code of Ethics and Conduct to assess its practicality
- reviewing how government entities provide guidance on the Code of Ethics and Conduct
- evaluating the training framework

To enable the monitoring and evaluation of the implementation of the Code of Conduct and Ethics and the Law of Responsibilities and to publish annual progress reports, clear and transparent indicators need to be developed.

At an organisational level and with respect to the Code of Conduct and Ethics itself, the monitoring exercises could be overseen by the UEEPCI, while the State Audit Institution (*Auditoría Superior del Estado de Coahuila*, ASEC) could generate the results of its annual reports and findings regarding disciplinary measures and reported disclosures. In turn, these findings and data could be compiled by SEFIR, which could assume the responsibility of generating clear and transparent indicators from which this monitoring process could evolve. Indicators could be collected and updated on a regular basis (e.g. quarterly).

To monitor and evaluate the implementation of the Code of Conduct and Ethics and the Law on Responsibilities, clear and transparent indicators would need to be developed (Box 2.15). The OECD recommends that the majority of indicators should have quantitative targets. Exactly how many and how resource-consuming indicators should be used depends on a balance between the need to measure progress on the one hand and the ability to devote resources for producing the data on the other hand. There is no single right set of indicators; SEFIR and other stakeholders should weigh needs versus possibilities and thus come to an appropriate judgment.

Box 2.15. **What makes good performance indicators**

Below is a list of recommendations regarding performance indicators based on a review of typical flaws found in the anti-corruption plans of different countries.

Indicators should be measurable:

- The indicator "media is better informed about a code of conduct" is not recommended because it itself needs an indicator. How does one know when something is better? Instead, the indicator should cite the number of publications that mention the code, because such specific information is measurable.

Indicators should be clear:

- The indicator "the ratio of cases related to the declaration of the property, income and interests considered by the Commission to the total number of cases considered" is unclear because it does not specify whether a higher or lower ratio shall count as an achievement.

Indicators should add meaning:

- The indicator "in accordance with the established procedure, carry out inspections of compliance" does not explain what is to be achieved. Instead, indicators should express expected results: the number of inspections, consequences such as rotation of officials following the inspections, number of proposed preventive measures based on the results of inspections, improved performance of the inspected institutions.

Link between goal and indicator:

- If the activity is an improvement of regulations related to the public officials' disciplinary responsibility, the indicator should not be the number of elaborated standards, instructions or legislative proposals. The indicator should rather focus on the improvement. For example, the indicator could focus us fuller coverage of typical wrongdoings by definitions of disciplinary violations.

Where possible, indicators should measure outcomes rather than just activities:

- If the task is to improve the system of filing complaints on administrative decisions, then training on handling complaints in itself is not a guarantee for better handling of complaints. The number of incomplete reviews of complaints (e.g. based on data from higher appeal instances) could be a better indicator.

Simplistic indicators may overshadow practice:

- Yes/no indicators are to be avoided. For example, a yes/no indicator on the availability of information in reception rooms about patient rights to receive state-funded health care should rather reflect degrees such as the percentage of reception rooms with displayed information or completeness of the information.

Quantitative indicators cannot express full essence of the matter:

- Qualitative analysis of case law in conflict-of-interest matters can be more telling than the sheer number of punished officials.

Box 2.15. **What makes good performance indicators** *(cont.)*

Danger of adverse incentives:

- If an institution that receives fewer complaints is entitled to a serious advantage, there is a risk that officials may discourage submitting complaints by persuasion, that they may conceal information about complaint procedures, or may even use intimidation. Paradoxically, expectation of total compliance may be an adverse incentive. For example, it should be generally acceptable for an institution to admit that it has managed to review only 90% of applications in due time. Otherwise, there is an incentive to avoid accurate reporting at all costs.
- Use multiple indicators for very important tasks but do not try to measure everything. Measuring spent resources and choice of measurements can be a legitimate way of reflecting the level of priority of activities.

Source: Kalnins, V. (2011), "Improving the designing of anti-corruption policies", Presentation at the Regional Workshop, 4 November, Strasbourg, OECD (2016), *The Implementation of the Palestinian Code of Conduct: Strengthening Ethics and Contributing to Institution-Building*, OECD Publishing, Paris. *http://dx.doi.org/10.1787/9789264256934-en.*

In addition, following these reviews and data gathering exercises, Coahuila could consider implementing, once amended, monitoring and evaluation of the implementation of the Law on Responsibilities. An annual report on the implementation and effectiveness of public ethics measures could help ensure that evaluation efforts are taken seriously and acted upon. The reports could be used by the Co-ordination Committee to discuss progress and amend the public integrity policy framework if necessary.

To monitor and evaluate the effectiveness of the asset declaration system, SEFIR could conduct a survey among the declarants and Internal Control Units to ensure user-friendliness and relevance of the requested information. Annual reports could be published to reassure the public of the effectiveness of the system.

Due to the fact that the disclosure system should take Coahuila's specific context and specific corruption risks into account, the disclosure system will need regular assessment and fine-tuning (World Bank, 2017). SEFIR could regularly review the disclosure system and the effectiveness of its implementation. This could be in the form of a survey, both of the declarants and the Internal Control Offices. Declarants could be surveyed on user-friendliness, such as ease of declaring information correctly or whether the system is perceived to be burdensome. The Internal Control Units should be consulted on a regular basis to ensure that the information gathered allows monitoring variations of wealth effectively and can help identify conflict-of-interest situations. In this way, the principles of user friendliness and relevance could be assessed.

SEFIR could also consider reporting annually on the effectiveness of the disclosure system by publishing statistics on complaints received, media reports, cases notified by other authorities, cases referred, cases with data being corrected, verification checks and audits, sanctions, open and closed investigations, and data on court decisions. The information on administered sanctions should differentiate between those sanctions for late or no submission and those for illicit enrichment. Similarly, the financial and human resources costs should be compiled to evaluate the cost-effectiveness of the system.

Proposals for Action

To conclude, this chapter recommends that Coahuila take the following actions to strengthen its integrity framework for the public administration.

Building a legal and policy framework for public ethics and conflict of interest to ensure coherence throughout the administration

- Following the model of the federal government, Coahuila could establish an ethics unit within SEFIR to harmonise existing policies across the administration. The ethics unit should have a counselling and guidance role.
- To ensure an effective implementation of integrity policies throughout the public administration, Coahuila could consider establishing Integrity Contact Points (or persons) within each public entity. The Integrity Contact Points should be responsible for public ethics and not for investigating breaches of integrity.
- The co-ordination agreement on collaboration on transparency and the fight against corruption between Coahuila and the federal Ministry of Public Function (SFP) could benefit from expertise on the federal level and could harmonise policies.

Harmonising the Law of Responsibilities of Coahuila

- The public integrity management framework could benefit from a more streamlined, duplication-free Code of Ethics and Conduct. Under the guidance of the Ethics Unit, Coahuila could consider the elaboration of manuals or guidance on practical examples and procedures for conflict-of-interest situations and ethical dilemmas.
- A common overarching integrity management framework opens the opportunity to elaborate codes of conduct on the organisational level in a participative way, and implementing them more effectively.
- SEFIR could develop specific guidelines for at-risk categories of public officials such as senior civil servants, auditors, tax officials, political advisors, and procurement officials.

Raising awareness and providing trainings

- A cross-departmental public ethics awareness campaign could be implemented as a shared and co-ordinated activity between the ethics unit, the Integrity Contact Points (or persons) and the human resources departments, including reaching out to the private sector, civil society, and citizens.
- Under the lead of the SEFIR Ethics Unit, a public integrity training programme could be developed based on the results of the survey on training needs (*Encuesta de Detección de Necesidades de Capacitación*) applied in 2014. A public ethics and conflict-of-interest training when joining the public service could be made mandatory for all public officials, while specific tailored trainings could be provided on an annual basis.
- The impact of the existing Network of Trainers (*Red Estatal de Instructores*) could be amplified by formalising the network and building a pool of trainers in each ministry. As a form of recognition for their efforts, trainers could receive a formal qualification and/or remuneration.
- The future Ethics Unit in SEFIR and Integrity Contact Points (or persons) in the entities could also consider to raise awareness of the conceptual overlap of managing a conflict-of-interest situation on an ad-hoc basis and the annual asset declaration.

Strengthening the asset disclosure system

- Adapting state regulations to the General Law on Administrative Responsibilities will entail modifications of the current asset disclosure system and will require all public officials to submit an asset declaration. Narrowing down the circle of public officials required to submit an asset declaration to those in senior positions and those representing a high corruption risk would ensure that no culture of distrust is created and would improve the system's cost-effectiveness.

- To detect illicit enrichment effectively, a systematic verification and audit process should be established. The electronic submission system could be leveraged by integrating the automatic verification of submission and automatic detection of "red flags".
- Coahuila could co-ordinate with other State Comptrollers' Offices through the National Permanent Commission of State-Federation Comptrollers (*Comisión Permanente de Contralores Estados-Federación*, CPCE-F) and the National Conference of Governors (*Conferencia Nacional de Gobernadores*, CONAGO) to establish agreements with other agencies to cross-check databases.

Ensuring effective monitoring and evaluation

- By designing tools and processes, including surveys, reviews of the guidance provided on the code and statistical data on the disciplinary sanctions, effective monitoring and evaluation could be facilitated.
- To enable the monitoring and evaluation of the implementation of the Code of Conduct and Ethics and the Law of Responsibilities and to publish annual progress reports, clear and transparent indicators need to developed.
- To monitor and evaluate the effectiveness of the asset declaration system, SEFIR could conduct a survey among the declarants and Internal Control Units to ensure user-friendliness and relevance of the requested information. Annual reports could be published to reassure the public of the effectiveness of the system.

References

Boehm, F., Isaza, C. and Villalba Díaz, M. (2015), "Análisis experimental de la corrupción y de las medidas anticorrupción. ¿Dónde estamos, hacia dónde vamos?" *Revista OPERA*, 17, 105-126.

Falk, A. & Kosfeld, M. (2006), "The Hidden Costs of Control", *The American Economic Review*, 96(5), 1611-1630.

Charness, G. & Sutter, M.(2012), "Groups Make Better Self-Interested Decisions", *Journal of Economic Perspectives*, 26(3):157–76

Anechiarico, F. & Jacobs, J.B. (1996), *The Pursuit of Absolute Integrity. How corruption control makes government ineffective*, University of Chicago Press.

Ariely, D. (2012), *The (honest) truth about dishonesty: How we lie to everyone–especially ourselves*, New York: Harper.

Camerer, C. (2003), *Behavioral Game Theory: Experiments in Strategic Interaction*, Princeton: Princeton University Press.

Fischbacher, U. & Föllmi-Heusi, F. (2012), „Lies in Disguise. An experimental study on cheating", Research Paper Series Thurgau Institute of Economics and Department of Economics no. 40, Konstanz: University of Konstanz.

Gino, F. & Bazerman, M. H. (2009), "When misconduct goes unnoticed: The acceptability of gradual erosion in others' unethical behaviour", *Journal of Experimental Social Psychology*, 45 (4), 708-719.

Gino, F., Ayal, S., and Ariely, D. (2009), "Contagion and Differentiation in Unethical Behavior", *Psychological Science*, 20 (3), 393-398

Kalnins, V. (2011), "Improving the designing of anti-corruption policies", Presentation at the Regional Workshop, 4 November, Strasbourg, OECD (2016), *The Implementation of the Palestinian Code of Conduct: Strengthening Ethics and Contributing to Institution-Building*, OECD Publishing, Paris, *http://dx.doi.org/10.1787/9789264256934-en*

Lambsdorff, J. (2015), "Preventing Corruption by Promoting Trust – Insights from Behavioral Science", University of Passau, Diskussionsbeitrag Nr. V - 69 – 15.

Lambsdorff, J. (2012), "Behavioral and Experimental Economics as a Guidance to Anti-corruption", In Serra, D. & Wantchekon, L., *New Advances in Experimental Research on Corruption Research in Experimental Economics*, Volume 15, Emerald Group Publishing Limited.

Liljenquist, K.,Chen-Bo Zhong, C-B., and Galinsky, A. D. (2010), "The Smell of Virtue: Clean Scents Promote Reciprocity and Charity", *Psychological Science*, 21 (3), 381-383

OECD (2009), "Towards a Sound Integrity Framework: Instruments, Processes, Structures and Conditions for Implementation", Global Forum on Public Governance, 4-5 May, Public Governance and Territorial Development Directorate, Public Governance Committee, GOV/PGC/GF(2009)1

OECD (2011), *Asset Declarations for Public Officials: A Tool to Prevent Corruption*, OECD Publishing, Paris, *http://dx.doi.org/10.1787/9789264095281-en*

OECD (2012), *Integrity Review of Brazil: Managing Risks for a Cleaner Public Service*, OECD Publishing, Paris, *http://dx.doi.org/10.1787/9789264119321-en.*

OECD (2014), "Renforcer l'Intégrité en Tunisie : L'Élaboration de Normes pour les Agents Publics et le Renforcement du Système de Déclaration de Patrimoine", OECD Publishing, Paris, *www.oecd.org/mena/governance/Renforcer-* Intégrité-Tunisie-Élaboration-Normes-Agents-Publics.pdf.

OECD (2015), *Government at a Glance 2015*, OECD Publishing, Paris, *http://dx.doi.org/10.1787/gov_glance-2015-en*

OECD (2016), *The Implementation of the Palestinian Code of Conduct: Strengthening Ethics and Contributing to Institution-Building*, OECD Publishing, Paris. *http://dx.doi.org/10.1787/9789264256934-en*

OECD (2017a), *Recommendation of the Council on Public Integrity*, Paris, *http://www.oecd.org/gov/ethics/Recommendation-Public-Integrity.pdf*

OECD (2017b), *OECD Integrity Review of Mexico: Taking a Stronger Stance Against Corruption*, OECD Publishing, Paris. *http://dx.doi.org/10.1787/9789264273207-en*

OECD (2017c), *OECD Integrity Review of Peru: Enhancing Public Sector Integrity for Inclusive Growth*, OECD Publishing, Paris. *http://dx.doi.org/10.1787/9789264271029-en*

Presidencia de la República (02.02.2015), *Anuncia el Presidente Entique Peña Nieto un conjunto de acciones ejecutivas para prevenir la corrupción y los conflictos de interés*, *www.gob.mx/presidencia/prensa/anuncia-el-presidente-enrique-pena-nieto-un-conjunto-de-acciones-ejecutivas-para-prevenir-la-corrupcion-y-los-conflictos-de-interes*

Schikora, Jan. (2010), "Bringing the Four-Eyes-Principle to the Lab", Beiträge zur Jahrestagung des Vereins für Socialpolitik, 2010, *www.econstor.eu/dspace/handle/10419/37465*, accessed Feb. 29, 2017.

Serra, D. & Wantchekon, L. (2012), "New Advances in Experimental Research on Corruption Research in Experimental Economics", Volume 15, Emerald Group Publishing Limited.

Schulze, G.G. & Frank, B. (2003), "Deterrence versus intrinsic motivation: Experimental evidence on the determinants of corruptibility", Economics of Governance, 4, 143–160.

Stevens, B. (2008), "Corporate Ethical codes: Effective instruments for influencing behaviour", *Journal of Business Ethics*, pp. 601-609

Rossi, I. M., Pop, L., and Berger, T. (2017), "Getting the Full Picture on Public Officials: A How To Guide for Effective Financial Disclosure". Stolen Asset Recovery (StAR) Series. Washington, DC: World Bank.

Ruxandra, B. et al. (2010), *Income and Asset Disclosure Systems: Establishing Good Governance thorugh accountability*, Poverty Reduction and Economic Management (PREM) Network, 17, June 2010.

Vargas, G and Schlutz, D (2016), *Opening Public Officials' Coffers: A quantative Analysis of the Impact of the Financial Disclosure Regulation on National Corruption Levels*, Hertie School of Governance, Berlin.

OECD Integrity Review of Coahuila, Mexico
Restoring trust through an integrity system

Chapter 3

Guaranteeing effective whistleblower protection in Coahuila

There is a general consensus among policymakers that effective whistleblower protection is needed to promote integrity, encourage transparency, and detect misconduct. To this end, many countries have introduced a dedicated whistleblower protection law. This chapter provides a review and analysis of Coahuila's whistleblower protection system. It addresses the need for Coahuila to enact a dedicated whistleblower protection law and make additional efforts to build trust in the protection system, enhance awareness, and systematically review and evaluate its whistleblowing system.

Introduction

A key pillar of an effective integrity system in the public sector is the existence of formalised mechanisms through which employees can disclose wrongdoing without fear of reprisals. Even if an organisation has preventive measures in place such as an ethics code or ethical training, wrongdoing cannot be avoided entirely. Employees have access to up-to-date information concerning their workplaces' practices and are usually the first to recognise wrongdoings (UNODC, 2015). Whistleblowers can be an invaluable source of exposing irregularities, fraud, mismanagement, and corruption. However, blowing the whistle can carry high personal risks, especially when there are no guarantees for legal protection for whistleblowers against retaliation such as dismissal or physical and psychological abuse.

The OECD *Recommendation on Public Integrity* (2017a) recommends that an effective public integrity system supports an open organisational culture that is responsive to integrity concerns and that encourages whistleblowers to report misconduct by ensuring visible support and positive reinforcement from the government and the organisational hierarchy. Clear guidance on reporting procedures, effective and comprehensive legal protection from all kinds of retaliation, and criteria for investigation are also needed. The right combination of all these measures promotes a culture of accountability and integrity and facilitates the reporting of misconduct, fraud, and corruption. Ultimately, the protection of whistleblowers deters and detects wrongdoing. As such, it is the ultimate line of defence for safeguarding the public interest.

In Coahuila, 83.5% of citizens perceive corruption as a frequent occurrence (INEGI, 2015). Given the high perception of corruption across all levels of government and the lack of a professional civil service scheme, it can be assumed that public officials and citizens alike do not feel confident about reporting crime for fear of reprisal and the assumption that reports will not be followed up upon. Only 39% of Mexicans say they would report crime (Instituto Nacional Electoral, 2015).). The main reason for not reporting crime is that it "is of no use" (63%), followed by a lack of trust in authorities (52%) (Figure 3.1). On-site interviews confirm that the situation may not be so different in the state of Coahuila.

Over the last decade, the majority of OECD countries have introduced whistleblower protection laws that facilitate the reporting of misconduct and protect whistleblowers from reprisals, not only in the private sector; but especially in the public sector. In OECD countries, such protections can be provided through several different laws such as anti-corruption laws, competition laws or laws regulating public servants, or through a dedicated public sector whistleblower protection law (Figure 3.2). In federal states, the laws at the state level are required to provide at least the same framework for protection as at the federal level.

Figure 3.1. **Reasons for not reporting**

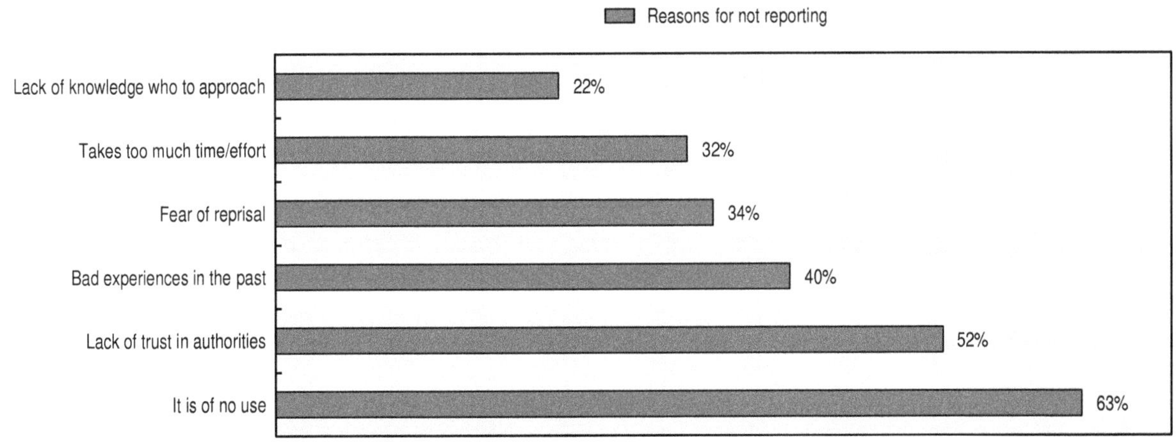

Source: Instituto Nacional Electoral (2015), Informe País sobre la calidad de la ciudadanía en México – Resumen ejecutivo,p.19, available from *http://portalanterior.ine.mx/archivos2/portal/DECEYEC/EducacionCivica/informePais/.*

Figure 3.2. **Legal protections for whistleblowers in the public sector in OECD countries**

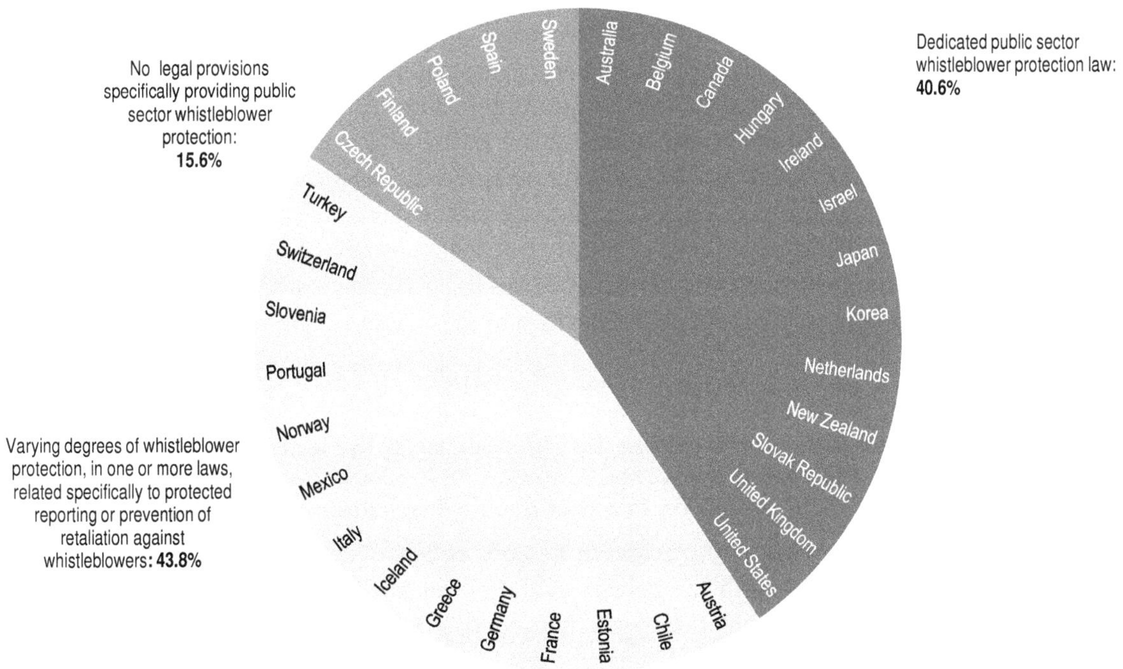

Source: OECD (2016), *Committing to Effective Whistleblower Protection*, OECD Publishing, Paris. *http://dx.doi.org/10.1787/9789264252639-en.*

Similar to the regulations at the federal level prior to the General Law on Administrative Responsibilities (*Ley General de Responsabilidades Administrativas*, LGRA), Coahuila does not have a dedicated whistleblower protection law, but relies on provisions in one or more laws, related specifically to protected reporting or prevention of retaliation against whistleblowers:

- Federal Criminal Code (*Código Penal*) provides that a crime of intimidation is committed when a civil servant, or a person acting on their behalf, uses physical violence or moral aggression to intimidate another person in order to prevent them from reporting, lodging a criminal complaint, or providing information concerning the alleged criminal act.

- Access to Information and Protection of Personal Data Law of Coahuila (*Ley de Acceso a la Información Pública y Protección de Datos Personales*) protects the anonymity of whistleblowers by classifying the information they provide as confidential (Article 39) and by classifying it as reserved information if there is a risk to the person's security (Article 30).
- Law to prevent and sanction corruption in public procurement procedures (*Ley para prevenir y sancionar las prácticas de corrupción en los procedimientos de contratación pública del Estado de Coahuila de Zaragoza y sus Municipios*) details the process to report misconduct. The authorities are obliged to protect the whistleblower's identity and rights. In order to guarantee the anonymity of the whistleblower, each case file is given a number. The whistleblower receives legal assistance and is protected from reprisals in the workplace, such as dismissal.

While this piecemeal approach is positive in the sense that it applies to the whole public sector, including state-owned enterprises, and offers a form of protection from the threat of reprisal, the extent of Coahuila's protection can be considered limited and insufficient. Besides the activity of public procurement, the legal provisions refer only to the obligation of public officials to refrain from inhibiting or preventing reporting by others – they do not provide specific protection for those who report.

Making use of the opportunity of the introduction of the local anti-corruption system and the necessary passing of secondary legislations, Coahuila could develop a whistleblower protection framework that is a strong shield behind which a whistleblower is kept safe from reprisals (Devine and Walden, 2013). In this way, Coahuila would go beyond the federal framework, which provides only limited protection. Specifically, Coahuila could strengthen protection, increase awareness, and conduct evaluations based on the following recommendations. For the purposes of this review, the focus will be on policies that seek to directly and indirectly protect whistleblowers in the workplace, which includes public servants, contractors, and suppliers, irrespective of their labour regime.

Guaranteeing strong protection for whistleblowers

To avoid fragmentation and to ensure the effectiveness of the whistleblower protection provisions spread throughout different laws, Coahuila could enact a dedicated whistleblower protection law that avoids duplication and ensures clarity.

Establishing the Local Anti-corruption System obliges Coahuila to harmonise the necessary secondary laws with the federal level. Despite further room for improvement, the legislation protecting whistleblowers has been strengthened at the federal level (OECD, 2017b). Public officials and citizens who disclose misconduct in the public sector are protected by the following:

- Mexico's new General Law on Administrative Responsibilities (*Ley General de Responsabilidades Administrativas*, LGRA), which requires investigative authorities of public organisations subject to the Law to adopt anonymous and confidential reporting channels to disclose misconduct and increase the accountability of recipients of disclosures of misconduct
- The General Law of the National Anti-corruption System (*Ley General del Sistema Nacional Anticorrupción*), which provides for a centralised electronic platform through which any citizen can disclose misconduct anonymously

Coahuila could adopt a dedicated whistleblower protection law based on the benchmarking of whistleblower protection laws in other countries (Box 3.1). Rather than strengthening the current fragmented piecemeal approach, a dedicated whistleblower protection would ensure universally applicable protection provisions, which would bring clarity and would make it easier to raise awareness of the existence of these provisions (Banisar, 2011). Translating whistleblower protection into a dedicated law legitimises and structures the mechanisms under which individuals can disclose actual or perceived wrongdoings, protects them against reprisals, and, at the same time, can help encourage them to come forward and report wrongdoing. However, Coahuila would need to ensure that the legislation's provisions are effectively implemented and that the measures are executed in a clear, unambiguous, and reassuring way.

Box 3.1. **Whistleblower protection in Alberta**

Alberta's whistleblower protection law came into force on 1 June 2013, with the enactment of the Public Interest Disclosure (Whistleblower Protection) Act (Section 1 and Part 6 of the Public Interest Disclosure [Whistleblower Protection] Act came into force on 24 April, 2013). The goal of the legislation is to protect public sector employees from job reprisal, such as termination, if they report wrongdoing. The new law applies to the Alberta public service, provincial agencies, boards and commissions, as well as to academic institutions, school boards, and health organisations.

The law also creates processes for the disclosure of wrongdoing and for the Office of the Public Interest Disclosure Commissioner to investigate and resolve complaints by public sector employees who report violations of provincial or federal law, acts, or omissions that create a danger to the public or environment, and gross mismanagement of public funds.

The penalty for offences under the Act is CAD 25 000 for the first conviction to a maximum of up to CAD 100 000 for subsequent offences.

Source: Public Interest Commissioner (2016), Public Interest Disclosure (Whistleblower Protection) Act, available from *https://yourvoiceprotected.ca/*.

Adopting a dedicated whistleblower protection law would send a strong message to public servants and citizens alike. With it, they would understand that they are expected to speak up and report wrongdoings, and that reprisals against whistleblowers are not to be tolerated. If drafted in a way that provides broad coverage and provides for the availability of reporting channels, such a law will likely contribute to establishing a culture of integrity in Coahuila that will be key in avoiding reprisals from occurring in the first place (*ex ante* protective measures).

However, there are times where such *ex ante* measures will not effectively protect whistleblowers. In some cases, it may be impossible to fully protect the identity of whistleblowers and therefore, the law will also need to comprise *ex post* protective measures to ensure that whistleblowers have appropriate remedies at their disposal to seek compensation from the individual or organisation that may have exercised reprisals (OECD, 2017b).

To mitigate the risk of having whistleblowers come forward with information that may not constitute protected disclosures, and to avoid potentially exposing them to unnecessary risks and overburdening the intake system with non-applicable cases, Coahuila could clarify the nature of a protected disclosure.

A whistleblower protection system ought to promote and facilitate the reporting of "illegal, unethical and dangerous" activities (Banisar, 2011). To ensure clarity and avoid incertitude surrounding the process, the precise classification of elements of disclosure that warrant protection is critical. The legal framework should provide a clear definition of the protected disclosures, specifying the acts that constitute violations to any code of conduct, regulation or law: gross waste or mismanagement, abuse of authority, dangers to the public health or safety, or corrupt acts. Clarifying the subject matter considered as a protected disclosure may be a deciding factor in whether an individual comes forward with a disclosure or keeps quiet due to uncertainty. Nevertheless, balance should exist between being overly prescriptive and thus making it difficult to disclose or requiring the discloser to have detailed knowledge of relevant legal provisions, and being overly relaxed, which allows for unlimited disclosures that in the end may not encourage internal resolution of issues within an organisation (Banisar, 2011).

The categories of wrongdoing, outlined in Figure 3.3 and extracted from existing whistleblower protection laws in OECD countries, encompass a broad range of subject matters which warrant the status of protected disclosures. Similar to most OECD countries, wrongdoings indicated by Coahuila in the interviews as constituting a protected disclosure are as follows:

- a violation of law, rule, or regulation
- a serious breach of a code of conduct
- a misuse of public funds or a public asset
- abuse of authority
- a criminal offence has been committed, is being committed, or is likely to be committed
- an act or omission that creates a substantial and specific danger to the life, health or safety of persons, or to the environment, other than a danger that is inherent in the performance of the duties or functions of a public servant
- types of wrongdoing that fall under the term "corruption" as defined under domestic law

To mitigate the eventuality of having whistleblowers come forward with information that may not be considered as a protected disclosure, potentially exposing them to unnecessary risks and overburdening the intake system with non-applicable cases, Coahuila may wish to consider a more detailed and balanced approach similar to the system in place in the United Kingdom. The UK legislation provides a balanced approach with a detailed definition including exceptions (Box 3.2).

Given the low trust in institutional safeguards, the possibility of anonymous reporting should be made available to facilitate the reporting of misconduct.

The Access to Information and Protection of Personal Data Law of Coahuila provides for the protection of whistleblowers' identities, which are kept confidential unless the whistleblower provides his or her consent for disclosure. However, it is important that confidentiality extends to all identifying information. The mechanisms in place in the United States, for example, prohibit the disclosure of identifying information of a federal sector whistleblower without consent, unless the Office of the Special Counsel (OSC) "determines that the disclosure of the individual's identity is necessary because of an imminent danger to public health or safety or imminent violation of any criminal law."[1] If the whistleblower's identity is disclosed, the whistleblower will be informed in advance (OECD, 2016).

Figure 3.3. **Categories of wrongdoing constituting a protected disclosure in OECD countries**

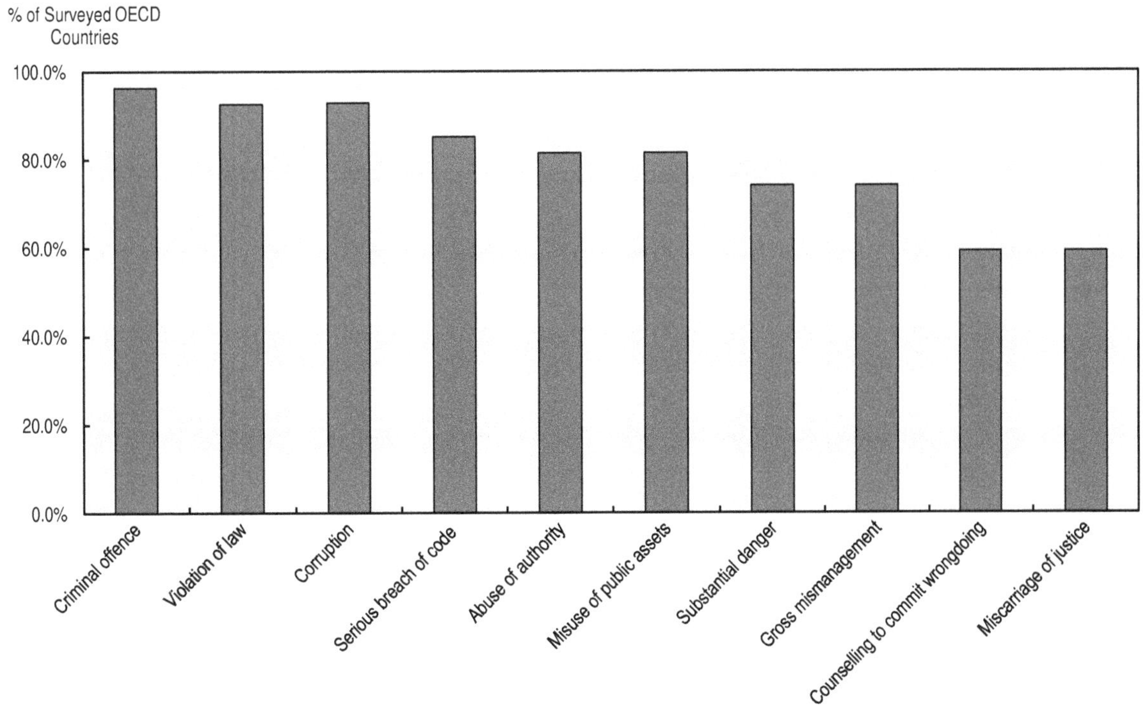

Source: OECD (2016), *Committing to Effective Whistleblower Protection*, OECD Publishing, Paris.*http://dx.doi.org/10.1787/9789264252639-en*

Beyond confidentiality, the possibility to disclose anonymously can encourage whistleblowers to come forward by providing a safe avenue to report. It may encourage reporting, especially where the institutional safeguards are non-existent or too weak to provide adequate protection.

Australia's whistleblower protection system allows for a public interest disclosure to be made anonymously as one of three options for reporting a public interest disclosure. In addition, it provides the option of making a public interest disclosure verbally or in writing, and without the discloser asserting that the disclosure is made for the purposes of the act. In Japan, anonymous reporting is protected by the interpretation of a number of articles within the Japanese Whistleblower Protection Act (WPA). In the Slovak Republic, employees may file an anonymous report to the internal disclosure handling system. A number of countries have established electronic intake systems and hotlines that cater to, among others, anonymous reporting. For example, the Netherlands has a national trustline where individuals can report suspected malpractices anonymously.

Mexico's new General Law on Administrative Responsibilities requires investigative authorities of public organisations to adopt anonymous and confidential reporting channels to disclose misconduct and increase the accountability of recipients of disclosures of misconduct. Pursuant to Article 109 of the National Code of Criminal Protection, victims and other injured parties have a right to anonymity when their safety is at risk. However, the right to anonymity for victims is not sufficient in the case of whistleblowers. The possibility to report anonymously should be made available to potential whistleblowers in Coahuila and it could be considered to introduce an anonymous reporting line, such as the trustline in the Netherlands.

Box 3.2. **A detailed definition of protected disclosures in the United Kingdom**

In the United Kingdom, the Public Disclosure Act defines a protected disclosure and provides clear criteria of the kind of disclosures that merits protection according to the law:

Part IV - A: Protected disclosures

43A: Meaning of "protected disclosure"

In this Act a "protected disclosure" means a qualifying disclosure (as defined by Section 43B) which is made by a worker in accordance with any of Sections 43C to 43H.

43B: Disclosures qualifying for protection

1. In this part a "qualifying disclosure" means any disclosure of information which, in the reasonable belief of the worker making the disclosure, tends to show one or more of the following:
   a. that a criminal offence has been committed, is being committed, or is likely to be committed,
   b. that a person has failed, is failing, or is likely to fail to comply with any legal obligation to which he is subject,
   c. that a miscarriage of justice has occurred, is occurring, or is likely to occur,
   d. that the health or safety of any individual has been, is being, or is likely to be endangered,
   e. that the environment has been, is being, or is likely to be damaged, or
   f. that information tending to show any matter falling within any one of the preceding paragraphs has been, is being or is likely to be deliberately concealed.
2. For the purposes of Subsection (1), it is immaterial whether the relevant failure occurred, occurs or would occur in the United Kingdom or elsewhere, and whether the law applying to it is that of the United Kingdom or of any other country or territory.
3. A disclosure of information is not a qualifying disclosure if the person making the disclosure commits an offence by making it.
4. A disclosure of information in respect of which a claim to legal professional privilege (or, in Scotland, to confidentiality as between client and professional legal adviser) could be maintained in legal proceedings is not a qualifying disclosure if it is made by a person to whom the information had been disclosed in the course of obtaining legal advice.
5. In this part "the relevant failure", in relation to a qualifying disclosure, means the matter falling within paragraphs (a) to (f) of Subsection (1).

Source: UK Public Disclosure Act of 1998, adding Part IV - A to Employment Rights Act of 1996.

Coahuila could consider clarifying the overlap between witness and whistleblower protection and ensuring that disclosures that do not lead to a full investigation or to prosecution are still eligible for legal protection.

There is a potential overlap between whistleblowers and witnesses as some whistleblowers may possess solid evidence and eventually become witnesses in legal proceedings (Transparency International, 2013a). When whistleblowers testify during court proceedings, they can be covered under the existing witness protection laws. The Mexican framework offers witness protection pursuant to Article 109 of the National Code of Criminal Procedures (*Código Único Nacional de Procedimientos Penales*), which applies to the state level and Coahuila's Victims Law.

However, if the subject matter of a whistleblower report does not result in criminal proceedings, or the whistleblower is never called as a witness, then witness protection will not be provided. Even if a whistleblower is entitled to witness protection due to eventual involvement in related criminal proceedings, the measures provided (such as relocation, changed identity, etc.) may not always be relevant. Also, given that whistleblowers are usually employees of the organisation where the reported misconduct took place, they may face specific risks which are normally not covered by witness protection laws, such as demotion or dismissal. Furthermore, in terms of remedies for retaliation, they may need compensation for salary losses and career opportunities. Witness protection laws are therefore not sufficient to protect whistleblowers (Transparency International, 2009).

Indeed, basing the eligibility for such protection on the decision to investigate disclosures and subsequently prosecute related offences decreases certainty surrounding legal protections against reprisals. This is because such decisions are often taken on the basis of considerations that remain inaccessible to the public. Indeed, it may be more effective, in terms of detecting misconduct, to implement facilitation measures through which whistleblowers may report relevant facts that could lead to an investigation or prosecution. Whistleblowers will be more likely to report relevant facts if they know they will be protected regardless of the decision to investigate or prosecute.

The provisions of a dedicated whistleblower law in Coahuila would therefore modify the National Code of Criminal Protection to establish protection for those disclosing information pertaining to an act of corruption that might not be recognised as a crime, but could be subject to administrative investigations.

Coahuila could provide more comprehensive protection to whistleblowers by specifically prohibiting dismissal of whistleblowers without a cause, or any other kind of formal or informal work-related sanction that has been exercised in response to the disclosure, if the information reported can reasonably be believed to be true at the time of the disclosure.

Whistleblowers face the risk of retaliation when exposing wrongdoing. Such retaliation usually takes the form of disciplinary action or harassment in the workplace. Whistleblower protection frameworks should provide protection against discriminatory or retaliatory personnel action. According to the United States' Project on Government Oversight, typical forms of retaliation include (Project on Government Oversight, 2005):

- taking away job duties so that the employee is marginalised
- taking away an employee's national security clearance so that he or she is effectively fired
- blacklisting an employee so that he or she is unable to find gainful employment
- conducting retaliatory investigations in order to divert attention from the waste, fraud, or abuse the whistleblower is trying to expose
- questioning a whistleblower's mental health, professional competence, or honesty
- setting the whistleblower up by giving impossible assignments or seeking to trap him or her
- reassigning an employee geographically so he or she is unable to do the job

Unlike the majority of OECD countries (Figure 3.4), Coahuila indicated that it does not provide protection from a broad range of reprisals. It does not protect whistleblowers from the following retaliatory action:

- dismissal, suspension, or demotion
- transfer or reassignment

- decisions concerning pay, benefits, awards, education or training
- significant change in duties, responsibilities, or working conditions such as harassment
- medical testing or examination

Figure 3.4. **OECD countries providing protection from all discriminatory or retaliatory personnel actions**

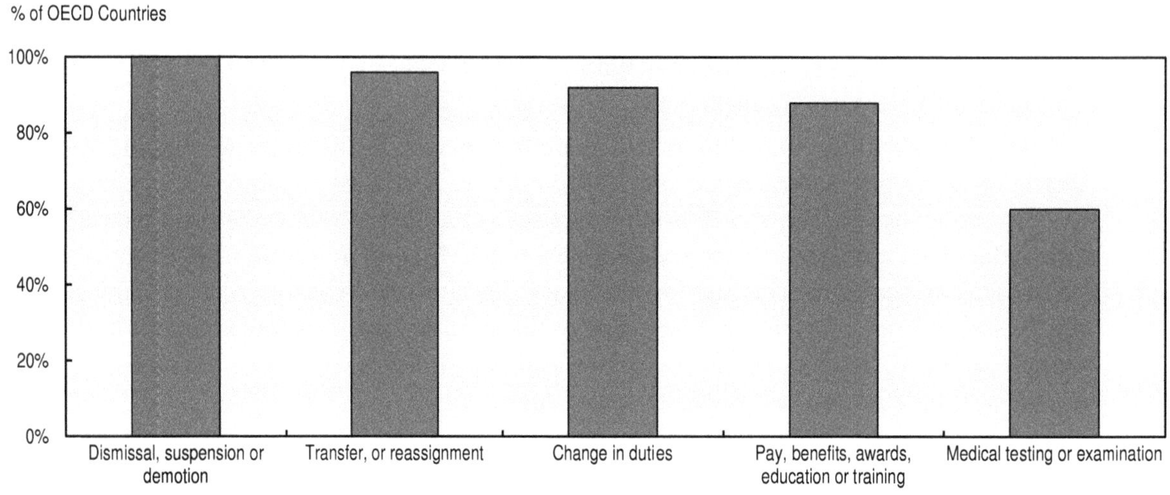

Source: OECD (2016), *Committing to Effective Whistleblower Protection*, OECD Publishing, Paris.*http://dx.doi.org/10.1787/9789264252639-en*.

Protection from reprisal in Coahuila's legislative framework is merely limited to protection from physical harm. A broader range of reprisals is necessary to protect whistleblowers from potential retaliation following a disclosure of wrongdoing. Anchoring these protections within the law will give whistleblowers more confidence in the procedures. For example, Korea's Protection of Public Interest Whistleblowers (PPIW) Act provides a comprehensive list of what disadvantageous measures whistleblowers should be protected against, including financial or administrative disadvantages such as the cancellation of a permit or license or the revocation of a contract (Box 3.3).

Concerning the protection from physical harm, in line with Article 64 of the LGRA, Coahuila will have to allow civil servants to request protective measures that are "deemed reasonable" (*medidas de protección que resulten razonables*) from the organisation providing the reporting channels. However, the lack of precision with respect to the protections that are contemplated under this article leave significant uncertainty as to the extent and scope of the protection that will be granted. Therefore, Coahuila should develop this provision further in its local regulations and set a benchmark for other states by including a non-exhaustive list of examples of measures that may be considered. Coahuila may consider specifically prohibiting dismissal without a cause of public and private sector whistleblowers, as well as other work-related reprisals such as demotion, suspension, and harassment. This protection may be limited in cases where tribunals have ruled that the whistleblower should have known that the disclosure was false or misleading at the time.

Such a list could be particularly useful in difficult and potentially hazardous situations when anonymity and confidentiality may not be sufficient, such as when the disclosed misconduct involves senior public officials, political staff, or organised crime, or when there are risks that the physical integrity of whistleblowers may be threatened.

Box 3.3. **Comprehensive protection in Korea**

In Korea, the term "disadvantageous measures" means an action that falls under any of the following items:

- removal from office, release from office, dismissal or any other unfavourable personnel action equivalent to the loss of status at work
- disciplinary action, suspension from office, reduction in pay, demotion, restriction on promotion, and any other unfair personnel actions
- work reassignment, transfer, denial of duties, rearrangement of duties, or any other personnel actions that are against the whistleblower's will
- discrimination in performance evaluation, peer review, etc. and subsequent discrimination in the payment of wages and bonuses
- the cancellation of education, training, or other self-development opportunities; the restriction or removal of budget, work force, or other available resources, the suspension of access to security information or classified information; the cancellation of authorisation to handle security information or classified information; or any other discrimination or measure detrimental to the working conditions of the whistleblower
- putting the whistleblower's name on a blacklist as well as the release of such a blacklist, bullying, the use of violence and abusive language towards the whistleblower, or any other action that causes psychological or physical harm to the whistleblower
- unfair audit or inspection of the whistleblower's work and disclosure of the results of such an audit or inspection
- the cancellation of a license or permit or any other action that causes administrative disadvantages to the whistleblower

Source: Korea's Act on the Protection of Public Interest Whistleblowers (2011), Act No. 10472, Mar. 29, 2011. Article 2 (6).

By creating greater certainty about the eligibility and the scope of protective measures, clarifying what measures may be available as well as the circumstances upon which these measures will be imposed, the effectiveness of the framework would be enhanced to encourage disclosures of misconduct.

Expanding the scope of the criminal prohibition to exercise reprisals on whistleblowers to a broader range of reprisals and to disclosures that are related to any breach of state laws could reinforce Coahuila's commitment to effective whistleblower protection and reassure potential whistleblowers.

To increase deterrence against the exercise of reprisals against whistleblowers, some OECD countries have implemented administrative and criminal prohibitions to exercise such reprisals. One of the strengths of the legal framework in Coahuila is that the Law of Responsibilities and the Criminal Code considers it an offence to take a reprisal against someone, to threaten reprisal, and to prevent a person from reporting. Threatening to take action can have the same effect on the whistleblower as actual retaliation. In this way, Coahuila has taken a positive step in including this provision in its legal framework.

While this provision certainly has a deterrent effect, its impact could be reinforced by broadening the scope of its application. The scope of the concept of "reprisals" is somewhat too narrow, as it only includes "acts of physical violence or moral aggression" that can intimidate the whistleblower in order to prevent him or her from reporting. However, there are several other ways to intimidate or threaten to exercise reprisals against whistleblowers in the civil service, including but not limited to the public disclosure of the identity of the whistleblower.

Another shortcoming of the prohibition is that it applies only to information that is linked to a criminal complaint or an alleged criminal act. As a result, an employer would not be prohibited from exercising reprisals against an employee who has disclosed misconduct that constitutes a contravention to any law, but that does not constitute a criminal offence.

Finally, the reprisals have to come from a civil servant or a person acting on his or her behalf in order to be sanctioned under the Criminal Code. Given that any citizen or corporation may disclose misconduct in the public sector, reprisals against whistleblowers could certainly be exercised by private sector representatives and other citizens. The deterrent effect of the Law of Responsibilities and the Criminal Code should also apply to reprisals that are exercised by individuals who do not work for the public sector and to other persons acting on their behalf.

Section 425.1 of Canada's criminal code, which also establishes a criminal prohibition to exercise reprisals against whistleblowers, does not include such limitations (Box 3.4). It applies to a broad range of reprisals including disciplinary measures against an employee such as demotion, termination, or otherwise adversely affecting the employment of such a whistleblower, or threatening to do so. It also applies to any employer or person acting on his behalf. Moreover, Section 425.1 of the Criminal Code applies to disclosures related to the breach of any federal or provincial law or regulation, and is therefore not limited to criminal offences.

Box 3.4. **Section 425.1 of the Canadian Criminal Code prohibiting reprisals against whistleblowers**

1. No employer or person acting on behalf of an employer or in a position of authority in respect of an employee of the employer shall take a disciplinary measure against, demote, terminate, or otherwise adversely affect the employment of such an employee, or threaten to do so,
   a. with the intent to compel the employee to abstain from providing information to a person whose duties include the enforcement of federal or provincial law, respecting an offence that the employee believes has been or is being committed contrary to this or any other federal or provincial Act or regulation by the employer or an officer or employee of the employer or, if the employer is a corporation, by one or more of its directors; or
   b. with the intent to retaliate against the employee because the employee has provided information referred to in paragraph (*a*) to a person whose duties include the enforcement of federal or provincial law.
2. Anyone who contravenes Subsection (1) is guilty of
   a. an indictable offence and liable to imprisonment for a term not exceeding five years
   b. an offence punishable on summary conviction.

Source: Criminal Code of Canada, R.S.C., 1985, c. C-46.

Consequently, similar to the OECD (2017b) recommendation given at the federal level, Coahuila could broaden the scope of the criminal prohibition to exercise reprisals on whistleblowers, extending its application to a broader range of reprisals from a broader range of individuals, and to disclosures that are related to any breach of laws. Disclosing the identity of a whistleblower can be another form of reprisal or intimidation. As such, Coahuila could consider it a criminal offence to disclose or threaten to disclose the identity of a whistleblower.

Coahuila could introduce sanctions on individuals who exercise reprisals against whistleblowers who have disclosed misconduct in accordance with applicable rules.

As discussed above, the federal criminal code sanctions public officials responsible for investigating, qualifying, and prosecuting administrative offences if they do not carry on their role in accordance with the law. The criminal code generally prohibits the obstruction of disclosures of misconduct by public servants. However, it remains ambiguous whether the exercise of reprisals following a disclosure of misconduct would be qualified as an "obstruction" to disclosing misconduct and if any sanctions for public officials who would exercise reprisals against whistleblowers apply.

This is contrary to international benchmarks. For example, Australia's whistleblower protection system calls for two years of imprisonment – or 120 penalty units[2], or both – in case of reprisal against whistleblowers[3]; in Korea, the punishment for retaliation varies depending on the type of reprisal that took place (Box 3.5).

In certain circumstances, some OECD countries, such as the United States, impose criminal sanctions on employers who retaliate against whistleblowers. The US Federal Criminal Code 18 U.S.C. §1513 (e) states that "whoever knowingly, with the intent to retaliate, takes any action harmful to any person, including interference with the lawful employment or livelihood of any person, for providing to a law enforcement officer any truthful information relating to the commission or possible commission of any Federal offense, shall be fined under this title or imprisoned not more than 10 years, or both."

Aligning the framework with international standards and OECD recommendations to Mexico's Federal Government (2017b), a dedicated whistleblower protection law could impose sanctions on civil servants who threaten to exercise or actually exercise reprisals on whistleblowers disclosing misconduct.

Coahuila could consider shifting the burden of proof to the employer to provide evidence that any sanction exercised against a whistleblower following a disclosure of misconduct is not related to that disclosure.

Whistleblower protection systems may reverse the burden of proof on the employer to prove that the conduct taken against the employee is unrelated to his or her disclosure of misconduct. This is in response to the difficulties an employee may face in proving that the retaliation was a result of the disclosure, "especially as many forms of reprisals may be very subtle and difficult to establish" (Chêne, 2009, p. 7). In Germany, to qualify for protection provided by the Civil Code, public servants are charged with the burden of proof and have to demonstrate that their disclosure was legally permissible, that discrimination took place, and that retaliation happened because of their disclosure. In the event that the employer has not explicitly mentioned this as the reason for termination, this type of proof has proven almost impossible to provide. To mitigate this, several whistleblower protection systems provide a more flexible approach to the burden of proof and assume that retaliation has occurred where adverse action against a whistleblower cannot be clearly justified by management on grounds unrelated to the disclosure (OECD, 2016).

Finally, allowing whistleblowers to introduce their own recourse before courts, instead of relying on the availability of resources of public authorities, could help to reinforce public trust in the whistleblowing framework and allow for a better use of enforcement authorities' limited resources. In this way, Coahuila could provide civil remedies for public servants who experience reprisals after disclosing misconduct as defined by the law.

Moreover, the availability of effective civil remedies may contribute to mitigating the professional marginalisation of whistleblowers by providing an opportunity for rehabilitation by civil courts. This role could be taken on by the Administrative Justice Tribunal (*Tribunal de Justicia Administrativa*), which will be established according to the governance of the Local Anti-corruption System. Such remedies could also compensate whistleblowers for prospective revenue losses. Combined with effective public awareness-raising campaigns, appropriate civil remedies can significantly improve public perceptions about whistleblowers, thus indirectly mitigating professional marginalisation and prospective financial losses (OECD, 2017c).

Ensuring effective review and investigation of reports

Coahuila could consider defining and formalising the communication channels for reporting misconduct to ensure public officials are fully aware of who they can contact if they decide to disclose misconduct, of how their anonymity or confidentiality will be protected, and of the remedies available to them if they experience reprisal.

International best practices recommend that the individual circumstances of each case should determine the most appropriate channel of disclosure (Council of Europe, 2014). These channels need to be clearly demarcated and facilitate disclosure to create confidence in the system and encourage reporting. As outlined by the UNODC *Resource Guide on Good Practices in the Protection of Reporting Persons* and the UNODC *Technical Guide to the United Nations Convention against Corruption*, channels of reporting should not be limited to a choice of reporting internally within the organisation, externally to a designated body or to the media or the public. Instead, all three levels should operate concurrently so that potential whistleblowers have a choice. If upon disclosing internally they were not provided with an adequate response within a certain timeframe, or if appropriate action was not taken, then the discloser should have the option of submitting the disclosure to an external body. In addition, potential whistleblowers should have direct access to external review agencies if they fear and have reason to believe that they would be reprimanded by their organisation's internal mechanism (OECD, 2016).

In Coahuila, the Attorney General's Office (*Procuraduría General de Justicia del Estado de Coahuila*, PGJE) and SEFIR are the authorities competent to receive and evaluate disclosures. In addition, each institution, as well as the *Procuraduría*, has installed an online reporting system that allows citizens and public servants to report corruption cases in the public administration. According to the LGRA, whistleblowers may report disclosures either to internal control bodies, present in each public organisation, or to national or subnational supreme audit institutions. Furthermore, according to the Law on the Anti-corruption System (*Ley del Sistema Anticorrupción del Estado de Coahuila de Zaragoza*), an information system will be established in Coahuila. Its information and data will be incorporated in the digital national platform, which includes a whistleblower reporting system. However, it is unclear how the state and national platform will co-ordinate to follow up on reports.

If a disclosure is made to an internal control body, SEFIR can conduct the preliminary assessment, the investigation, and it can impose sanctions if the disclosure is related to a non-serious offence. If during the preliminary assessment, the conclusion is reached that the disclosure is related to a criminal offence, SEFIR must complete its investigation and submit it to the Attorney's Office.

However, on-site interviews revealed that neither the existence of the various channels nor the procedure for following up on a report are clear to the majority of public officials. In addition, a strong reluctance to report any misconduct to superiors or other bodies was evident due to previous negative experiences and a lack of trust. In accordance with the recommendation given at the federal level by the OECD (2017b), Coahuila could add additional channels through which protected disclosures can be made. These could include internal disclosures made to a Senior Officer for Disclosure, external disclosures to a designated body, and external disclosures to the public or to the media.

To provide an increased variety of disclosure channels and offer whistleblowers the opportunity to discuss potential misconduct with their direct supervisor, Coahuila could also consider formalising a channel for disclosure of misconduct to supervisors. This would place a stronger responsibility on senior officials to actively create a culture in which employees come forward to management with disclosures of wrongdoing, questions and advice, and that the latter would, in turn, follow the measures in place to protect them and investigate the allegations accordingly. Furthermore, by being receptive to disclosures and encouraging this as a method of detection, management could mitigate the reputational damage that may ensue. In addition, the proposed Integrity Contact Point (see Chapter 2) could be an additional channel that receives, records, and reviews disclosures of wrongdoing and refers them to the appropriate authority to investigate the claims.

For example, in Canada, employees have three different options in terms of disclosing misconduct. Their first option is to make protected disclosures to their supervisors. In addition, they can disclose misconduct to their organisation's designated Senior Officer for Disclosure who receives, records, and reviews disclosures of wrongdoing, leads investigations of disclosures, and makes recommendations to the chief executive regarding any corrective measures to be taken in relation to the wrongdoing found. Senior Officers for Disclosure also have key leadership roles in the providing information and advice to employees and supervisors on the act (Box 3.7).

Finally, in Canada, if employees prefer not to use internal reporting channels, they may also disclose externally to the independent Public Sector Integrity Commissioner, who protects the identity of whistleblowers and acts upon allegations of misconduct made by federal civil servants.

These channels for disclosure need to be clearly demarcated and facilitate disclosure, as whistleblowers may lack confidence in the system, or may not be comfortable or persistent in coming forward. The sheer availability of channels is not sufficient to render a confusing process clear. Instead, this process should be accompanied by an explanation of the steps to follow and the processes to abide by in order to ensure that whistleblowers are not only well informed regarding whom to disclose to, but also of the potential repercussions of doing so, which can depend on the party that is disclosed to and the subject matter at hand. Information campaigns should also include a component that explains appropriate procedures as to how the anonymity or confidentiality of whistleblowers will be protected.

Box 3.7. **Options for making a protected disclosure of wrongdoing in Canada**

What are your options for making a protected disclosure of wrongdoing? Know your options.

Ask yourself...

Who do I feel comfortable approaching if I want to make a disclosure?

Does my organisation have internal policies on how to make an internal disclosure?

My Supervisor / Manager	My Senior Officer	The Office of the Public Sector Integrity Commissioner
I can go directly to my supervisor/ manager to make an internal disclosure.	I can find the co-ordinates of my Senior Officer on my organisation's intranet or I can consult the Treasury Board list of Senior Officers (www.tbs-sct.gc.ca). If my organisation has not identified a Senior Officer, I can make a disclosure to the Office of the Public Sector Integrity Commissioner.	I can go directly to the Office at any time. I do not have to exhaust internal mechanisms before making a disclosure to the Office.

Source: Office of the Public Sector Integrity Commisioner of Canada, Decision-making Guide, available from *http://psic-ispc.gc.ca/eng/resources/decision-making-guide*.

Establishing clear follow-up mechanisms and communication procedures between the whistleblower and the receiving agency would ensure the effective management of reports. This could include information about the receipt of the report, regular updates on the status of investigation, and the final outcome or explanation of reasons why an investigation has not been undertaken.

Allowing whistleblowers to follow up on the outcome of their disclosure of misconduct promotes the accountability of recipients of whistleblower allegations, who are often the internal audit, compliance, legal, or investigation divisions of an organisation. The ability to follow up on disclosures may also lead to better communication between whistleblowers and disclosure recipients in cases of unclear or insufficient information (OECD, 2017c).

The LGRA defines a follow-up mechanism through which whistleblowers are kept informed of the proceedings. In addition, according to Sections 102 to 110 of the LGRA, whistleblowers can reinforce accountability by enabling whistleblowers to appeal a decision made by internal control bodies with respect to the investigation, qualification, and prosecution of administrative offences, and participate in the proceedings.

Utilising the future electronic platform, Coahuila could consider strengthening the process foreseen by the LGRA by clearly detailing the procedural steps that are to be taken by the receiving agency to inform the whistleblower. The following steps could be made obligatory:

1. acknowledging the receipt of information
2. indicating the period of time to undertake a preliminary review to determine whether an investigation will be launched
3. if no investigation is launched, informing the whistleblower of the reasons why no investigation was undertaken
4. if an investigation is launched, keeping the whistleblower informed of the formal status of the case and the conclusion

To strengthen trust in the procedures and guarantees of the whistleblower protection framework, Coahuila could create an independent agency mandated to receive and investigate reports on misconduct and provide remedies as necessary.

The on-site interviews showed even if there were strong legal protections guaranteed for whistleblowers, public officials would not necessarily feel comfortable to come forward to report misconduct due to mistrust and the lack of a civil service scheme. Although enacting a dedicated whistleblower protection law may increase awareness of the importance of encouraging whistleblowing and assuring protection, this will not necessarily translate into the dedication of specific resources.

Therefore, in the long term, Coahuila could send a strong signal that the protection of whistleblowers and fight against corruption is a priority. To do so, Coahuila could create an independent body with the capacity to receive, investigate, and provide remedies for complaints related to retaliation. Best practice when setting up an oversight and enforcement agency is to ensure that it is independent, that it has sufficient budgetary resources to enable it to operate effectively, and that it meets the objectives of the law.

Several best practices on the federal level could inform the introduction of such a body. In the United States, the Office of the Special Counsel (OSC) is an independent federal investigative and prosecutorial agency that protects federal employee whistleblowers. It receives, investigates, and prosecutes appeals from whistleblowers who claim to have suffered reprisals. In addition, the Merit Systems Protection Board, an independent quasi-judicial agency with the power to adjudicate decisions, was established to protect federal employees against political and other prohibited personnel practices and ensure that there is adequate protection from abuse by agency management[5]. In Canada, the Public Sector Integrity Commissioner of Alberta is required to report annually to parliament and has the power to give recommendations to the heads of public offices (Box 3.8). The Public Servants Disclosure Protection Tribunal is in charge of determining remedies and sanctions when violations of whistleblowers' rights occur (Banisar, 2011).

Box 3.8. **Office of the Public Interest Commissioner in Alberta**

The Office of the Public Interest Commissioner is an independent office of the Alberta Legislature providing advice and investigating disclosures of wrongdoing and complaints of reprisals made by employees of jurisdictional public entities covered by the Public Interest Disclosure Act of Alberta. The Public Interest Commissioner is a nonpartisan officer of the Legislature appointed by the Lieutenant Governor in Council on the recommendation of the Legislative Assembly for a term of five years with the possibility of reappointment. On its website, the Office provides clear guidance on who the whistleblower legislation applies to, what is defined as a wrongdoing, what a reprisal is, and how public officials are protected. An online disclosure form is made available through the website.

The Office of the Public Interest Commissioner also gives advice to public entities by providing examples of whistleblower policies and procedural guidelines and checklists. The Office also provides recommendations on legislation and possible improvements.

Its annual budget in 2014-15, which is approved by the legislative assembly, was CAD 1 196 000.

Source: Public Interest Commisioner (2016), "About us", available from *https://yourvoiceprotected.ca/about-us/#role-of-the-commissioner*.

Alternatively, if adequate financial resources cannot be guaranteed due to budget constraints, Coahuila could introduce an anti-corruption commissioner or trust attorney that allows whistleblowers to report anonymously. Coahuila could follow the model of several German states (Box 3.9). This would provide individuals with a channel for disclosing wrongdoing that they may feel more comfortable with than alternatives. In some cases, hotlines or online platforms provide potential whistleblowers with the option of disclosing information anonymously, a practice that should be coupled with the allocation of a unique identification number to callers that allows them to call back later, and anonymously, to receive feedback or answer follow-up questions from investigators (Banisar, 2011).

Box 3.9. **External reporting channels in German states**

German states have established different external channels to facilitate reporting:

- **Schleswig-Holstein's Anti-corruption Commissioner**: In 2007, the government of Schleswig-Holstein, Germany, set up a contact point for combating corruption (KBK-SH), which was established as a permanent institution after a two-year pilot phase. The KBK-SH has been created as a point of contact for whistleblowers and is independent from the administration. An Anti-corruption Commissioner for the state of Schleswig-Holstein was appointed to carry out the tasks. The Anti-corruption Commissioner acts as an independent mediator between whistleblowers, the administration, and law enforcement agencies. Whistleblowers can report to him anonymously or under confidentiality. The Anti-corruption Commissioner is obliged to maintain total discretion and to protect fully the identity of the whistleblowers. Reports not within the area of responsibility of the KBK-SH are forwarded to the respective responsible office. The Anti-corruption Officer can be contacted by telephone, e-mail, or post. Detailed information is made available on the website of the state government of Schleswig-Holstein.
- **Lower Saxony's Internet-based information system**: Since 2003, the State Office of Criminal Investigation has been using an Internet-based information system to receive anonymous reports of corruption and economic crime (BKMS system). It is also possible to use a virtual mailbox to communicate anonymously with the police officer and answer follow-up questions on the report.
- **Baden-Wuerttemberg's trust attorney:** In September 2009, the position of trust attorney was introduced to improve the handling of reports of corruption. The attorney can be contacted as an independent contact point outside the administration to receive corruption-relevant reports. The attorney accepts anonymous reports and examines them for their credibility and criminal relevance. In the event of sufficient evidence of misconduct of employees or third parties at the expense of the state government, the report will be referred to the highest state authority. The authority will be in charge of further investigations and may, if necessary, ask the attorney to forward questions to the whistleblower. If the report does not fall under the purview of the authority, it will be referred to the respective local authority unless employees of the local authority are accused. It is then sent to the next higher-ranking body. In addition, the State Office of Criminal Investigation operates an Internet-based dialogue system.

Source: Denny Mueller (2012), *Korruptionsbekaempfung in Deutschland: Institutionelle Ressourcen der Bundesländer im Vergleich*, Transparency International, available from *www.transparency.de/fileadmin/pdfs/Themen/Justiz/Korruptionsbekaempfung_web.pdf*, accessed 27 February 2017.

Strengthening awareness

To implement the law effectively, Coahuila could consider promoting a broad communication strategy and undertaking increased awareness efforts through various channels.

Strengthening the legal and institutional framework to protect whistleblowers is only one component of an effective whistleblower protection framework. On its own it is not sufficient to promote a culture of openness and integrity in which public officials trust that their reports will be followed up and that they will be protected from reprisals. As such, whistleblower protection legislation needs to be validated by awareness-raising, communication, training, and evaluation efforts. Assuring whistleblowers that their concerns are being heard and that they are supported in their choice to come forward is paramount to the integrity of an organisation, and to how whistleblowers are viewed by society as a whole. There are multiple measures organisations can take to encourage the detection and disclosure of wrongdoing. These measures would contribute to an open organisational culture and help reinforce trust, working relationships, and boost staff morale.

Led by SEFIR, all institutions within the administration could introduce awareness-raising campaigns which underscore the role of whistleblowers in promoting the public interest by shedding light on misconduct that harms the effective management and delivery of public services, and ultimately, the fairness of the whole public service. Such campaigns will repudiate any perceptions that blowing the whistle is a sign of lack of loyalty to the organisation. Well-targeted campaigns make clear that civil servants' loyalty belongs first and foremost to the public interest, and not to their managers. For example, the Public Interest Commission of Alberta designed a series of posters and distributed them to public entities to be displayed in employee work spaces. The posters show messages such as "Make a change by making a call. Be a hero for Alberta's public interest." In this respect, reporting structures and internal rules should be designed so that civil servants feel they should be loyal to the public interest, and not to public officials who have been appointed by the government of the day. The UK Civil Service Commission suggests including a statement in staff manuals to assure them that it is safe to raise concerns (Box 3.10). Coahuila may consider similar statements and materials.

Box 3.10. **Example of a statement to staff reassuring them to raise concerns**

"We encourage everyone who works here to raise any concerns they have. We encourage 'whistleblowing' within the organisation to help us put things right if they are going wrong. If you think something is wrong, please tell us and give us a chance to properly investigate and consider your concerns. We encourage you to raise concerns and will ensure that you do not suffer a detriment for doing so."

Source: Civil Service Commission (2011), Whistleblowing and the Civil Service Code, available from *http://civilservicecommission.independent.gov.uk/wp-content/uploads/2014/02/Whistleblowing-and-the-Civil-Service-Code.pdf.*

By introducing and implementing such measures, Coahuila can facilitate awareness of whistleblowing and whistleblower protection, which will not only enhance understanding of these mechanisms, but will also help to improve the often negative and misguided perceptions linked to the term "whistleblower". By expanding these communication efforts, the public view of whistleblowers as important safeguards for the public interest can be improved. Furthermore, communicating the importance of whistleblowers and showing how they are protected in practice can help restore trust in the government. In the United Kingdom, the way the public understands the term "whistleblower" changed considerably since the adoption of the Public Interest Disclosure Act in 1998 (Box 3.11).

Box 3.11. **Change of cultural connotations of "whistleblower" and "whistleblowing": The case of the UK**

In the UK, a research project commissioned by Public Concern at Work from Cardiff University examined national newspaper reporting on whistleblowing and whistleblowers covering the period from 1 January 1997 to 31 December 2009. This includes the period immediately before the introduction of the Public Interest Disclosure Act and tracks how the culture has changed since then. The study found that whistleblowers were overwhelmingly represented in a positive light in the media. Over half (54%) of the newspaper stories represented whistleblowers in a positive light, with only 5% of negative stories. The remainder (41%) was neutral. Similarly, a study by YouGov found that 72% of workers view the term "whistleblowers" as neutral or positive.

Source: Public Concern at Work (2010), *Where's whistleblowing now? 10 years of legal protection for whistleblowers*, Public Concern at Work, London, p. 17, YouGov (2013), YouGov/PCAW Survey Results, YouGov, London, page 8.

In Peru, CAN launched in 2013 the campaign "*Yo denuncio la Corrupción*" (I report corruption). In parallel, a Whistleblower Manual was developed with clear and easily understandable information on the specific mechanisms for administrative complaints in government agencies. In addition, the "Whistleblower Counselling Centre" was implemented to facilitate communication with whistleblowers via e-mail, phone, or mail. This initiative provides for a free hotline, distribution of leaflets containing basic information as well as stickers and pins, and an advertisement campaign was launched. More recently, training and awareness-raising activities were held by relevant authorities at different public entities in 2015 and 2016 in order to publicise the scope of the Peruvian Whistleblowing Law (OECD, 2017c).

Moreover, Coahuila could tailor its awareness-raising efforts similar to the US Office of Special Counsel (OSC). Specifically, the OSC has a Certification Programme developed under section 5 U.S.C. § 2302(c), which has made efforts to promote outreach, investigations, and training as the three core methods for raising awareness. The OSC offers training to federal agencies and non-federal organisations in each of the areas within its jurisdiction, including reprisal for whistleblowing. To ensure that public officials understand their whistleblower rights and how to make protected disclosures, agencies must complete OSC's programme to certify compliance with the Whistleblower Protection Act's notification requirements (Box 3.12). In Coahuila, SEFIR could oversee annual trainings and notices to public officials regarding their rights and available protections under the whistleblower legislation.

Box 3.12. **The United States' approach to increasing awareness through the Whistleblower Protection Enhancement Act (WPEA)**

Under 5 U.S.C. § 2302(c) of the WPEA is the stipulation that "the head of each agency shall be responsible for the prevention of prohibited personnel practices, for the compliance with and enforcement of applicable civil service laws, rules, and regulations, and other aspects of personnel management, and for ensuring (...) that agency employees are informed of the rights and remedies available to them under (...), including how to make a lawful disclosure of information that is specifically required by law or Executive order to be kept classified in the interest of national defense or the conduct of foreign affairs to the Special Counsel, the Inspector General of an agency, Congress, or other agency employee designated to receive such disclosures."

Furthermore, Section 117 of the Act "designates a Whistleblower Protection Ombudsman who shall educate agency employees:

(i) about prohibitions on retaliation for protected disclosures; and

(ii) who have made or are contemplating making a protected disclosure about the rights and remedies against retaliation for protected disclosures."

Source: American Bar Association, Section of Labor and Employment Law, "Congress Strengthens Whistleblower Protections for Federal Employees", November-December 2012.

Conducting evaluations and increasing the use of metrics

Coahuila could consider including a mandate to review periodically its whistleblower protection scheme in the corresponding legislative bill so that the state government could evaluate the relevance of its objectives, implementation, and effectiveness.

Similar to the recommendation on the federal level by the OECD (2017b), Coahuila could consider reviewing on a periodic basis the Law of Responsibilities and, if enacted, the dedicated whistleblower protection legislation, as well as any other additional whistleblower protection laws that may be adopted in the future, to assess whether the mechanisms in place are meeting their intended objectives and whether the law is adequately implemented. If necessary, the framework can then be amended to reflect the results of the evaluation. Provisions regarding the review of effectiveness, enforcement, and impact of whistleblower protection laws have been introduced by a number of OECD countries such as Australia, Canada, Japan, and the Netherlands. The Japanese Whistleblower Protection Act specifically outlines that the Government must take the necessary measures based on the findings of the review. In Canada and Australia, the review must be presented before the House of Commons or Parliament (OECD, 2017c).

To evaluate the effectiveness of the whistleblower framework, Coahuila could consider systematically collecting data and establishing robust indicators.

Coahuila could gather information on 1) the number and types of disclosures received; 2) the entities receiving most disclosures; 3) the outcomes of cases (i.e. if the disclosure was dismissed, accepted, investigated, and validated, and on what grounds); 4) whether the misconduct came to an end as a result of the disclosure; 5) whether the organisation's policies were changed as a result of the disclosure if gaps were identified; 6) whether sanctions were exercised against wrongdoers; 7) the scope, frequency and target audience of awareness-raising mechanisms; and 8) the time it takes to process cases (Transparency International, 2013a; Apaza and Chang, 2011; and Miceli and Near, 1992).

This data, particularly information on the outcomes of cases, can be used in the review of a government whistleblowing framework in order to assess its impact on public sector organisations. Furthermore, employee surveys can review staff awareness, trust, and confidence in whistleblowing mechanisms. In Colombia, for example, the National Statistics Department (*Departamento Administrativo Nacional de Estadística*) conducts surveys with public officials which include questions on why a public official would not report corruption, whether there is knowledge of the existence of protection mechanisms, and if public officials would seek protection. Such efforts play a key role in assessing progress – or lack thereof – in implementing effective whistleblower protection systems.

To measure the effectiveness of protective measures for whistleblowers, additional data could be collected on cases where whistleblowers claimed having experienced reprisals. Such data could include whether allegations of reprisals were investigated, by whom, and how reprisals were exercised, whether and how whistleblowers were compensated, the grounds for underlying these decisions, the time it takes to compensate whistleblowers, and whether they were employed during the judicial process (OECD, 2017c).

Proposals for Action

Integrity and openness are important features of any administration and efforts to encourage employees to express their concerns without fear of persecution should be made. Legitimising and structuring the mechanisms under which public officials can disclose actual or perceived wrongdoings is essential to this approach. An organisational culture built on integrity and open communication not only detects, but also prevents corruption. To ensure that Coahuila's whistleblower system is effective in facilitating the reporting of wrongdoing and protecting against reprisals, the following measures could be considered: strengthening protections, increasing the accountability of the recipients of whistleblower allegations, raising awareness, conducting evaluations and increasing the use of metrics.

Guaranteeing strong protection for whistleblowers

- To avoid fragmentation and ensure the effectiveness of the whistleblower protection provisions spread throughout different laws, Coahuila could enact a dedicated whistleblower protection law that avoids duplication and ensures clarity.
- To mitigate the risk of having whistleblowers come forward with information that may not constitute protected disclosures, and to avoid potentially exposing them to unnecessary risks and overburdening the intake system with non-applicable cases, Coahuila could clarify the nature of a protected disclosure.
- Given the low trust in institutional safeguards, the possibility of reporting anonymously should be made available to facilitate the reporting of misconduct.
- Coahuila could consider clarifying the overlap between witness and whistleblower protection and ensuring that disclosures that do not lead to a full investigation or to prosecution are still eligible for legal protection.
- Coahuila could provide more comprehensive protection to whistleblowers by specifically prohibiting dismissal of whistleblowers without a cause, or any other kind of formal or informal work-related sanction that has been exercised in response to the disclosure, if the information reported can reasonably be believed to be true at the time of the disclosure.

- Expanding the scope of the criminal prohibition to exercise reprisals on whistleblowers to a broader range of reprisals and to disclosures that are related to any breach of state laws could reinforce Coahuila's commitment to effective whistleblower protection and reassure potential whistleblowers.
- Coahuila could introduce sanctions on individuals who exercise reprisals against whistleblowers who have disclosed misconduct in accordance with applicable rules.
- Coahuila could consider shifting the burden of proof to the employer to provide evidence that any sanction exercised on a whistleblower following a disclosure of misconduct is not related to that disclosure.
- Providing express civil remedies for civil servants who experience reprisals after disclosing misconduct as defined by the Law would add a further layer of protection to the whistleblower protection framework.

Ensuring effective review and investigation of reports

- Coahuila could consider defining and formalising the communication channels for reporting misconduct to ensure public officials are fully aware of who they can contact if they decide to disclose misconduct, of how their anonymity or confidentiality will be protected, and of the remedies available to them if they experience reprisal.
- Establishing clear follow-up mechanisms and communication procedures between the whistleblower and the receiving agency would ensure the effective management of reports. This should include information about the receipt of the report, regular updates on the status of investigation, and the final outcome or explanation of reasons why an investigation has not been undertaken.
- To strengthen trust in the procedures and guarantees of the whistleblower protection framework, Coahuila could create an independent agency mandated to receive and investigate reports on misconduct and provide remedies as necessary.

Strengthening awareness

- To implement the law effectively, Coahuila could consider promoting a broad communication strategy and undertaking increased awareness efforts through various channels.

Conducting evaluations and increasing the use of metrics

- Coahuila could consider including a mandate to review periodically its whistleblower protection scheme in the corresponding legislative bill so that the state government could evaluate the relevance of its objectives, implementation, and effectiveness.
- To evaluate the effectiveness of the whistleblower framework, Coahuila could consider systematically collecting data and establishing robust indicators.

Notes

1. See the United States' Whistleblower Protection Act 1989; 5 U.S.C. § 1213(h).
2. In Australia, penalty units are used to describe the payable for fines under commonwealth laws. By multiplying AUS Dollar equivalent of one penalty unit, the fine for an offence is set.
3. Australia's Public Interest Disclosure Act, Subdivision B, Part 2 – Section 19.
4. See for example the United States' Whistleblower Protection Act, Subchapter III Section 1221(h)(1); the United States' False Claims Act 31 U.S.C. §3730(h)).
5. The MSPB and the OSC were set up under the Civil Service Reform Act (CSRA) of 1978.

References

American Bar Association (2012), "Congress Strengthens Whistleblower Protections for Federal Employees", November-December 2012 (accessed 23 July, 2015), *www.americanbar.org/content/newsletter/groups/labor_law/ll_flash/1212_abalel_flash/lel_flash12_2012spec.html.*

Banisar, D. (2011), "Whistleblowing: International Standards and Developments" in Sandoval, I. (editor), Corruption and Transparency: Debating the Frontiers between State, Market and Society, World Bank-Institute for Social Research, UNAM, Washington, D.C., *http://papers.ssrn.com/sol3/papers.cfm?abstract_id=1753180.*

Chêne, M. (2009), *Good Practice in Whistleblowing Protection Legislation (WPL)*, U4 Anti-Corruption Resource Centre, Bergen. *www.u4.no/publications/good-practice-in-whistleblowingprotection-legislation-wpl/.*

Devine, T. and Walden, S. (2013), *International Best Practices For Whistleblower Policies*, Government Accountability Project, Washington, DC.

Government Accountability Project website, *www.whistleblower.org/*, accessed 23 Feb, 2017.

Morehead Dworkin, T. (2002) "Whistleblowing, MNCs and Peace", William Davidson Working Paper Number 437, February 2002.

Project on Government Oversight (2005), *www.pogo.org/*, accessed 20 Jan 2017.

OECD (2017a), *Recommendation of the Council on Public Integrity*, Paris, *www.oecd.org/gov/ethics/Recommendation-Public-Integrity.pdf*

OECD (2017b), *OECD Integrity Review of Mexico: Taking a Stronger Stance Against Corruption*, OECD Publishing, Paris. *http://dx.doi.org/10.1787/9789264273207-en*

OECD (2017c), *OECD Integrity Review of Peru: Enhancing Public Sector Integrity for Inclusive Growth*, OECD Publishing, Paris. *http://dx.doi.org/10.1787/9789264271029-en*

OECD (2016), *Committing to Effective Whistleblower Protection*, OECD Publishing, Paris. *http://dx.doi.org/10.1787/9789264252639-en*

OECD (2014a), *OECD Survey on Public Sector Whistleblower Protection*, OECD, Paris (unpublished document).

OECD (2014b), *Open Government in Latin America*, OECD Publishing, Paris. *http://dx.doi.org/10.1787/9789264223639-en*

OECD (1998), *Recommendation of the Council on Improving Ethical Conduct in the Public Service Including Principles for Managing Ethics in the Public Service*, 23 April 1998, Paris.

Public Concern at Work (2010), "Where's whistleblowing now? 10 years of legal protection for whistleblowers", London, *www.pcaw.org.uk/files/PIDA_10year_Final_PDF.pdf.*

Transparency International (2013a), "Whistleblowing in Europe: Legal protections for whistleblowers in the EU", Transparency International, Berlin. *www.transparency.org/whatwedo/publication/whistleblowing_in_europe_legal_protections_for_whistleblowers_in_the_eu*, accessed 23 January 2017.

Transparency International (2013b), "International Principles for Whistleblower Legislation: Best Practices for Laws to Protect Whistleblowers and Support Whistleblowing in the Public Interest", Berlin. *www.transparency.org/whatwedo/pub/international_principles_for_whistleblower_legislation*, accessed 23 January 2017.

UNODC (2015), "Resource Guide on Good Practices in the Protection of Reporting Persons", United Nations, Vienna.

Vandekerckhove,W (2006), *Whistleblowing and Organizational Social Responsibility: A Global Assessment*, Ashgate Publishing, Ltd., Hampshire

OECD Integrity Review of Coahuila, Mexico
Restoring trust through an integrity system

Chapter 4

Strengthening Coahuila's internal control and risk management framework

This chapter discusses how Coahuila could strengthen its internal control and risk management framework to better safeguard integrity in public sector organisations and enable effective accountability. It highlights the value of ensuring a strategic approach to risk management, which Coahuila could cultivate by encouraging implementation of the existing framework through guidance, training, and capacity building. The chapter also focuses on the role of the internal audit function in providing reasonable assurance over risk management and internal control processes, stressing the need to gradually appoint internal control units in all ministries and to scale up professionalism and capacities to fulfil the investigative attributions that the Ministry for Audit and Accountability (SEFIR) will undertake within the Local Anti-corruption System with respect to non-serious offences of public officials.

Introduction

An effective internal control and risk management framework is essential in public sector organisations to safeguard integrity, improve accountability, and prevent corruption. This framework should include internal control measures, risk management, and internal audit and be designed to provide reasonable assurance about the achievement of the organisation's objectives with regard to reliability of financial reporting, effectiveness, and efficiency of operations and compliance with applicable rules, regulations, and legislation.

Internal controls are the policies, structures, procedures, and processes that enable an organisation to identify and appropriately respond to risks, whether these are internal or external and strategic, operational, financial, or compliance. Internal controls are checks and balances that are the responsibility of management and are carried out by staff as part of their everyday activities. An effective internal control and risk management framework helps an organisation comply with its mandate and any relevant legislation, safeguard its assets, and facilitate internal and external reporting. It also helps ensure greater accountability, better management and increased cost-effectiveness, because controls help organisations to run more smoothly, reduce costs, avoid waste, hold officials to account for their actions, and report to the public and oversight institutions on the performance and value for money achieved.

While senior managers are primarily responsible for implementing internal controls and monitoring their effectiveness, all officials in a public organisation – from the most senior to the most junior – play a role in identifying risks and deficiencies and ensuring that internal controls address and mitigate these risks. Every staff member should be encouraged to contribute continually to the development of better systems and procedures that enhance the organisation's integrity and its resistance to corruption.

A mature internal control and risk management framework needs to include a strategic approach to risk management that effectively identifies the likelihood of events occurring that may hamper the operations of an organisation and the achievement of its objectives and sets up adequate controls to mitigate them. Risk assessment plays a key role in the selection of appropriate internal control measures.

Internal audit is another key element of an internal control and risk management framework. Internal audit provides objective assurance that risk management and internal controls are functioning properly. An effective internal audit monitoring and assurance function ensures that internal control deficiencies are identified and communicated in a timely manner to those responsible for taking corrective action. The monitoring process involves establishing risk-based monitoring procedures, assessing and reporting results, and following up on corrective action where necessary.

In Coahuila, the Ministry for Audit and Accountability (*Secretaría de Fiscalización y Rendición de Cuentas*, or SEFIR) is the state-level entity, within the Executive, responsible for developing and overseeing policies, standards, and tools on internal control including risk management and internal audit functions in the state administration. Its activities are carried out within the framework governing the internal control system in Coahuila—the General

Standard for Internal Control (*Norma General de Control Interno*)—which was published in August 2013. It is based on five standards set by the Committee of Sponsoring Organizations of the Treadway Commission's (COSO) Internal Control Integrated Framework (Figure 4.1).

Figure 4.1. **Coahuila's general standard for internal control**

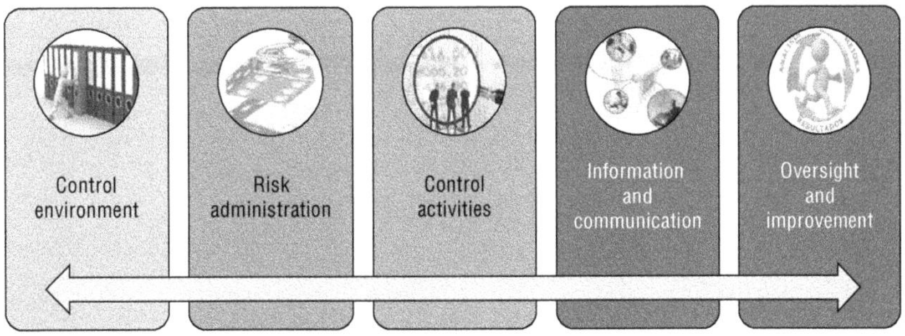

Source: SEFIR presentation, July 2016 (translation by OECD).

This chapter examines Coahuila's internal control and risk management framework as defined by the COSO Internal Control Integrated Framework, focusing on areas where the implementation gap is most significant and emphasising the extent its risk management framework safeguards integrity in public sector organisations. The analysis is informed by internationally-recognised standards such as the COSO Internal Control Integrated Framework (COSO, 2013) and the INTOSAI Guidelines for Internal Control Standards for the Public Sector (INTOSAI, 2004), as well as by the OECD *Recommendation on Public Integrity* (OECD, 2017a), which calls states to "ensure a strategic approach to risk management that includes assessing risks to public integrity, addressing control weaknesses (including building warning signals into critical processes), and building an efficient monitoring and quality assurance mechanism for the risk management system."

Demonstrating high-level commitment to integrity objectives and risk management

The risk administration framework in Coahuila

Risk assessments are key to understanding risk exposure and allowing public organisations to reach informed risk management decisions. COSO defines entity risk management as "a process affected by an entity's board of directors, management and other personnel, applied in strategy setting and across the entity, designed to identify potential events that may affect the entity and manage risk to be within its risk appetite, to provide reasonable assurance regarding the achievement of entity objectives" (COSO, 2004). This broad definition may also be applied in the public sector, where the concept of operational risk management would encompass the systems, processes, procedures, and culture that facilitate the identification, assessment, evaluation, and treatment of risks in order to help public sector organisations successfully pursue their strategies and performance objectives (OECD, 2013).

Operational risk management begins with establishing the context and setting an organisation's objectives and continues with the identification of events—related to both internal and external factors—that might have an impact on their achievement. Those events that may have a negative impact represent risks. Risk assessment is a three-step process that starts with risk identification and is followed by risk analysis, which includes developing an understanding of each risk, its consequences, the likelihood of those consequences occurring, and the risk's severity. The third step is risk evaluation, which involves determining the tolerability of each risk and whether the risk should be accepted or treated. Risk treatment is the process of adjusting existing internal controls or developing and implementing new controls to bring a risk's severity to a tolerable level (Figure 4.2).

Figure 4.2. **Risk management cycle according to ISO 31000: 2009**

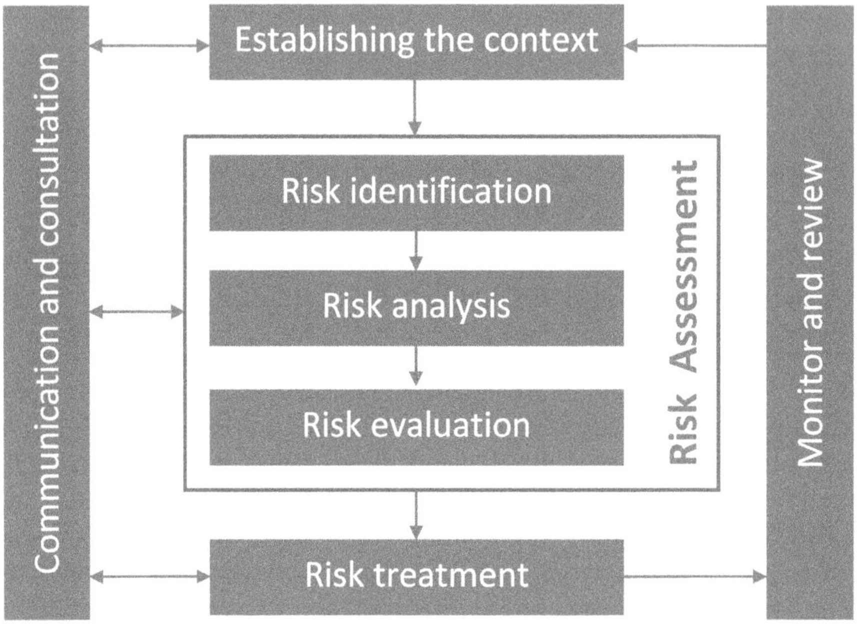

Source: Adapted by OECD from ISO 31000: 2009; OECD (2013), *OECD Integrity Review of Italy: Reinforcing Public Sector Integrity, Restoring Trust for Sustainable Growth*, OECD Publishing, Paris, *http://dx.doi.org/10.1787/9789264193819-en*.

The process of establishing the context and assessing and treating risk is linear, while communication and consultation, monitoring, and reviewing are continuous. Communication and consultation with internal and external stakeholders is, where practicable, a key step towards securing their input into the process and giving them ownership of the outputs of risk management. It is also important to understand stakeholders' concerns about risk and risk management so that their involvement can be planned and their views taken into account in determining risk criteria. Finally, monitoring and reviewing support the identification of new risks and reassessment of existing ones that result from changes either in the organisation's objectives or in the internal and external environment where they are pursued. This involves scanning for possible new risks and learning lessons about risks and controls from the analysis of successes and failures (OECD, 2013).

The risk management framework in Coahuila is outlined in the General Standard for Internal Control. Although all officials in the organisation are responsible for communicating and reporting risks, the framework assigns specific responsibilities to the following actors, who should follow minimum steps and requirements in line with the process described in Figure 4.3:

- the head of the public entity (*titular de dependencia/entitdad*) oversees compliance with the risk administration process
- the internal control co-ordinator (*coordinador de control interno*) co-ordinates the risk administration process and communication between the head of the entity and the liaison officer for risk management
- the liaison officer for risk management (*enlace de administración de riesgos*) links the internal control co-ordinator with all the administrative and operational areas of the organisation;

supports the managers and the staff throughout the different steps of the process; reviews and analyses their inputs to elaborate risk administration-related documents; and follows up the Programme of Work for Risk Management (*Programa de Trabajo de Administración de Riesgos*, PTAR), whose primary objective is to monitor and assess the execution of the mitigating strategies and controls aiming to address risks.

Figure 4.3. **Coahuila's risk administration framework**

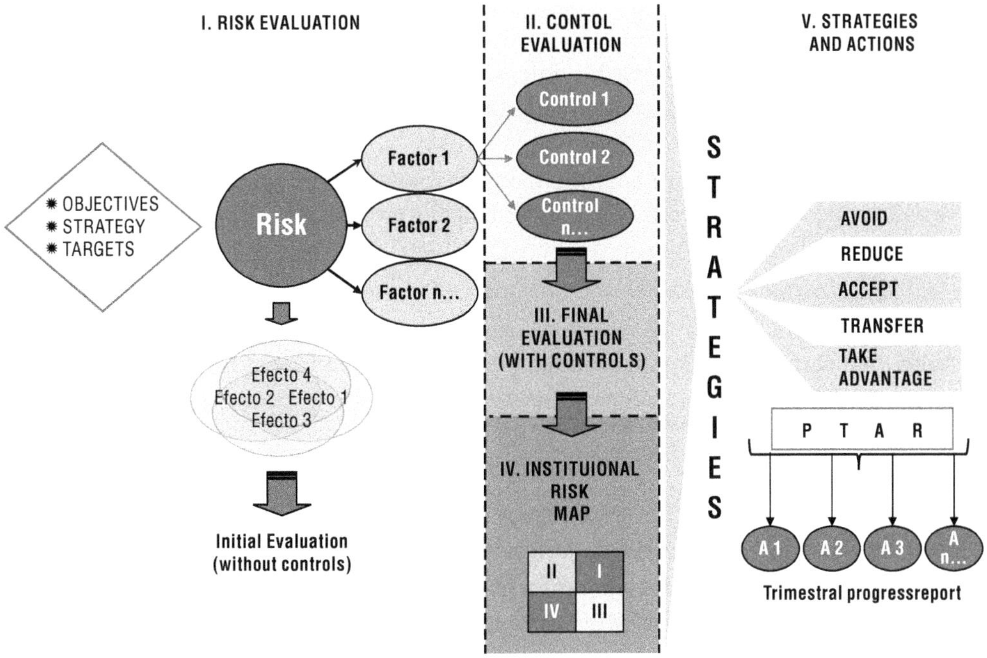

Source: SEFIR presentation, July 2016 (translation by OECD).

Coahuila could strengthen standards and policies in order to place greater emphasis on corruption and fraud as it relates to risk management and to clarify how and when to undertake risk assessments.

Developing a dedicated risk management framework for corruption and fraud risks is crucial in increasing awareness of those risks and in detecting and mitigating the different types of corruption that may take place within public entities. Such risks impact on resource allocation and decision making. They also affect the integrity of public policies and the public's trust in government.

Although 44% of the population think corruption is very frequent in state institutions in Coahuila (INEGI, 2015), there is currently no dedicated policy to manage fraud and corruption risks. In particular, the risk administration framework does not include a specific process for addressing these kinds of risks, which impairs the government's ability to mitigate them.

Considering the adverse impact that corruption and fraud have on carrying out government policies and building public trust, SEFIR could gradually introduce specific guidance, processes, and responsibilities to address those risks in its standards and policies. In the short term, SEFIR could integrate the existing internal control and risk management framework with additional guidance and information on dealing with corruption risks. To do so, it could follow the model of the Independent Commission Against Corruption (ICAC) in the Australian state of New South Wales (Box 4.1).

Box 4.1. **Corruption risk management guidance in New South Wales (Australia)**

The Independent Commission Against Corruption (ICAC) established by the government of New South Wales in 1988 has, among its functions, the task to actively prevent corruption through advice and assistance. Through its website, it provides guidance and information to help identify the risks of corruption and to develop strategies to manage these risks effectively. This is considered "the first step in preventing corruption." In particular, four topics are dealt with by the ICAC:

- The risk management approach addresses the importance of risk management for preventing corruption and recognizes the specificities of corruption risks compared to other risks.
- Identifying corruption risks includes methods for identifying such risks such as using existing information/experience/skills and having recourse to external professionals or techniques.
- Managing corruption risks illustrates treatment options and corruption risk plans.
- Internal audit illustrates the role and options of internal auditors in assisting agencies with their corruption risk management process, also by means of a case study.

Source: ICAC website section on Corruption Risk Management: *www.icac.nsw.gov.au/preventing-corruption/corruption-risk-management*, accessed 1 June 2017.

In the medium term, SEFIR could then consider aligning to the Standard Model of Internal Control adopted by the federal Ministry of Public Administration (*Secretaría de Función Pública*, or SFP) in 2016, which introduces for the first time a principle dedicated to managing corruption risks (*Gestión de riesgos de corrupción*) and illustrates specific methodologies, risk factors, and mitigation strategies to address them (*Acuerdo por el que se emiten las Disposiciones y el Manual Administrativo de Aplicación General en Material de Control Interno*, MAAG-CI, November 2016). Lastly, as a long-term objective, SEFIR could consider adopting a set of dedicated procedures, standards, and tools to effectively prevent, detect, and respond to risks of fraud and corruption in the manner of the United States and Colombia (Box 4.2).

Box 4.2. **Dedicated fraud and corruption risk management frameworks: the United States and Colombian examples**

A. United States Government Accountability Office (GAO): A framework for managing fraud risks in federal programmes

The framework encompasses the control activities as well as structures and environmental factors that help managers to mitigate fraud risks. The framework consists of the following four components for effectively managing fraud risks:

1. Commit: Demonstrate commitment to combating fraud by creating an organisational culture and structure conducive to fraud risk management.
2. Assess: Plan regular fraud risk assessments and assess risks to define a fraud risk profile.
3 Design and implement: Design and implement a strategy with specific control activities to mitigate assessed fraud risks and collaborate to help ensure effective implementation.
4. Evaluate and adapt: Evaluate outcomes using a risk-based approach and adapt activities to improve fraud risk management.

Box 4.2. **Dedicated fraud and corruption risk management frameworks: the United States and Colombian examples** *(cont.)*

In addition, the framework reflects activities related to monitoring and feedback mechanisms, which include ongoing practices that apply to all four concepts above.

B. Colombia: Guide for Corruption Risk Management

In Colombia, anti-corruption risk management became obligatory for all public entities in 2011 with Law 1474, the Anti-corruption Statute. Corruption risk identification and assessment started as an add-on exercise in 2012, promoted by the Transparency Secretariat (*Secretaría de Transparencia*, or ST). From the beginning the methodology was widely based on the existing internal control model (i.e. *Modelo Estándar de Control Interno*, or MECI). Taking stock of the experience of the latter exercise, a second version of the methodology highlighting the inherent characteristic of corruption risks versus the institutional risks of public organisations and aligning even better and more explicitly with the MECI was issued in 2015. As a result, Colombian public organisations must develop two different risk maps following standardised procedures and templates.

A system with two separate risk management exercises based on the same methodological model has both positive and negative attributes. On the one hand, it may be seen as burdensome and bureaucratic, duplicating efforts and wasting valuable resources. On the other hand, this exercise could raise awareness among senior management and staff of the importance of having a sound anti-corruption policy with risk activities distinct from the mainstream financial control and risk activities.

The following figure depicts the Colombian methodology for corruption risk management:

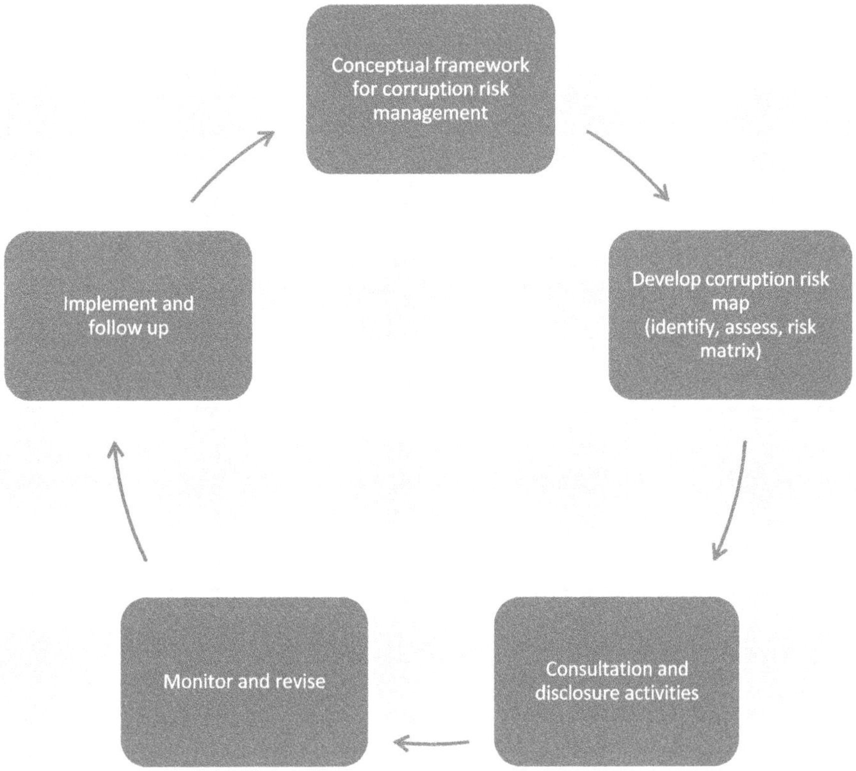

Source : US GAO (2015), *A Framework for Managing Fraud Risks in Federal Programs*, Washington, GAO-15-593SP, *www.gao.gov/products/GAO-15-593SP* and Colombia Transparency Secretariat (2015), *Guía para la Gestión de Riesgo de Corrupción*, *www.anticorrupcion.gov.co/SiteAssets/Paginas/Publicaciones/guia-gestion-riesgo-anticorrupcion.pdf*.

Coahuila could strengthen its "tone at the top" and its leadership's commitment to integrity and effective control environment.

In order to manage fraud and corruption risks effectively, an additional fundamental step is to create an internal control environment where organisations demonstrate commitment to integrity, and where managers and senior public officials demonstrate the right tone at the top. Indeed, the "tone at the top" – which refers to entity-wide attitudes of integrity and control consciousness as exhibited by the most senior executives of an organisation (Association of Certified Fraud Examiners-ACFE, 2006) – is a crucial component in the promotion of ethics. In this context, although every public official has a role in creating and maintaining an internal control environment aligned with institutional objectives and values, including their adherence to integrity, managers are primarily responsible for modelling ethical behaviour and creating an environment that demonstrates the entity's commitment to ethical values.

In Coahuila, interviews during the fact-finding mission indicated minimal commitment of senior managers in setting the tone to create a sustainable and functional control environment. This seems to be consistent with Coahuila's existing General Standard for Internal Control, which only requires those responsible for the internal control's strategic level to create and update and diffuse Coahuila's Codes of Ethics and Conduct and to design and implement the corresponding controls (Article 13(I)(b) and (c)).

However, as noted in Chapter 2, commendable initiatives have been developed by SEFIR's Deputy Ministry of Government Auditing and Administrative Development (*Subsecretaría de Auditoría Gubernamental y Desarrollo Administrativo*) aimed at raising awareness and which include:

- posters with the values in each ministry and government entity
- dissemination through the internal network: in SEFIR, for example, the value of the month is displayed on the computer screen
- buttons with the slogan "With ethics and values, better public officials" (*Con Ética y Valores, Funcionarios Mejores*) for officials interacting directly with the public
- banners with the values and principles as established in the code of conduct and ethics, which are set in visible places in each ministry and government entity
- leaflets with specific information about the values and responsibilities of public officials

To improve its internal control environment, Coahuila could consider, as a starting point, revising its general standard in line with the Standard Model of Internal Control (*Modelo Estándar de Control Interno*) adopted by the SFP in 2015 and codifying the principle that "the organisation demonstrates a commitment to integrity and ethical values", including the following subset of elements substantiating it:

1. Sets the tone at the top: The board of directors and management at all levels of the entities demonstrate through their directives, actions, and behaviour the importance of integrity and ethical values to support the functioning of the system of internal control.
2. Establishes standards of conduct: The expectations of the board of directors and senior management concerning integrity and ethical values are defined in the entities' standards of conduct and understood at all levels of the organisations and by outsourced service providers and business partners.

3. Evaluates adherence to standards of conduct: Processes are in place to evaluate the performance of individuals and teams against the entities' expected standards of conduct.
4. Addresses deviations in a timely manner: Deviations from the entity's expected standards of conduct are identified and remedied in a timely and consistent manner (OECD, 2017b).

Furthermore, Coahuila could ensure that its control environment is part of planning, daily operations, and standard evaluation and monitoring processes. It could thus consider the measures compiled by the European Union to create an optimal anti-corruption control environment (Box 4.3).

Lastly, Coahuila could emphasise the value of role models and the tone at the top for promoting ethical behaviour among managers and could consider the following initiatives:

- screening managers on traits favouring ethical behaviour and testing ethical compliance during management selection procedures
- seminars and awareness campaigns on ethics and values for management both collectively and individually
- self-assessment tools for managers (evaluation questionnaires) including ethical aspects
- complete evaluations for senior managers as well as managers in high-risk positions (with evaluations including ethical aspects)
- communicating concrete compliance actions, for example, high-ranking officials giving up gifts (OECD, 2017d)

Box 4.3. **Key measures towards developing an environment non-conducive to corruption**

- all management plans, regardless of level, should reflect the organisation's values and ethics
- requiring an individual "ethical contract'" or code of conduct to be signed between recruiter and recruit at the moment of first entry into service and periodical (e.g. annual) re-signing
- dilemma training during which the organisation's values are explained in very concrete situations (for all levels of the organisation, including management)
- workshops on ethics and values including some especially for senior and middle management
- HR procedures for hiring, evaluation and dismissal must reflect and openly support the organisation's mission and values
- the organisation's values are included in function profiles and job descriptions
- ethical clauses in procurement processes and in contracts with external suppliers
- ethics co-ordinators with specific responsibilities to promote and enhance awareness of ethics
- the key values of the organisation are publicly displayed
- developing a process to report suspected violations of the organisation's code of conduct

Source: Public Internal Control Systems in the European Union, Position Paper 2015.

Overcoming implementation gaps for improved risk management

SEFIR could help improve management ownership and awareness of the internal control system and risk management by developing awareness-raising activities on risk-based approaches and could also work to provide enhanced capacity-building initiatives, additional guidance, and training.

Many OECD member and partner countries face challenges in closing the implementation gap between their conceptual internal control and risk management frameworks and the actual internal control activities and risk management functions that need to take place on a daily basis. There are four basic stages of a maturity towards achieving the integration of internal control and risk management processes into the organisation's overall governance and management systems (Figure 4.4).

Figure 4.4. **Maturity levels of integrating internal control and risk management**

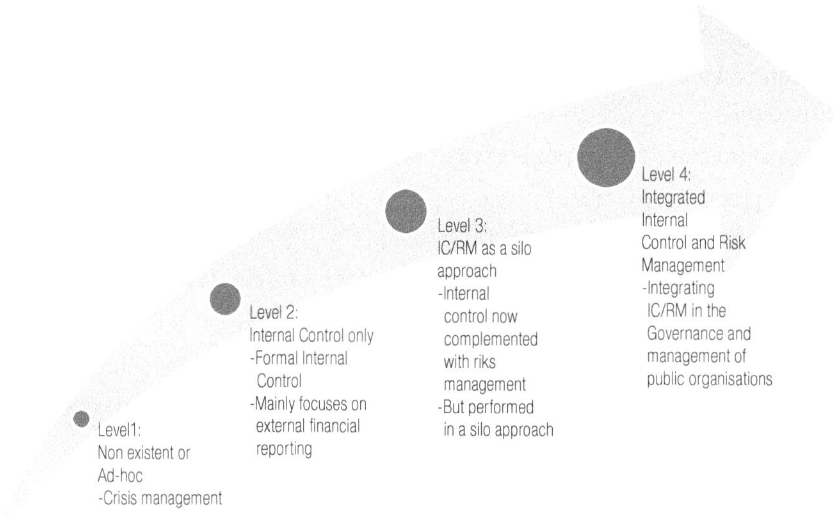

Source: OECD (2017d), Integrity Review of Colombia.

One of the major issues in linking internal control with the governance and management systems of public organisations is that politically-appointed personnel, public managers, and staff may not fully understand the added value of internal control in improving performance and achieving institutional objectives. Many do not appreciate that internal controls can help organisations to run more smoothly, reduce costs, and avoid waste, as well as to help hold officials to account for their actions and to report to the public and oversight institutions on the performance and value-for-money achieved (OECD, 2017d).

Public managers have key responsibilities in relation to establishing and maintaining sound internal control processes and activities. In particular, senior managers are primarily responsible for implementing internal controls and monitoring their effectiveness consistent with the three-lines-of-assurance model of the Institute of Internal Auditors (2013) (Table 4.1), which differentiates between the following three core functions:

1. **Management (First Line)**: Functions responsible for designing, developing, implementing, and executing controls, processes, and practices to deliver services and objectives and to drive intended results (i.e., outcomes). This line may also be referred to as "programme

management" and is responsible for the effective and efficient management of the service delivery and the daily operations of the entity. Because oversight and independent assurance cannot compensate for weak management or control, these functions generally have the greatest influence on entity-wide risk management.

2. **Oversight (Second Line)**: Functions responsible for overseeing and monitoring line management and front desk activities. These groups may include (but are not limited to) functions responsible for financial control/oversight, privacy, security, risk management, quality assurance, integrity, and compliance. Oversight functions also inform decision makers with objective perspectives and expertise, and provide continuous monitoring to strengthen risk management.
3. **Internal Audit (Third Line)**: A professional, independent, and objective appraisal function that uses a disciplined, evidence-based approach to assess and improve the effectiveness of risk management, control, and governance processes. Internal Audit may provide consulting, assurance, or a combination of both to inform key decisions and support good and accountable public governance.

Table 4.1. **The three lines of assurance model**

1st line of assurance	2nd line of assurance	3rd line of assurance
Operational level: • Own and manage the risks • Good policy and performance data • Monitoring statistics • Risk registers	Independent from delivery units • Compliance assessments or reviews • Programme and project management • Direct reporting line to senior management and the minister	Independent internal audit function • Assess and provide assurance over the effectiveness of the 1st and the 2nd lines arrangements • Risk-based approach on addressing gaps or inefficiencies in the assurance system

Source: OECD (2017c), *Integrity Review of Peru*, OECD Publishing, Paris. *http://dx.doi.org/10.1787/9789264271029-en*.

While the conceptual framework defined in the General Standard for Internal Control shows that a risk management strategy is developing in Coahuila, interviews during the fact-finding mission highlighted limitations in the implementation of corresponding processes and tools throughout the state. In particular, the OECD found that the internal control and risk management processes in Coahuila are still not part of the organisation's overall management system, but are rather seen as a formal administrative exercise. As such, the processes add up to a number of administrative commitments rather than to a process to prevent risks and achieve objectives and value for money more effectively. Similarly, the risk management exercise is seen as the responsibility of a specific group of people who are separate from the operational units where real risks are present. This inhibits an entity's ability to identify, address, and mitigate a range of risks that could threaten the achievement of the entity's objectives.

In order to build greater ownership within Coahuila's public administration over internal control and risk, the roles and responsibilities of managers in this context could be clarified. As a first step, SEFIR could release an official communication framing the content of managerial responsibility in line with the circular adopted by the United States Office of Management and Budget (Box 4.4).

As a following step and as an objective on the longer term, Coahuila could take into account the approach of the Belgian Public Federal Service of Budget and Management Control, which completely integrates the risk cycle and, by extension, the maintenance of the internal control system into the four phases of the Deming's management cycle (Plan – Do – Check – Act) (Box 4.5).

Box 4.4. **United States Office of Management and Budget (OMB) Circular A-123: Management's responsibility for internal control**

The circular states the office policy as:

1. Management is responsible for establishing and maintaining internal control to achieve the objectives of effective and efficient operations, reliable financial reporting, and compliance with applicable laws and regulations.
2. Management shall consistently apply the internal control standards to meet each of the internal control objectives and to assess internal control effectiveness.
3. When assessing the effectiveness of internal control over financial reporting and compliance with financial laws and regulations, management must follow the OMB's outlined assessment process.
4. Annually, management must provide assurances on internal control in its Performance and Accountability Report, including a separate assurance on internal control over financial reporting, along with a report on identified material weaknesses and corrective actions.

Actions required by the circular indicate agencies and individual Federal managers must take systematic and proactive measures to:

- develop and implement appropriate, cost-effective internal control for results-oriented management
- assess the adequacy of internal control in federal programmes and operations
- separately assess and document internal control over financial reporting consistent with the process
- identify needed improvements
- take corresponding corrective action
- report annually on internal control through management assurance statements

Source: OMB Circular A-123, *https://obamawhitehouse.archives.gov/sites/default/files/omb/memoranda/2016/m-16-17.pdf*; and *https://www.kscpa.org/writable/files/Self-Study/FGE/updated_managers_responsibility_for_internal_control-_article.pdf*.

Box 4.5. **Leveraging internal control over the Deming's management cycle**

A public entity's scope and activities are determined and influenced by factors such as:

- political strategic goals
- annual policy priorities
- citizen expectations
- resource limitations

The head of a public entity is accountable for managing available resources to meet stakeholders' expectations in the most effective way. To this end, he or she is responsible for:

- evaluating what was accomplished against what was planned
- taking action to improve the situation
- anticipating changes and possible new risks

Deming's cycle illustrates the need to integrate internal control processes within the daily management operation.

Box 4.5. **Leveraging internal control over the Deming's management cycle** *(cont.)*

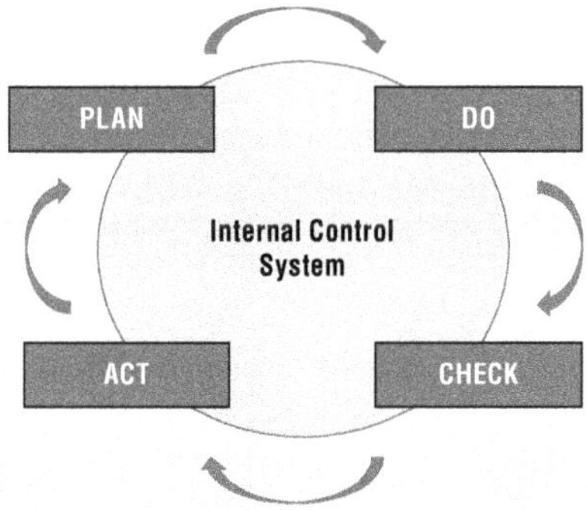

The Belgian Public Federal Service for Budget and Management Control has adopted an approach that completely integrates the risk cycle and, by extension, the maintenance of the internal control system into the four phases of the management cycle (Plan – Do – Check – Act, cf. Deming), in twelve steps.

- During the planning phase (Plan), the organisation defines periodic expectations concerning the services to be provided and the necessary resources. The measuring system, comprised of a set of indicators and reports, takes into account the results of the periodic monitoring.
- The execution phase (Do) includes the "regular" activities of the organisation. During this phase, basic information is collected in order to be examined in the analysis phase. The management ensures the proper execution of activities and the adequate application of the measuring system.
- During the analysis phase (Check), results obtained are assessed and discussed. This is one of the most important aspects of management control. In this stage, the internal control system begins to be updated based on the events that occurred during the execution phase. To this end, Management Support created an intuitive tool, *Diabolo*, which serves as a process sheet and contains a complete risk module. It facilitates the identification and assessment of risks. The control measures can then be evaluated, which reduces the organisation's vulnerability to risks. Risk exposure is an indication of the possible need to deal with a priority risk.
- During the reaction phase (Act), appropriate measures are developed so as to address a risk. Good support is required to ensure that the measures taken are properly implemented.

Policy-related risks have to be indicated separately because they are related to longer-term objectives in the management plan or the governmental agreement. Their monitoring requires a lower frequency than the monitoring of management risks. They can be estimated during the planning phase by means of a SWOT (strengths, weaknesses, opportunities, and threats) analysis, with a view to possible strategic or operational rectifications. Periodic reporting from the management cycle provides a valuable contribution in this case.

Source: Public Internal Control Systems in the European Union and Practical Guide for the Development and maintenance of an Internal control System by the Belgian Public Federal Service for Budget and Management Control.

In addition, since internal control is an "integral process effected by the entity's management and personnel" (EU Commission, 2015), Coahuila could also consider developing further guidance and training not only for senior and middle management, but for all staff in general. The inclusion of operational staff would help to clarify the tasks and responsibilities within the internal control and risk management system and would contribute to closing the implementation gap. It could also motivate staff to link operational objectives and associated risks to the higher level management plans and organisational-level risks.

Specific training is currently provided in Coahuila to 54 Internal Control Committees and 38 municipalities through the Network of Trainers (*Red Estatal de Instructores*), which relies on volunteer work from public officials trained by SEFIR (see Chapter 2). Although the Network of Trainers is a valuable model for training staff in charge of the internal control function, SEFIR could consider building on these activities and develop further initiatives such as:

- e-learning modules on principles, roles, and responsibilities within the risk management process
- dilemma training scenarios underpinning the attributes of a sound internal control environment
- workshops on the added value of internal controls in improving management and governance systems, including some especially designed for senior and middle management
- training modules and awareness campaigns focusing on bridging the gap between organisational objectives, daily operations, and internal control activities

Furthermore, there is little evidence that SEFIR or single ministries in Coahuila are promoting awareness among all staff of the internal control and risk management framework and its developments. As a consequence, some measures and initiatives could also be considered to help raise awareness, including:

- using awareness campaigns or events on the importance of integrating the internal control and risk management activities into daily business as a tool to influence public perception and enhance the accountability, and therefore the legitimacy, of public entities
- communicating with all staff (e.g. by videos, electronic messages, newsletters) good practices and individual achievements in integrating and using internal control as a management tool
- providing regular feedback about the linkages between a sound internal control environment and the achievement of the entity's objectives by using periodic messages (e.g. newsletters, videos, etc.) from senior management to highlight progress and achievements on improving the actual implementation and integration of the internal control requirements and activities
- linking issues such as budget allocation, expenditure limits, staff and payroll ceilings, especially at the municipal level, with the progress made in mainstreaming internal control and risk management into daily operations
- reflecting the organisation's mission and ethical values within human resources procedures
- introducing concrete tasks and responsibilities in relation to allocation of internal control functions (OECD, 2017b)

Findings from the fact-finding mission in July 2016 and the workshop in December 2016 also highlighted that the limitations in implementing internal control and risk management processes and tools throughout the state seemed to be due to the difficulties in understanding the rationale and in integrating such a process in each entity. In order to address this issue, SEFIR could complement the general guidelines provided through the Manual for General Application on Internal Control (*Manual Administrativo de Aplicación*

General en Materia de Control Interno) released in November 2016 with ad-hoc guidance on risk-management arrangements, tools, and methodology, which could support public sector entities in better understanding, and eventually integrating, risk management in daily tasks and operations. For this purpose, such guidance could contain graphs and tables illustrating the process in line with the Manual, as well as narrative explanations of the objectives, concepts, and processes in accessible language. In these efforts, Coahuila could follow the example of the documents released by State of Victoria in Australia and by Colombia's Administrative Department of Public Function (*Departamento Administrativo de la Función Pública*, or DAFP) (Box 4.6). Such guidance could also support entities in using the Matrix and Risk Analysis Map (*Matriz y Mapa de Analisis de Riesgos Institucionales*), which was provided by SEFIR and which follows the model shared by the General Comptroller Office of the Baja California State within the Commission of State and Federal Comptrollers (*Comisión Permanente de Contralores Estados Federación*, or CPCE-F).

Box 4.6. **Practical guidance for risk administration in Victoria (Australia) and Colombia**

In the State of Victoria (Australia) the Victorian Managed Insurance Authority (VMIA) has developed a Practice Guide to the Victorian Government Risk Management Framework with the aim to support the agencies in implementing it and meeting related obligations. The Guide provides a practical explanation of the framework, presenting risk management requirements, principles, and concepts in a practical and synthetic way. In order to further assist agencies in dealing with the risk management processes, the Guide also includes figures and graphs as well as practical tips and case studies. The final section of the Guide provides a list of the templates to fulfil the steps of the risk management process, in particular on the risk management policy, communication plan, risk assessment, risk register, sources of risk, risk rating criteria, and risk treatment plan.

On the other hand, the Risk Administration Guide of Colombia's DAFP is a document that provides guidance and clarifications in relation to the risk administration methodology applying in Colombia's public administration. For this purpose, it does not only mention objectives, policies, and the legal framework, but it also addresses introductory questions (what is risk? what does it mean to manage risks?) as well as basic concepts for each of the steps of the process (e.g. context, identification, analysis, and evaluation). The document is written in plain language but includes concrete examples, tables, and graphs.

Source: State of Victoria (2016), *Victorian Government Risk Management Framework. Practice Guide*, Melbourne, Australia, *www.vmia.vic.gov.au/~/media/internet/content-documents/risk/risk-tools/risk-management-guide/vmia-practice-guide.pdf*; DAFP (2011), *Guía para la administración del riesgo*, Bogotá, Colombia, *www.funcionpublica.gov.co/documents/418537/506911/1592.pdf/73e5a159-2d8f-41aa-8182-eb99e8c4f3ba*.

SEFIR could make better use of data to identify and address integrity risks, and thereby improve the quality of its institutional risk maps and mitigation strategies. It could develop an action plan and use the Local Digital Platform to be established within the Local Anti-corruption System, which will allow the interconnectivity of several datasets.

An effective risk management function relies on the capacity and the knowledge of the staff involved but also on the quality of the data and input used to inform each phase of the activities, including risk identification and assessment, evaluation of the effectiveness of existing controls, and identifying patterns and historical trends.

Considering the increasing amount of data produced by public administrations, governments have been developing data analytics, which are the techniques and tools to extract information from data by revealing the context in which they are embedded, their organisation, and their structure (OECD, 2015). In this sense, governments are increasingly improving the analytical process to extract insights from operational, financial, and other forms of electronic data internal or external to the organisation. The outcome of this process can also lead to the production of risk-focused analysis on a number of issues such as controls effectiveness, fraud, waste, abuse, and policy/regulatory non-compliance.

Data analytics can therefore help detect operational risks, improper transactions, and integrity breaches such as corruption events, either before they are manifested or after they occur. By incorporating data analytics practices into the risk management function, organisations can monitor performance through risk sensitivity analysis, model key risk event scenarios, and become more risk-intelligent in developing intervention and mitigation strategies (OECD, 2017b). This could be particularly helpful in the state of Coahuila, where the risk management function needs to be further implemented and integrated in daily operations, and where there is room to improve the understanding over the potential impact of corruption risks (Box 4.7).

Coahuila's General Standard for Internal Control includes the concept of "self-control" (*autocontrol*), which encompasses the assessment/evaluation mechanisms, actions, and practices that operate automatically through digital systems and allow risks to be identified, prevented, or mitigated, as well as any other condition limiting or hindering the achievement of objectives. At the same time, open government is an emerging theme in Coahuila's political agenda and its institutions are producing an increasing amount of open data, which could be exploited for analytical and anti-corruption purposes (cf. Chapter 5).

In spite of the theoretical framework and work on open data, the use of data analytics is not a common practice in the internal control system and the risk management function of Coahuila. Considering the potential impact of data analytics in identifying, preventing, and mitigating corruption risks, SEFIR, in co-operation with all other relevant institutions and stakeholders, could consider implementing the "self-control" element of its General Standard for Internal Control by developing a concrete action plan to promote data quality and the use of data analytics tools for effective risk management. In this context, SEFIR could leverage the Local Digital Platform to be created within the CLACS (cf. Chapter 1) and connect various databases to provide relevant information for preventing corruption including, for instance:

- database of assets, conflict of interests, and tax declarations
- database of public officials involved in public procurement contracts
- database of sanctioned public officials and individuals
- information and communications system of the Local Anti-corruption System and the Local Auditing System
- database of public complaints related to corruption (both administrative and criminal)
- database of public procurement contracts

Furthermore, Coahuila could consider one of the recommendations emerging from civil society organisations (IMCO and *Transparencia Mexicana*, or TM) which, among the priorities of the Local Anti-corruption System, identifies the need to create a specialised intelligence unit within state comptrollers such as SEFIR. This unit would have with access to all the information needed for auditing and investigating purposes and could co-ordinate with similar areas around the executive through formal agreements (IMCO/TM, 2016) (see Chapter 2).

Box 4.7. **Leveraging data analytics for managing corruption risks**

The 2016 Global Fraud Study of the Association of Certified Fraud Examiners (ACFE) report identifies proactive data monitoring and analysis as the most effective tool for anti-corruption control in helping reduce corruption losses and corruption scheme duration. More specifically, the 36.7% of victim organisations that used proactive data monitoring and analysis techniques as part of their anti-fraud programme suffered fraud losses that were 54% lower and detected fraud in half the time compared to organisations that did not use this technique.

Furthermore, according to the Institute of Internal Auditor's Global Technology Audit Guide (IPPF-Practice Guide), data analysis can help internal auditors meet their auditing objectives relating to the efficiency of risk management arrangements. Analysing data within key organisational processes enables internal auditors to:

- identify instances of fraud, errors, inefficiencies, or noncompliance, with data driven from 100 percent of relevant transactions and diverse sources
- detect changes, vulnerabilities, and weaknesses that could expose the organisation to undue or unplanned risk
- identify changes in organisational processes and ensure that it is auditing today's risks and not yesterday's

A number of specific analytical techniques have been proven highly effective in analysing data for wrongdoing and anti-fraud auditing purposes:

- calculation of statistical parameters (e.g., averages, standard deviations, highest and lowest values) to identify outlying transactions
- classification to find patterns and associations among groups of data elements
- stratification of numeric values to identify unusual (i.e. excessively high or low) values
- digital analysis using Benford's Law to identify statistically unlikely occurrences of specific digits in naturally occurring data sets
- joining different data sources to identify inappropriately matching values such as names, addresses, and account numbers in disparate systems
- duplicate testing to identify simple and/or complex duplications of organisational transactions such as payments, payroll, claims, or expense report line items
- gap testing to identify missing numbers in sequential data
- summing of numeric values to check control totals that may have errors
- validating data entry dates to identify postings or data entry times that are inappropriate or suspicious

Sources: ACFE, *Report to the nations on occupational fraud and abuse*, 2016 and IIA Global Technology Audit Guide, IPPF-Practice Guide, 2011.

In its efforts to embrace the use of data analytics and therefore the processes of inspecting, cleaning, transforming, and modelling data with the goal of highlighting useful information, suggesting conclusions, and supporting decision making in internal control and risk assessment, Coahuila could take the example provided by several OECD countries, which are moving towards more advanced use of data analytics for anti-corruption purposes and could represent a model for the long-term strategy of Coahuila in this field (Box 4.8).

Box 4.8. Data analytics and data sharing for managing fraud and corruption risks in the United Kingdom and United States

Data Analytics and Data Sharing: With the growing sophistication of corruption, many public sector organisations in the UK are looking to take a more proactive approach to verifying and validating transactions in order to uncover potential and actual corruption. Common approaches have included real-time credit reference and other data checks, online verification techniques, data matching with data held by other public and private sector organisations, and predictive/innovative analytics, which involves developing a model to score data for potential fraud and error. This model can then forecast probabilities of fraud and error to an acceptable level of reliability.

A. The UK example:

The National Fraud Initiative was launched as the UK's largest data matching exercise in relation to fraud. The Serious Crime Act of 2007 enabled bodies other than those that have a mandatory requirement to provide data for the National Fraud Initiative to volunteer to participate by providing data to the Audit Commission (and after March 2015, the Cabinet Office). The following figure shows how the Department for Work and Pensions, the Driver and Vehicle Licensing Agency, and HM Revenue & Customs use data matching to detect evasion acts and how the BBC and the NHS Counter Fraud Service have used data mining for the same purpose.

1. The Department for Work and Pensions has a dedicated Database and Matching Service to identify possible fraud and error. It matches data across benefit systems, between other government departments and Department for Work and Pensions data, for other government departments, and for Local Authorities on Housing and Council Tax Benefits. It also works to tackle internal fraud.
2. The Driver and Vehicle Licensing Agency uses data matching to detect vehicle excise duty evasion.
3. The HM Revenue & Customs application of data matching has identified people who may have received income from property but have not disclosed it.
4. The BBC uses data mining software tools to match details of licensable places with external commercially available data to identify specific places or segments of the population for targeted enforcement activity.
5. The NHS Counter Fraud Service uses data mining and analysis software to examine pharmaceutical and dental data. The software is capable of advanced data analysis that establishes data profiles and highlights anomalies. These can indicate potential fraud for further investigation.

B. The US example:

The US Bureau of Fiscal service has created the Do Not Pay (DNP) Business Center which is a multi-functional analytics tool and one-stop data shop.

DNP's mission is to protect the integrity of the government's payment process by assisting agencies in mitigating and eliminating improper payments in a cost-effective manner while safeguarding the privacy of individuals.

DNP allows government agencies to check various data sources for pre-award, pre-payment eligibility verification, at the time of payment and any time in the payment lifecycle. It allows them to verify eligibility of a vendor, grantee, loan recipient, or beneficiary. This will help prevent, reduce, and stop improper payments, as well as prevent fraud, waste, and abuse.

- DNP offers a centralised system (the DNP portal) that agencies can use at no cost to isolate and identify the potential for improper payments.
- DNP will benefit the federal agency that enters into a financial transaction with a person or entity.
- DNP is NOT a list of entities or people that should not be paid.
- DNP centralises many data sources that agencies can use to verify eligibility.
- DNP is committed to providing quality data, more data sources, continuous system development, cutting edge data analytics, and customised agency outreach.

Box 4.8. **Data analytics and data sharing for managing fraud and corruption risks in the United Kingdom and United States** *(cont.)*

Overview of data source functions:

Data Sources	Function
Credit Alert System (CAIVRS) inputs from Department of Justice (DOJ), Education, Small Business Administration (SBA), Department of Housing and Urban Development (HUD), Department of Agriculture (USDA) & Department of Veterans Affairs (VA)	Verify whether an individual is a delinquent federal borrower
Department of Health and Human Services' (HHS) List of Excluded Individuals & Entities (LEIE)	Verify whether payments are to entities excluded from participating in federal health care programmes
General Services Administration's (GSA) System for Award Management (SAM) Entity Registration Records	Verify that a vendor seeking to do business with the federal government has registered, in accordance with the Federal Acquisitions Regulation (FAR)
GSA SAM Exclusion Records	Verify whether payments are to debarred individuals
Treasury's Office of Foreign Assets Control (OFAC)	Verify whether an individual or entity is prohibited from entering into financial transactions with U.S. financial institutions and the U.S. government
Social Security Administration's (SSA) Death Master File (DMF)	Verify whether a payee is deceased
Treasury Offset Program (TOP) Debt Check	Verify whether payee owes delinquent non-tax debts to federal government (and participating states)

Source: HM Treasury & National Audit Office, *Good Practice Guide on Tackling External Fraud*, and HM Treasury, London, 2008, HM Treasury, *Tackling Internal Fraud*, London, 2011 and United States Government, "Do Not Pay List" *http://donotpay.treas.gov/*.

Strengthen the presence and impact of internal audit in Coahuila

In order to strengthen the internal audit function and improve the effectiveness of governance, risk management, and internal controls, SEFIR could gradually ensure that all ministries have an internal control unit. A corruption risk assessment could be conducted and a priority list created to start the appointment of internal control units in the ministries with the greatest need first.

According to the three lines of assurance model (Table 4.1), internal auditors provide the governing body and senior management with comprehensive assurance based on the highest level of independence and objectivity within the organisation. Accordingly, the Institute of Internal Auditors defines internal auditing as "an independent, objective assurance, and consulting activity designed to add value and improve an organisation's operations. It helps an organisation accomplish its objectives by bringing a systematic, disciplined approach to evaluate and improve the effectiveness of risk management, control, and governance processes." (Institute of Internal Auditors, 2017a)

The audit function on government and public procurement activities in Coahuila is carried out by SEFIR, whose Internal Regulation (*Reglamento Interior de la Secretaría de Fiscalización y Rendición de Cuentas del Estado de Coahuila de Zaragoza*) gives the head of such Ministry the responsibility to appoint the internal control units (*Órganos Internos de Control*, or OICs) within Coahuila's ministries and entities upon proposal of the Deputy Minister for Government Audit and Administrative Development (*Subsecretaría de Auditoría Gubernamental y Desarrollo Administrativo*). However, it emerged that only few ministries have OICs, while audit activities for the rest of the ministries are currently carried out directly by other areas such as legal and administrative departments. As a result, the degree of accountability in the latter entities is diminished insofar as the audit activity is not carried out by dedicated staff having specific responsibilities and resources to devote to the auditing activity in a continuous manner and in close co-ordination with SEFIR. Furthermore, in both cases, relevant personnel is appointed by the entity, thereby posing the risk that its activity may not be carried out independently.

In order to provide closer assurance to senior management and better support entities in implementing their risk-management process, SEFIR could implement its Internal Regulation and appoint internal control units which could be designed in line with the model established at the federal level (Box 4.9). The creation of OICs could begin in selected ministries after carrying out a risk-based assessment. For example, news sources from Coahuila and experience in other countries point out that health and infrastructure are two areas which are exposed to a number of risks and where those units could be first integrated.

Box 4.9. **Offices of Internal Control (*Órganos Interno de Control*) at the federal level in Mexico**

The current model of the OICs consists of four different areas including internal audit, complaints management, investigation and disciplinary activities, and performance evaluation issues. The relevant institutional arrangements and roles are described in Articles 76 and 80 of the Internal Regulation of the SFP as well as in the "*Acuerdo por el que se adscriben orgánicamente las unidades administrativas de la Secretaría de la Función Pública y se establece la subordinación jerárquica de los servidores públicos previstos en su Reglamento Interior*", which was published in the Official Gazette on 9 December 2015.

With regards to auditing functions, OICs have the following responsibilities: co-operating in carrying out the functioning of the control system; monitoring compliance with the internal control standards; analysing and proposing regulations and guidelines to strengthen internal control within entities; planning and carrying out audits, revisions and inspections; and following up on observations made during SFP audits.

Source: OECD (2017b) and SFP Internal Regulation (most recently revised in January 2017), *www.gob.mx/cms/uploads/attachment/file/182651/21_RI_SFP_v_12012017_vf.pdf.*

Considering increased competence to conducting administrative proceedings for non-serious offences of public officials within the CLACS, SEFIR could improve the internal audit function with regards to fraud and corruption investigations by scaling up professionalism and ensuring adequate capacities and resources.

Internal auditors should have a role in fighting corruption, although such responsibility should be limited to evaluating the existing situation and submitting proposals to improve governance in order to promote the right ethical values and principles inside the entity (Institute of Internal Auditors, 2017b). In particular, the auditors should act to identify fraud and corruption indicators that can be recognised in most of the core business processes relying on their technical experience, professional judgment, and good understanding of how potential fraud and corruption acts can be committed. Audit strategy could focus on areas and operations prone to fraud and corruption by developing and applying effective high risk indicators. Box 4.10 provides an example of the internal audit's role in combatting fraud and corruption.

According to SEFIR's Internal Regulation (*Reglamento Interior de la Secretaría de Fiscalización y Rendición de Cuentas del Estado de Coahuila de Zaragoza*), SEFIR is currently responsible for administrative disciplinary cases based on the findings from audits or related to the lack of compliance with public officials' obligations. However, interviews during the OECD fact-finding mission made clear that the enforcement of integrity-related obligations in Coahuila is limited because of the lack of capacity and expertise to carry out investigations. This is confirmed by the fact that no sanctions have been issued for conflict-of-interest cases. This challenge is likely to become more relevant in the future, because in the context of the CLACS reform process, Coahuila will have to revise its State Responsibilities Law. Similarly to the federal model adopted in July 2016, this law will increase SEFIR's responsibility to conduct administrative proceedings in relation to non-serious administrative offences.

Box 4.10. **Fraud and Corruption - Internal Audit's Role**

Internal audit's primary role is not to detect fraud and corruption, rather it exists to provide an independent opinion based on an objective assessment of the framework of governance, risk management, and control. In doing so, internal auditors may:

- review the organisation's risk assessment seeking evidence on which to base an opinion that fraud and corruption risks have been properly identified and responded to appropriately (i.e. within the risk tolerance)
- provide an independent opinion on the effectiveness of prevention and detection processes put in place to reduce the risk of fraud and/or corruption
- review new programmes and policies (and changes in existing policies and programmes) seeking evidence that the risk of fraud and corruption had been considered where appropriate and providing an opinion on the likely effectiveness of controls designed to reduce risks
- consider the potential for fraud and corruption in every audit assignment and identify indicators that crime might have been committed or control weaknesses that might indicate a vulnerability to fraud or corruption
- review areas where major fraud or corruption has occurred in order to identify any system weaknesses that were exploited or controls that did not function properly and make recommendations about strengthening internal controls where appropriate
- assist with or undertake investigations on management's behalf: internal auditors should only investigate suspicious or actual cases of fraud or corruption if they have the appropriate expertise and understanding of relevant laws to allow them to undertake this work effectively, and investigation work is undertaken, management should be made aware that the internal auditor is acting outside of the core internal audit remit and of the likely impact on the audit plan
- provide an opinion on the likely effectiveness of the organisation's fraud and corruption risk strategy (e.g. policies, response plans, whistleblowing policy, codes of conduct) and if these have been communicated effectively across the organisation; management has primary responsibility for ensuring that an appropriate strategy is in place and the role of internal audit is to review the effectiveness of the strategy.

Source: United Kingdom, HM Treasury, *Fraud and the Government Internal Auditor*, January 2012.

Considering the existing limits and the prospective responsibilities in sanctioning integrity breaches, SEFIR would need to increase their technical expertise and capacity as well as allocate adequate resources and expertise to fulfil its duties. With regards to capacity-building and training needs, there could also be a state-wide certification policy for internal control and audit professionals linked with training and capacity-building activities. Recent reviews and relevant data from Latin America and the Middle East and North Africa (MENA) region document that there is a low percentage of practitioners who have acquired certifications such as the IIA's Certified Internal Auditor (CIA) or Certified Government Auditing Professional (CGAP).

In order to address the issues of weak professional expertise and capacity, Coahuila could include the development of customised training modules in co-operation with the Network of Trainers, the Supreme Audit Institution of the State of Coahuila (*Auditoría Superior del Estado de Coahuila*, or ASEC), local professional chambers (i.e. public accountants, associations, and universities). Furthermore, Coahuila could consider the key elements of the Canadian internal auditor recruitment and development programme (IARD) and the training for internal auditors in the public sector (TIAPS) programme, which are two different approaches to improving the capacity and the skills of internal auditors in public organisations (Box 4.11).

Box 4.11. **Professionalization and capacity-building of the internal audit service**

A. The Canadian Internal Auditor Recruitment and Development Programme (IARD Programme)

I. Benefits of the Internal Audit Recruitment and Development Programme

In addition to coaching, mentoring, and professional development courses, the Internal Audit Recruitment and Development (IARD) Programme offers:

- the experience and on-the-job training needed to pursue a Certified Internal Auditor (CIA) designation
- a development plan designed to help recruits succeed including competency-based work objectives and support from senior staff
- unique on-the-job learning opportunities where recruits will learn the profession of internal audit in the government of Canada
- professional development sessions offered by the Institute of Internal Auditors that are related to the position and CIA certification
- potential for promotion

II. Internal Audit Recruitment and Development Programme work experience

Recruits will work under general supervision, providing support and performing assigned tasks within each of the phases of an audit engagement as a member of an audit team. Audit teams typically report to the Internal Audit Principal or the Director of Internal Audit.

Audit teams are designed to:

- provide departmental senior management with opinions on the effectiveness and adequacy of risk management, control, and governance processes
- report on the results of risk-based audits

III. The Comptroller General of Canada has developed Internal Audit Competency Profiles and Dictionary as a tool of the overarching Internal Audit (IA) Human Resources Management Framework (HRMF).

The IA HRMF aims to support and enable a self-sufficient, quality IA community across the federal public sector. It provides an excellent infrastructure along with tools and support services to position the IA community as professionals who perform unique, high value-added work within the government of Canada.

The IA competency profiles and dictionary are the main building blocks of competency-based management (CBM). They allow organisations to focus on how someone undertakes his or her job based on the skills, abilities, and knowledge required to perform the work. CBM is the application of a set of competencies to the management of human resources (i.e., staffing, learning, performance management, and human resources planning) to achieve excellence in performance and results that are relevant to organisations.

Box 4.11. **Professionalization and capacity-building of the internal audit service** *(cont.)*

B. Training for Internal Auditors in the Public Sector (TIAPS)

The Training for Internal Auditors in the Public Sector (TIAPS) initiative provides an example of public-sector-oriented internal audit certification that merges international best practices with localised regulatory concerns, delivered in the host country's language.

I. Scope and key characteristics

The idea behind TIAPS started in Slovenia in 2002. The TIAPS Programme was developed to strengthen qualifications in internal audit processes in the public sector while devoting special attention to requirements introduced by the accession processes of the European Union. The mandatory and recommended guidelines issued by the IIA have long been viewed as private-sector centric and unable to address comprehensively the concerns of the public sector.

One of the ways TIAPS addresses such gaps is to include a customisable module on legislation and taxation, written by experts from the participating country. The way in which standards and practices are taught is different from the IIA in that it is more rules-based than principles-based. TIAPS clearly outlines what should be done and how, as opposed to guidance issued by the IIA, which leaves room for interpretation.

TIAPS targets public sector employees who hold a Bachelor's degree and already have practical experience in areas such as accounting, financial oversight, and control. The programme comprises seven modules – divided into two levels, certificate, and diploma – of which all but the module on National Legislation and Taxation were developed by CIPFA.

II. Challenges

The biggest hurdle for implementing TIAPS is also its greatest strength—localising the curriculum. This requires involved institutions to do significant preparation work prior to the delivery of the programme, which includes translating training material and coaching the local tutors who will deliver the content of modules in local languages.

A related issue is the need to find and hire experts to create the legislation and taxation modules. The programme-implementation team engages translators with sound knowledge of the material, and the initial translation is checked by an editor/proofreader who makes language revisions in line with standard terminology in each country.

Despite being a relatively young programme, TIAPS provides specialisations. These, however, have yet to achieve the total level of equivalence to directly replace specialised certifications such as the Certified Information Systems Auditor (CISA), provided by the Information Systems Audit and Control Association (ISACA). However, there are plans of achieving these equivalence levels in the medium term.

The programme also does not have a way to monitor and ensure that its certified practitioners stay informed of evolving audit trends, which both IIA and ISACA do, through their continuing professional education requirements.

Source: Office of the Comptroller General of Canada: IARD Post-Secondary Recruitment; *https://emploisfp-psjobs.cfp-psc.gc.ca/psrs-srfp/applicant/page1800?poster=941922&toggleLanguage=en* ; IARD Program; *www.tbs-sct.gc.ca/ip-pi/job-emploi/ford-rpaf/benefitsiard-avantagesrpai-eng.asp* ; Training for Internal Auditors in the Public Sector-An Alternative Approach for State Internal Auditors, Knowledge Showcases, Asian Development Bank, 2016.

Proposals for Action

Coahuila has a ministry responsible for audit and accountability (SEFIR), which is tasked with developing and overseeing policies, standards, and tools on internal control, risk management, and internal audit. These activities are to be carried out within Coahuila's framework for governing the internal control system. This framework is called the General Standard for Internal Control (*Norma General de Control Interno*).

Although Coahuila has an internal control framework in place, it is having difficulty integrating and implementing this framework, raising awareness about the framework among all levels of staff, setting an appropriate tone at the top, and assessing and mitigating fraud and anti-corruption risks. To face these challenges, the OECD recommends that Coahuila consider taking the following actions:

Demonstrating high-level commitment to integrity objectives and risk management

- Coahuila could strengthen standards and policies in order to place greater emphasis on corruption and fraud as it relates to risk management and to clarify how and when to undertake risk assessments.
- Coahuila could strengthen its "tone at the top" and its leadership's commitment to integrity and effective control environment.

Overcoming implementation gaps for improved risk management

- SEFIR could help improve management ownership and awareness of the internal control system and risk management by developing awareness-raising activities on risk-based approaches and could also work to provide enhanced capacity-building initiatives, additional guidance, and training.
- SEFIR could make better use of data to identify and address integrity risks, and thereby improve the quality of its institutional risk maps and mitigation strategies. It could develop an action plan and use the Local Digital Platform to be established within the Local Anti-corruption System, which will allow the interconnectivity of several datasets.

Strengthen the presence and impact of internal audit in Coahuila

- In order to strengthen the internal audit function and improve the effectiveness of governance, risk management, and internal controls, SEFIR could gradually ensure that all ministries have an internal control unit. A corruption risk assessment could be conducted and a priority list created to start the appointment of internal control units in the ministries with the greatest need first.
- Considering increased competence to conducting administrative proceedings for non-serious offences of public officials within the CLACS, SEFIR could improve the internal audit function with regards to fraud and corruption investigations by scaling up professionalism and ensuring adequate capacities and resources.

References

Colombia Transparency Secretariat (2015), *Guía para la Gestión de Riesgo de Corrupción*, *www.anticorrupcion.gov.co/SiteAssets/Paginas/Publicaciones/guia-gestion-riesgo-anticorrupcion.pdf*.

Committee of Sponsoring Organizations of the Treadway Commission (COSO) (2004), Enterprise Risk Management.

Committee of Sponsoring Organizations of the Treadway Commission (COSO) (2013), *Internal Control-Integrated Framework*.

DAFP (2011), *Guía para la administración del riesgo*, Bogotá, Colombia. *www.funcionpublica.gov.co/documents/418537/506911/1592.pdf/73e5a159-2d8f-41aa-8182-eb99e8c4f3ba*.

EU Commission (2015), *Public Internal Control Systems in the European Union. Principles of Public Internal Control*. Position Paper No. 1: Public Internal Control. An EU Approach, Ref. 2015-1, *http://ec.europa.eu/budget/pic/lib/docs/2015/CD02PrinciplesofPIC-PositionPaper.pdf*.

IMCO/TM (2016), *Guía de Implementación para los Sistemas Locales Anticorrupción*, *http://imco.org.mx/politica_buen_gobierno/ruta-de-implementacion-para-los-sistemas-locales-anticorrupcion/*.

INEGI (2015), Encuesta Nacional de Calidad e Impacto Gubernamental 2015, *http://www.beta.inegi.org.mx/proyectos/enchogares/regulares/encig/2015/*.

Institute of Internal Auditors (2013), *The Three Lines of Defense in Effective Risk Management and Control*, IIA's Position Paper, Altamonte Springs, Fla., USA, *https://na.theiia.org/standards-guidance/Public%20Documents/PP%20The%20Three%20Lines%20of%20Defense%20in%20Effective%20Risk%20Management%20and%20Control.pdf*.

Institute of Internal Auditors (2017a), Definition website, *www.theiia.org/guidance/standards-and-guidance/ippf/definition-of-internal-auditing/?search%C2%BCdefinition*.

Institute of Internal Auditors (2017b), *International Standards for the Professional Practice of Internal Auditing*, *https://na.theiia.org/standards-guidance/Public%20Documents/IPPF-Standards-2017.pdf*.

INTOSAI (2013), INTOSAI GOV 9100 – *Guidelines for Internal Control Standards for the Public Sector*, *www.intosai.org/issai-executive-summaries/view/article/intosai-gov-9100-guidelines-for-internal-control-standards-for-the-public-sector.html*.

OECD (2013), *OECD Integrity Review of Italy: Reinforcing Public Sector Integrity, Restoring Trust for Sustainable Growth*, OECD Publishing, Paris, *http://dx.doi.org/10.1787/9789264193819-en*.

OECD (2015), *Data-Driven Innovation: Big Data for Growth and Well-Being*, OECD Publishing, Paris, *http://dx.doi.org/10.1787/9789264229358-en*

OECD (2017a), *Recommendation of the Council on Public Integrity*, Paris, *www.oecd.org/gov/ethics/Recommendation-Public-Integrity.pdf*

OECD (2017b), *OECD Integrity Review of Mexico: Taking a Stronger Stance Against Corruption*, OECD Publishing, Paris. *http://dx.doi.org/10.1787/9789264273207-en*.

OECD (2017c), *OECD Integrity Review of Peru: Enhancing Public Sector Integrity for Inclusive Growth*, OECD Publishing, Paris. *http://dx.doi.org/10.1787/9789264271029-en*

OECD (2017d), *OECD Integrity Review of Colombia: Investing in Integrity for Peace and Prosperity*, OECD Publishing, Paris. *http://dx.doi.org/10.1787/9789264278325-en*.

State of Victoria (2016), *Victorian Government Risk Management Framework. Practice Guide*, Melbourne, Australia, *www.vmia.vic.gov.au/~/media/internet/content-documents/risk/risk-tools/risk-management-guide/vmia-practice-guide.pdf*.

U.S. GAO (2015), *A Framework for Managing Fraud Risks in Federal Programs*, Washington, GAO-15-593SP, *www.gao.gov/products/GAO-15-593SP*.

OECD Integrity Review of Coahuila, Mexico
Restoring trust through an integrity system

Chapter 5

Enhance transparency and participation for effective accountability in Coahuila

The present chapter considers Coahuila's transparency framework as well as mechanisms to engage stakeholders in developing and implementing public policies, and assesses the extent to which they promote integrity, accountability, and the public interest. On the one hand, this chapter acknowledges recent efforts which led to the establishment of a solid institutional and legal framework, but also underlines that the data and information created by public entities in Coahuila could lead to greater accountability through visualisation tools and the use of a single portal. On the other hand, this chapter analyses the extent to which existing mechanisms for stakeholder participation are used in practice, and proposes additional measures Coahuila could take to improve constructive dialogue and monitor public entities' commitments to transparency.

Introduction

Open and transparent institutions are essential in ensuring accountability at all stages of public life. Disclosing information to the public and giving stakeholders the possibility to contribute to the decision-making processes does not only allow citizens to monitor the integrity of public institutions and deter corrupt behaviours by public officials, but also strengthens democratic processes and, eventually, improves trust in public institutions.

While a necessary condition, transparency is not enough to guarantee greater accountability, especially if it merely makes public a flow of complex information without a tool to understand it or a mechanism with which stakeholders could effectively engage with public institutions in shaping the public debate and the decision-making process. In this sense, a government may disclose significant volumes information and yet remain opaque, while other governments may publish a more limited set of information but be more accountable, because they provide tools to make the information accessible and encourage forms of stakeholder participation.

The idea that transparency and participation frameworks should be designed to promote accountability is also reflected in the OECD *Recommendation on Public Integrity* (OECD, 2017a), whereby states are recommended to encourage transparency and stakeholder engagement at all stages of the political process and policy cycle to promote accountability and the public interest. The present chapter assesses the framework and the activities undertaken in the latter context and, in particular, whether they effectively promote transparency and an open government, and whether they facilitate stakeholder access in the development and implementation of public policies.

Leveraging information and data for more accountable institutions

Over the last several years, Coahuila has built one of the most advanced transparency frameworks among Mexican states.

Through a series of reforms undertaken in recent years, Coahuila has developed one of the most advanced legal frameworks among Mexican states in transparency matters. In 2015, Coahuila was the first state to harmonise its legal framework with the General Transparency and Access to Information Law (*Ley General de Transparencia y Acceso a la Información*, or General Transparency Law), which, among other accomplishments, created the National Transparency System. Similarly to the National Anti-corruption System (see Chapter 1), the System aims to co-ordinate all institutions in Mexico to improve overall transparency in the country (Box 5.1).

The drive for transparency in Coahuila is led by the Institute for Access to Public Information of Coahuila (*Instituto Coahuilense de Acceso a la Información Pública*, or ICAI), which is the state entity empowered by the Constitution of Coahuila (the Constitution) to guarantee the fundamental right of all citizens to share, investigate, and request public information (Article 7). In particular, the Constitution gives ICAI the leadership in the following areas:

- access to public information
- culture of transparency
- personal data
- elaborating statistics, polls, surveys, and any other public opinion instrument

Box 5.1. **The Mexican National Transparency System**

The National Transparency System is the mechanism which will lead the co-ordination, collaboration, and promotion of the efforts among all the relevant institutions at the three levels of government and will eventually contribute to generating better quality, management, and processing of information. According to the General Transparency and Access to Information Law, this mechanism will facilitate the knowledge and assessment of public management, the access to public information, the dissemination of a culture of transparency and accessibility, and more effective audit and accountability.

According to this law, the National Transparency System consists of the following institutions:

- National Institute for Transparency and Access to Information (*Instituto Nacional de Transparencia, Acceso a la Información y Protección de Datos Personales*, INAI), which leads and co-ordinates the system
- the entities in charge of guaranteeing access to information and personal data protection at the state-level (including ICAI)
- the Superior Audit Institution (*Auditoría Superior de la Federación*, ASF)
- the General National Archive (*Archivo General de la Nación*)
- the National Institute for Statistics and Geography (*Instituto Nacional de Estadística y Geografía*, INEGI)

For the state of Coahuila, ICAI is the representative in the National Transparency System and takes also part in the North regional group of the system together with the states of Baja California, Baja California Sur, Chihuahua, Durango, Nuevo León, Sinaloa, Sonora, and Tamaulipas.

Source: General Transparency and Access to Information Law (*Ley General de Transparencia y Acceso a la Información Pública*), *http://www.diputados.gob.mx/LeyesBiblio/pdf/LGTAIP.pdf.*

ICAI, which was created in 2004, is given political, legal, administrative, budgetary, and financial autonomy. Its members are appointed by Coahuila's Congress through a majority vote (at least two-thirds of the assembly) pursuant to Coahuila's Access to Information Law (*Ley de Acceso a la Información Pública y Protección de Datos Personales para el Estado de Coahuila de Zaragoza*, or Transparency Law - lastly reformed in March 2016), which also spells out its activities as well as the transparency obligations for all state entities. An Internal Regulation (*Reglamento Interior*) regulates ICAI's internal organisation and functioning.

The current Transparency Law obliges public entities to make public more than 70 sets of information concerning the organisation, their relationship with other actors, and the legal framework (Articles 21-22; 25-28; 30-38; and 43-47). It also provides for a comprehensive mechanism to access information with the following features:

- no subjective limitation on those who can request information
- all state branches of government, entities, and municipalities are subject to the law

- exceptions to the rights to access to information include:
  - personal data
  - public order, crimes prosecution
  - where there is a risk to the health or security of citizens
  - when tax collection is impeded.
- exceptions apply only to those parts of requested information/document related to the latter grounds of refusal
- requests can be anonymous, oral, or written
- costs may be incurred when the requested document exceeds 20 pages
- the ICAI may be challenegd in cases of request denial or neglect

The advanced level of Coahuila's legal framework is confirmed by several national rankings, which regularly assess different aspects of Mexican states' attitude toward transparency and which place Coahuila among the best Mexican states based on several indicators (Table 5.1).

Table 5.1. **Coahuila in National Transparency Rankings**

Indicator	Position	Ranking organization
Access to information law	1st	FUNDAR/IDAIM (Right to access information index)
Budget information	1st	IMCO (Mexican Institute for Competitiveness)
Guaranteeing institution	1st	CIDE (Centre for Economic Research and Teaching)
Simulated customer	1st	CIDE
Institutional capacities	1st	CIDE
Transparent state	3rd	CIDE
Legal framework	4th	CIDE
National index of institutions guaranteeing the right to access information	5th	Artículo 19 and México Infórmate
Transparency and availability of tax information of State entities Index	7th	ARegional
Transparency portal	13th	CIDE

Source: ICAI presentation, July 2016; idaim.org.mx/.

Given that Coahuila is currently developing policies on open government, it could better exploit the data and information currently produced by public entities by improving data socialisation and developing online visualisation tools.

A relatively recent trend undertaken by many countries to increase transparency and accountability of public institutions is to make their data available to the public and allow the use, reuse, and free distribution of datasets through the so-called open data format. The OECD has been analysing such an increasingly relevant phenomenon and has identified the potentials of the extraordinary quantity of data collected by governments, which can increase transparency and awareness but also improve performance, encourage public participation, and improve the decision making of governments and individuals (Ubaldi, 2013).

In 2013, G8 countries adopted an Open Data Charter, which represented the first international instrument designed to guide the implementation of open government data strategies. The Charter laid out five principles (G8, 2013):

1. Open data by default;
2. Optimised quality and quantity of data;
3. Data should be usable by all;

4. Releasing data for improved governance; and
5. Releasing data for innovation.

The OECD has elaborated a pilot Index on Open Government Data (OECD OURdata Index) which assesses governments' efforts to implement open data in three dimensions based on its methodology and structured around the following principles of the G7 Open Data Charter: 1) Data availability on the national portal; 2) Data accessibility on the national portal; and 3) governments' support to innovative re-use and stakeholder engagement. As shown in Figure 5.1, Mexico scores above the OECD average.

The OECD OURdata Index assesses governments' efforts to implement open data in the three critical areas: openness, usefulness, and re-usability of government data. Data for the index is taken from member countries and focuses on government efforts to ensure public sector data availability and accessibility and to spur greater re-use. The Index is based on OECD methodology and the guidelines of the G8 Open Data Charter. Figure 5.1 illustrates a composite index where 0 is lowest and 1 highest.

Figure 5.1. **OECD OURdata Index: Open, Useful, Reusable Government Data, 2014***

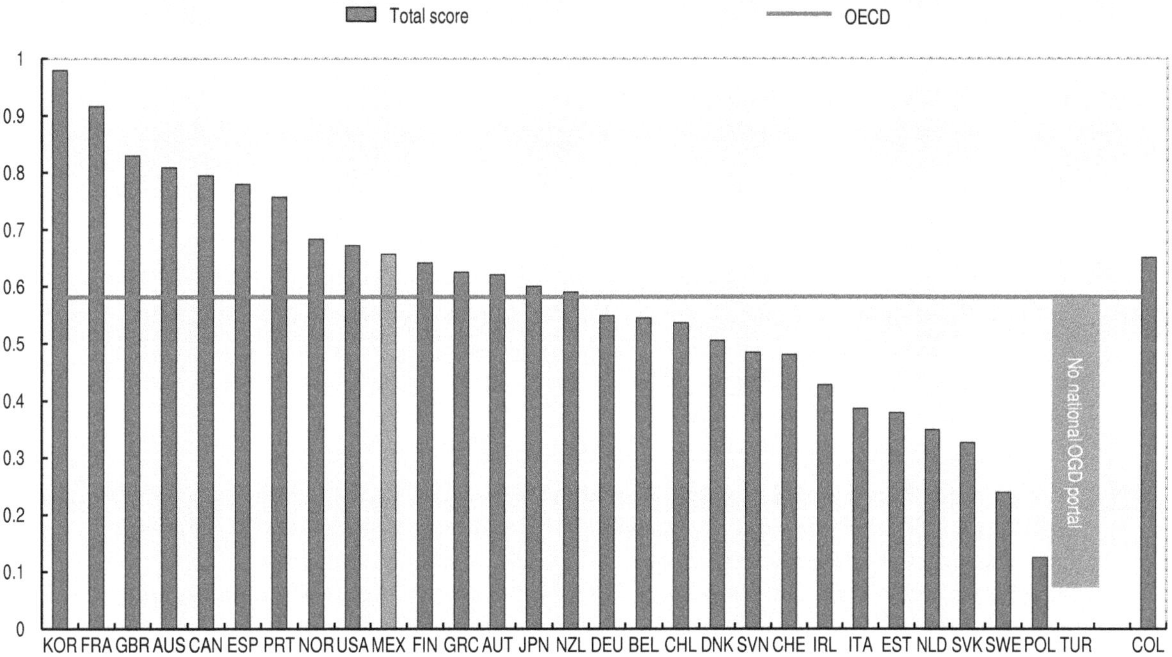

Source: OECD (2015), *Government at a Glance 2015*, OECD Publishing, Paris. *http://dx.doi.org/10.1787/gov_glance-2015-en*.
*Data for the Czech Republic, Hungary, Iceland, Israel, and Luxembourg are not available.

Countries have become increasingly aware of the potential of open data to enhance integrity and tackle corruption. In particular, the OECD *Recommendation on Public Integrity* (OECD, 2017a) calls states to encourage transparency and stakeholders' engagement "promoting transparency and an open government, including ensuring access to information and open data, along with timely responses to requests for information." In 2015, the G20 adopted six Anti-corruption Open Data Principles that identify open data as a tool to prevent and tackle corruption insofar as they shed light on government activities, decisions, and expenditures. In addition, they increase accountability and allow citizens and government to better monitor the flow and use of public money within and across borders (Box 5.2).

Box 5.2. G20 Anti-Corruption Open Data Principles

Principle 1: Open Data by default

Access to information has been widely accepted as a tool to increase transparency and fight corruption. Open data by default goes a step beyond transparency, as it promotes the provision of reusable data from its source, without requiring requests for information and increasing access in equal terms for everyone; while at the same time, assuring the necessary protection to personal data in accordance to laws and regulations already established in G20 countries.

Principle 2: Timely and comprehensive

Releasing comprehensive data sets - which are accurate, timely and up to date, published at a disaggregated level, adequately documented, and following internationally agreed upon standards, metadata and classifiers - is crucial to increase data use for anti-corruption means. Such data openness will allow a better understanding of government processes and policy outcomes in as close to real-time as possible.

Principle 3: Accessible and usable

Lowering unnecessary entry barriers, and by publishing data on single window solutions such as central open data portals increases the value of data, as more citizens and organisations are able to find and use it to reduce opacity in government institutions.

Principle 4: Comparable and interoperable

Enabling the comparison and traceability of data from numerous anti-corruption-related sectors increases its potential to inform decisions and feedback between decision-makers and citizens.

Principle 5: For improved governance and citizen engagement

Open data empowers citizens and enables them to hold government institutions into account. Open data can also help them understand, influence and participate directly in the decision-making processes and in the development of public policies in support of public sector integrity. This is paramount to build trust and strengthen collaboration between governments and all sectors of society.

Principle 6: For inclusive development and innovation

Open data, through reinforced transparency and integrity, can promote greater social and economic benefits by providing actionable information to build effective, accountable, and responsive institutions; this alone can increase economic output and efficiency in government operations. Furthermore, while preventing corruption, open data facilitates the development of new insights, business models and digital innovation strategies at a global scale.

Source: G20 (2015), G20 Anti-Corruption Open Data Principles.

Open government is an emerging theme in Coahuila's political agenda and its institutions are producing an increasing amount of open data. This is reflected in Coahuila's Transparency Law, which requires public entities to publish the information available to the public as open data and provides for specific open government obligations to increase citizen participation, transparency, and improve accountability (Article 50). Furthermore, it envisages the creation of an Open Government Secretariat in charge of promoting best practices for citizen participation, co-operating in the implementation and the evaluation of Coahuila's digital policy in the realm of open data, and elaborating specific indicators on relevant themes. The Secretariat (*Secretariado Técnico Tripartita Local de Gobierno Abierto*) was created in 2015 and comprises the President of ICAI, the Minister of SEFIR, and a co-ordinator representing the civil society contact points of the five regions of the state. In August 2016, after a broad public consultation process involving all of the state's regions, the STGA presented an open government action plan (*Plan de acción de Gobierno Abierto para el Estado de Coahuila de Zaragoza 2016-2017*) which set a number of commitments and a detailed timetable on the identified deliverables (STGA, 2016).

In spite of the remarkable efforts displayed so far by Coahuila in setting up the adequate legal framework and requiring public institutions to publish a significant amount of data and information, interviews during the fact-finding mission in July 2016 suggested that their actual use is limited. Despite the stated goal of the open data initiative, citizens are not the prime users of existing transparency mechanisms. This state of affairs raises doubts about the data's effectiveness for accountability. In order to make the best out of data that are being created by public entities and elevate the experience of Coahuila as a best practice at the international level, Coahuila should not only create databases presenting data in disaggregated formats for technical analysis and evaluation as laid out in the principles of G8 Open Data Charter, but it could also make data more intelligible by presenting them in a plain, aggregated, and simplified format. Data visualisation does not only help to make public information more comprehensible, but it also stimulates the public interest in areas not commonly accessible to the public (HATVP, 2016).

In practice, in order to improve data socialisation and develop online visualisation tools, Coahuila could consider the open data projects and portals developed in other OECD countries, such the one set up by the city of Montreal in Canada (Box 5.3) to consult all of its contracts (*Vue sur les contrats*) as well as the ones created by the Italian government to access and monitor data on public spending data (*SoldiPubblici*), infrastructure projects (*Opencantieri*) and the 2015 Universal Exposition of Milan (Box 5.4). The latter examples could also be taken into consideration to improve existing efforts to make open data user and citizen-friendly, such as the SITODEM Portal (*Sistema de Información y Transparencia de Obras para el Desarrollo Metropolitano; [http://sitodem.sefircoahuila.gob.mx/]*), which presents a number of useful information items linked to the Integral System of Public Investment including the names of approved public works, their cost, the amount already spent, the responsible departments, beneficiaries and auditors. This portal, however, does not ensure that this information is made available in real time and does not provide an user-friendly visualisation of the evolution of projects and related contracts (see also Chapter 6).

Box 5.3. **Montreal's "View on the Contracts" (*Vue sur les contrats*) platform (Canada)**

Following a series of corruption scandals at the beginning of the 2010s, the city of Montreal identified transparency as crucial element in its efforts to improve integrity and become a "smart city". In June 2015 it therefore launched the platform "View on the Contracts" (*Vue sur les contrats*), which makes available for public consultation contracts signed by the city. The contracts may be visualised in an intuitive way according to several criteria including dates, amount, typologies, authorising entity, area, and keyword. In this way, the platform does not only provide easily-understandable information for the average user, but it also represents a portal for more expert users to analyse and use the specific data in greater detail.

Source: HATVP (2016); Website of the city of Montreal, *https://ville.montreal.qc.ca/vuesurlescontrats/*,.

Box 5.4. **Open data portals with visualisation tools in Italy**

SoldiPubblici

The SoldiPubblici initiative provides open data and data visualisation tools on public spending at all levels of government in order to enhance transparency, improve participation, and provide comparable data to administrators. The corresponding website (*http://soldipubblici.gov.it/it/home*) includes an interactive visualisation tool allowing users to search and compare public spending data by geographical area and institution.

Opencantieri

Opencantieri is a project managed by the Ministry of Infrastructure and Transportation (*Ministero delle infrastrutture e dei trasporti*, or MIT) to provide open, complete, and updated information on ongoing public infrastructure projects. The platform website contains the available data and provides syntheses as well as specific insights on issues such as financing, costs, timing, and delays. All the information is publicly accessible and can be downloaded through the MIT's open data website.

OpenExpo

OpenExpo was the portal set up for the 2015 Universal Exposition of Milan. It deals with several data and transparency issues including the following sections:

- Why OpenExpo
- Expo Barometro
- Open Data
- Expo2015 Works
- reporting
- transparent administration
- Visit Expo
- use cases

The Open Data section, in particular, contains all data related to the exhibition. Datasets can be searched for using a search engine that filters data, or by browsing datasets per description tag. The licence used is Creative Commons - Attribution 4.0 International (CC BY 4.0). The website provides exhaustive information on the format of the data and contains a section with examples of reuse of OpenExpo datasets (available in Italian only).

Source: Soldipubblici's website: *http://soldipubblici.gov.it/it/home*; Opencantieri's website, *http://opencantieri.mit.gov.it/*; OpenExpo's website, *http://dati.openexpo2015.it/en*.

In developing data visualisation tools, Coahuila should take into consideration the different levels of digital literacy across the state. The latter emerged as a significant challenge during fact-finding interviews, especially in rural areas. In consequence, tools to make information and data more friendly and understandable could be coupled with awareness-raising and capacity-building initiatives to narrow the digital divide and achieve the effective use of open data in line with the G20 Anti-Corruption Open Data Principles (Box 5.2).

In order to avoid gaps or overlaps and allow citizens and civil society to have comprehensive access to all the information and data provided by public institutions, Coahuila may wish to identify a single portal to consult and request information.

The potential of transparency as a tool to increase accountability also depends on the accessibility of the information, i.e. on how easily citizens can obtain the desired information. If, for instance, an institution discloses a significant amount information but it is not clear where it is published or how to consult a certain database, the usefulness of transparency as an accountability tool is diminished. This issue is also stressed by the G20, which acknowledges the importance of making open data "easily discoverable and accessible" and invites states to publish open data on "central portals, or in ways that can increase its accessibility, so that it can be easily discoverable and accessible for users" (G20, 2015).

In Coahuila, the significant amount of information produced by public entities can be consulted or requested through several websites:

- Coahuila Transparente (*www.coahuilatransparente.gob.mx/*), which centralises all the information to be published by public entities
- ICAI's website (*www.icai.org.mx:8282/ipo/*), which provides links to the websites of public with the information to be disclosed according to the law as well as the link to the portal to request information
- Infomex Coahuila (*www.infocoahuila.org.mx/*), the website used to submit a request for information
- Coahuila Todo Transparente (*www.coahuilatodotransparente.gob.mx/*), Coahuila's open data portal
- SEFIR's website (*www.sefircoahuila.gob.mx/*), which also seems to function as a "database of databases" insofar as it displays the link to SITODEM, and to other databases such as the ones on public officials' asset declarations and state budget reports.

The simultaneous existence of several platforms to access information in Coahuila does not allow potential users to unambiguously identify the main source of information in Coahuila, and this may deter them from looking into information. This is confirmed by the relatively low score of Coahuila in the Transparency Portal Indicator developed by CIDE (Table 5.1). In order to encourage people in accessing and using public information and data, Coahuila could consider using one single portal, as suggested in Chapter 6 in relation to public procurement. This would not only enable better understanding and communicability on the entry point to access all available information, but it could also allow institutions to focus their efforts on one single portal, thereby minimising the risks of gaps and overlaps, as well as saving resources needed to keep updated and relevant multiple databases and information at the same time. In designing a single and comprehensive database containing the latter features, Coahuila may consider the model adopted by Spain, which provides a comprehensive and user-friendly transparency portal with high level of usability and reusability of information in co-ordination with the Spanish central open data portal (*www.datos.gob.es*) (Box 5.5).

Box 5.5. **The Transparency Portal of Spain**

The Transparency Portal (*Portal de la Transparencia*) set up by the government of Spain is organised around four main components, namely:

- categories, where information is organised around four categories (Institutional data; Regulations; Budgeting, monitoring and reporting; Contracts, agreements and grants) and a number of sub-categories (e.g. remuneration of senior officials and authorisations provided to civil servants to exercise private activity after leaving senior public positions; planning and execution and audit reports; bills, laws, and regulations; data on public procurement; grants to political parties; subsidies and public properties)
- ministries

Box 5.5. **The Transparency Portal of Spain** *(cont.)*

- right to access information, where users can submit a request, consult the status of requests, as well as receive information about statistics or how to use such tool
- open government and citizen participation, which provides information and relevant link to access open government data and tools for participation

In addition, the portal includes sections providing a comprehensive picture of information and data in Spain, including one on Spanish regions (*Comunidades Autónomas*) with a list of links to relevant databases, laws, and institutions for each region, as well as one on public institutions (*Instituciones públicas*) where one may find links to the transparency pages of institutions that are not part of the executive, such as the parliament and national courts pages.

Source: Spain Transparency Portal, *http://transparencia.gob.es/*.

Improving stakeholders' engagement to promote transparency and the public interest

Although the legal framework of Coahuila offers tools for stakeholder participation and oversight, they have not been regularly used in the past. In order to improve their effectiveness, mechanisms could be introduced to improve awareness and enable active engagement in innovative and interactive ways.

Transparency, while a necessary condition, does not in itself guarantee oversight and effective citizen engagement. Public officials and institutions are accountable to the public not only when their activities and information are made available for public scrutiny, but also when citizens and stakeholders are able to participate in public life and actively contribute to the decision-making process.

Building on country experiences and practices, the OECD found that civic engagement enhances a government's policy performance by working with citizens, civil society organisations, businesses, and other stakeholders to deliver improvements in policy and the quality of public services (Box 5.6). More important for the present review, stakeholders' engagement is a meaningful tool to enable public integrity and effective accountability as stressed by the OECD *Recommendation on Public Integrity*, which calls upon states to grant "all stakeholders – including the private sector, civil society and individuals – access in the development and implementation of public policies" (OECD, 2017a). As stressed in Chapter 1, stakeholder engagement is also crucial to embrace a whole-of-society approach to public integrity, and therefore specific forms of participation should be designed to engage them in the development, regular update, and implementation of the public integrity system.

Box 5.6. **OECD Guiding Principles for Public Participation in Policy Making**

The experience of OECD member countries indicates open and inclusive policy making can help governments better understand and respond to the changing needs of society, use ideas and resources from civil society and business to confront complex policy challenges, lower costs and improve policy outcomes, and reduce administrative burdens on policy implementation and service delivery.

As such, the OECD has created a set of guiding principles designed to help governments strengthen open and inclusive policy making as a means to improve their policy performance and service delivery. A summary of the principles is provided here:

Box 5.6. **OECD Guiding Principles for Public Participation in Policy Making** *(cont.)*

1. **Commitment:** leadership and strong commitment to open and inclusive policy making is needed at all levels – politicians, senior managers, and public officials.
2. **Rights:** citizens' rights to information, consultation and participation in policy must be grounded in law. Government obligations to respond to citizens must be clearly stated. Independent oversight arrangements are essential to enforcing these rights.
3. **Clarity:** objectives for and limits to information, consultation, and participation should be well clarified. The roles and responsibilities of all parties must be clear. Government information should be complete, objective, reliable, relevant, and easy to find and understand.
4. **Time:** public engagement should be undertaken as early in the policy process as possible and adequate time must be available for consultation and participation to be effective.
5. **Inclusion:** citizens should have equal opportunities and channels to access information, be consulted and participate. Every reasonable effort should be made to engage with as wide a variety of people as possible.
6. **Resources:** adequate financial, human and technical resources for effective public information, consultation and participation. Government officials must have access to appropriate skills, guidance and training, as well as an organisational culture that supports both traditional and online tools.
7. **Co-ordination:** initiatives to inform, consult and engage civil society should be co-ordinated within and across levels of government to ensure policy coherence, avoid duplication, and reduce the risk of "consultation fatigue."
8. **Accountability:** governments have an obligation to inform participants how they use inputs received through public consultation and participation.
9. **Evaluation:** governments need to evaluate their own performance. To do so effectively will require efforts to build the demand, capacity, culture, and tools for evaluating public participation.
10. **Active citizenship:** societies benefit from dynamic civil society and governments can facilitate access to information, encourage participation, raise awareness, strengthen citizens' civic education and skills, as well as support capacity-building among civil society organisations. Governments need to explore new roles to effectively support autonomous problem-solving by citizens, CSOs, and businesses.

In increasing citizen engagement in policy making, public officials must be careful to ensure that engagement processes are fit for purpose and protect against potential conflict of interests and policy capture (OECD 2014). The type and level of engagement used for a particular matter should reflect the intended purpose of that engagement. The nature of the legislative scheme and the regulatory style adopted will affect the nature of any engagement. For example, advisory bodies can be effective in providing insights from industry or the community as to how to most effectively change behaviour or anticipate developments which may warrant a change (OECD, 2009). Whatever style of engagement is chosen, opportunities to increase dialogue and exchange information in order to ensure informed decision making and confidence in the system should be maximised.

Engagement must not be used as a tool to favour certain particular interests, as this would compromise the regulators' ability to achieve broader outcomes (OECD, 2014). Instead, engagement must be inclusive (unless this would compromise the intended outcome) and transparent. Inclusive consultation allows any interested stakeholder to contribute or comment on proposals, rather than just representative groups, building confidence that all interests are heard. Similarly, transparent engagement involves publicly documenting who has been consulted and what their input has been and the release of the policy maker's responses to the main issues. This can protect the regulator from suggestions of capture or failure to listen to the range of views, and also builds confidence in the regulatory process.

Sources: OECD (2017b), *OECD Integrity Scan of Kazakhstan: Preventing Corruption for a Competitive Economy*, OECD Publishing, Paris. *http://dx.doi.org/10.1787/9789264272880-en*; OECD (2009), Focus on Citizens: Public Engagement for Better Policy and Services, OECD Publishing, Paris, *http://dx.doi.org/10.1787/9789264048874-en*; OECD (2014a), *The Governance of Regulators*, OECD Publishing, Paris, *http://dx.doi.org/10.1787/9789264209015-en*.

Coahuila adopted a specific Law on Civic Participation in 2001 (*Ley de Participación Ciudadana para el Estado de Coahuila de Zaragoza*), which aims to support Coahuila's citizens' right to participate in public life and to promote policies for community development. In this sense, it provides for a number of different tools for civic participation and consultation (Articles 4-5), namely:

- plebiscite (*plebiscito*)
- referendum (*referendo*)
- popular initiative (*iniciativa popular*)
- popular consultation (*consulta popular*)
- community collaboration (*colaboración comunitaria*)
- public hearing (*audiencia pública*)
- citizen Participation Councils (*Consejos de Participación Ciudadana*)
- community Participation Councils (*Consejos de Participación Comunitaria*)

In practice, the latter tools are only used rarely, as evidenced by Montemayor (2016) who, after presenting requests to information to all relevant institutions in Coahuila, found that in the last years 149 public hearings have been organised (2004-2016), while 12 legislative proposals were presented in front of the Congress (2004-2015) and 7 to the Executive (2012-2016, out of 181). On the other hand, various initiatives have been taken by institutions in Coahuila to engage citizens, youth, universities and NGOs, mostly consisting of monitoring or social audit activities (Table 5.2).

Table 5.2. **Monitoring or social audit initiatives in Coahuila**

Initiative	Stakeholder involved
Citizens Observatory in Local Conciliation and Arbitration Councils (*Observatorio Ciudadano en Juntas Locales de Conciliación y Arbitraje*)	Citizens
Citizens Observatory Guardians of the Urban Forest (*Observatorio Ciudadano Vigilantes del Bosque Urbano*)	Children and youth
Citizens Observatory for the Conservation of the Las Vacas River (*Observatorio Ciudadano para la Conservación del Arroyo Las Vacas*)	Youth
Social Audit days with the University of Coahuila (*Jornadas de Contraloría Social*)	Students and universities
Transparency in Short Film Competition (*Concurso de Transparencia en Corto*)	Youth
Social Audit Competition (*Concurso de Contraloría Social*)	Citizens
Social Witnesses in General Hospital (*Testigo Social en el Hospital General*)	Hospital customers
Social Witnesses in Electoral Protection (*Testigo Social en el Blindaje Electoral*)	Citizens, NGOs, universities
Transparency Rally (*Rally por la Transparencia*)	University students

Source: SEFIR presentation, 6 July 2016, *www.contraloriasocial.gob.mx/*.

Although the latter initiatives reveal significant efforts to stimulate stakeholder oversight in public life, the minimal use of institutional tools for civic participation clearly points to a low level of citizen participation in the public life of Coahuila, which in turn signals the scarce use of stakeholder engagement mechanisms to encourage accountability. Considering the increasing use of web portals to consult and access information (Figure 5.2), Coahuila could consider leveraging ICTs to promote the engagement of society as done by Colombia (Box 5.7), as well as improving the understanding of available tools by devoting a specific section of its future single portal to explain and describe them following the example provided by Spain (Box 5.8).

Figure 5.2. **Visits to Coahuila's online transparency portals**

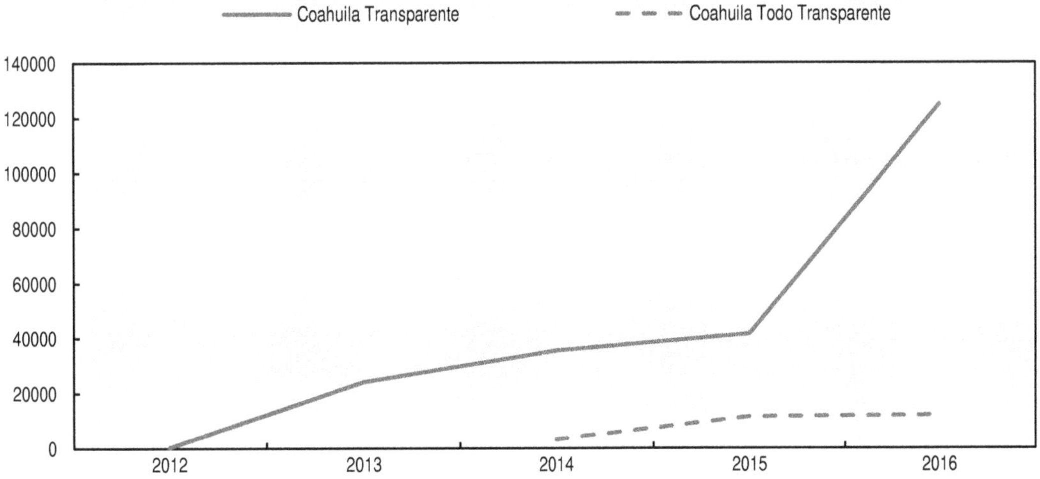

Source: Montemayor (2016) and SEFIR.

Box 5.7. **Colombia's Crystal Urn (*Urna de Cristal*)**

Crystal Urn (*Urna de Cristal*) is the Colombian government's leading initiative of electronic citizen participation and government transparency strategy. Since its launch in October 2010, *Urna de Cristal* has consolidated a multi-channel platform, which integrated traditional communication channels such as radio and television with digital channels such as social media, SMS, and web sites. Through these channels, Colombians can learn about government results, progress and initiatives, address their concerns directly with the government bodies, and participate and interact on subjects of state administration and public services and policies, thus creating a binding relationship between citizens and a state truly committed to service. More than three million Colombians have visited the *Urna de Cristal* website to access government information and to get involved in one of the 28 participation exercises or the more than 300 awareness campaigns carried out in 2014. More than 50 000 questions were raised by Colombians in 2014. The *Urna de Cristal* team is in charge together with the Online Government strategy team and the ICT Ministry of the initiative rollout and operation.

Source: OECD (2013), *Colombia: Implementing Good Governance*, OECD Publishing, Paris. *http://dx.doi.org/10.1787/9789264202177-en*, and *www.oecd.org/gov/colombia-urna-cristal.pdf*.

Box 5.8. **Public participation in draft regulations in Spain**

Most ministries in Spain provide for a channel for citizens to participate in their decision-making processes. The objective of these mechanisms is to gather the views of citizens and stakeholders before the elaboration of a legal instrument and to receive opinions on drafts under discussion from those who are directly involved. As a consequence, two procedures for stakeholders to participate are envisaged:

- preliminary public consultation (*consulta pública previa*), which concerns opinions from citizens, organisations, and associations before the elaboration of a draft instrument
- public hearing and information (*audiencia e información pública*), which allows those citizens (or representative organisations) having a legitimate interest or whose rights are affected by a draft instrument under discussion to provide views and improve the text

Box 5.8. **Public participation in draft regulations in Spain** *(cont.)*

Although the list of instruments which are subject to the latter procedures are available on the ministry websites, Spain's Transparency Portal provides for a clearly identifiable section on Civic Participation presenting the available tools and containing links to the relevant ministry pages.

Source: Spain Transparency Portal, Civic Participation Section: *http://transparencia.gob.es/transparencia/transparencia_Home/index/GobiernoParticipacion/ParticipacionCiudadana/ParticipacionProyectosNormativos.html*; Law 39/2015 and Law 50/1997.

Coahuila could make its transparency framework more responsive to society by introducing mechanisms to improve stakeholder engagement through a demand-drive approach based on dialogue, consultation, and on data collaboration and interoperability.

The institutional and legal framework of Coahuila on transparency has evolved significantly in the last years, creating the basis for a transparent public system. However, the typologies of relevant information and the usability and availability of data change over time according to the evolving socio-economic context and technological developments. Furthermore, public institutions are not always aware of which data interests the public, nor how such data could be used for the public interest. In consequence, the significance of transparency frameworks and platforms depends very much on their dynamism and capacity to evolve along technology developments and social needs.

Institutions in Coahuila are well aware of the need to keep the legal framework up-to-date: indeed, the Transparency Law, first enacted in 2003, has been amended several times since (in 2008, 2012, 2014, 2015, and 2016). Over these years, for instance, the categories of general information to be disclosed by all public entities increased from 19 to 101 (Montemayor, 2016). Similarly, some websites and portals have created sections to receive comments or make proposals, as it is the case for ICAI's website forum (*Foro*) and the section "Citizen Observer" in the "Coahuilatodotrasparente" portal. However, the former contains only a few outdated comments and the latter only presents pictures and videos uploaded by users with comments describing misconduct by public authorities or problems in public buildings.

Considering the importance in involving stakeholders in determining the most relevant and priority data for the promotion of public integrity (HATVP, 2016), Coahuila could introduce further mechanisms to allow stakeholders to contribute effectively in building a dynamic transparency framework and environment. On the one hand, relevant institutions and social actors could gather periodically to identify typologies of information which could potentially enhance the transparency and accountability of public institutions. Considering the inclusiveness and diversity of actors represented in the Open Government Secretariat, this could take place in such context. After that, ICAI – which has the legal mandate to submit legislative proposals in the realm of transparency pursuant to Article 59(7) of the Constitution of Coahuila – could submit a draft to the Congress of Coahuila to amend or introduce obligations set by the existing legal framework. On the other hand, Coahuila could consider creating a simple and user-friendly platform to submit ideas on transparency as done in Colombia, and could take better advantage of its open data platform, allowing users to enrich it with new datasets following the examples of France and Finland (Box 5.9). In order to encourage data co-creation and collaboration as well as to enable data re-use that produces value (Ubaldi, 2013), Coahuila should also ensure the availability, quality, and interoperability of public datasets, the latter being essential prerequisites for open data to "play a key role to dismantle corruption networks" (Open Data Charter, 2016).

Box 5.9. **Citizen engagement mechanisms to improve transparency and open data portals**

Colombia

The Transparency Council of Colombia developed a platform called "*Ideas.Info: Tus ideas en Transparencia*" to improve citizen participation in public affairs through visions and ideas, as well as to facilitate each person's right to present a request to public authorities. For this purpose, citizens are invited to propose ideas – in the form of good practices or legislative improvements – concerning the scope of action of the Transparency Council and issues of general public interest. If accepted, petitions become public, where they can be openly discussed and supported by other users. Once the petition obtains 1 000 supporters, the Transparency Council's Director General will issue an official opinion on the corresponding subject matter.

France

The French national open data portal enables data prosumers to add new datasets to the portal directly. In order to publish open data (datasets, APIs, etc.), data contributors are requested to fill out an online form which collects information related to data licensing, granularity, and a description of the overall data content, among others. The French open data portal also enables data prosumers to publish and showcase examples of open data reuse (OGD or not) and to monitor the use of the datasets they publish. In addition, the French government used the portal to launch the *Base Adresse Nationale* project, which is a multi-stakeholder collaboration initiative aiming to crowdsource a unique national address database fed by the data contributions from private, public, and non-profit organisations.

Finland

In Finland, the national open data portal has been enabled as a platform where citizens can publish open data and interoperability tools (i.e. guidelines to ease the interaction between user datasets and other data formats or platforms). Users are required to register on the portal in order to publish datasets. As in France, uploading open data on the Finnish portal requires filling in an online form where users can provide a detailed description of the data. This description includes, for instance, information on the data's licensing model (i.e. Creative Commons) and the data validity timeframe. Users can also browse the profiles of other users using the portal and can explore their activity and the datasets they have published. The portal also provides users with the possibility of subscribing to specific organisations in order to receive updates on new datasets, comments, etc.

Sources: "Ideas.Info" Portal, *www.ideasinfo.cl/Peticion/Inicio.aspx*; OECD (2016), *Open Government Data Review of Mexico: Data Reuse for Public Sector Impact and Innovation*, OECD Digital Government Studies, OECD Publishing, Paris. *http://dx.doi.org/10.1787/9789264259270-en*; *www.data.gouv.fr/fr*; *www.avoindata.fi*.

Coahuila could improve oversight over the transparency commitments of its institutions by developing an easily accessible index measuring compliance and implementation of state- and municipal-level institutions.

Stakeholders' engagement to improve transparency and the public interest does not only take place through direct consultative processes and mechanisms, but can also be exercised by means of public mechanisms that help to oversee and monitor public institutions' commitment to openness and transparency. The value of developing benchmarks and indicators on the level of implementation, as stressed by the OECD Recommendation (OECD, 2017a) in relation to public integrity systems, can be transferred to the realm of transparency, where the frequent updates and developments highlighted in the previous section require a responsive approach from public entities.

A useful tool which could be deployed by Coahuila to favour stakeholder monitoring is to introduce a transparency index providing easily accessible evidence and visualisation of improvements made in implementing the relevant framework and, at the same time, point out good practices as well as weak areas and institutions where further efforts are most needed. This could be particularly effective in the Mexican context, where rankings receive high visibility and therefore provide incentives to administrators to improve over the years. On the other hand, considering the legalist approach which often emerged during the fact-finding mission's interviews, such an index should be carefully designed in order not to lead to a formal "check-the-box" activity disregarding the level of actual implementation and creating a mere compliance exercise.

In Coahuila, ICAI is in charge of measuring compliance of public entities with transparency obligations and making public the corresponding results pursuant to Articles 18 and 34(7) of the Transparency Law. Although ICAI carries out such task on a trimestral basis, accessing the corresponding results is not straightforward as one may find them only after searching the subfolders of ICAI's transparency obligations page (*información pública de oficio*) [*www.icai.org.mx/*]. Furthermore, such information is provided through power point presentations without any possibility to use data or to do customised comparison between institutions and across time. Coahuila could therefore leverage the data which are already being collected and improve their socialization by creating a transparency index, which should be made widely public and easily accessible to the public. Furthermore, it should provide visualisation tools and customisation options as well as include indicators not only related to compliance with the Transparency Law but also its implementation and effectiveness. In this context, Coahuila could consider the example provided by Transparency International Slovakia, which regularly develops Open Local Government indexes (*Otvorená samospráva*) assessing the level of transparency in Slovakian regions and municipalities. Although the latter consider transparency in a broad sense, they represent a valuable reference for Coahuila in so far as they deal with subnational entities (including municipalities), they consider several indicators and provide graphs and visualisation tools to understand, assess, and compare scores in a clear, customisable and interactive way (Box 5.10).

Box 5.10. **Local Transparency Indexes for Regions and Municipalities in Slovakia**

The Open Local Government Indexes are developed by the Transparency International Slovakia (TIS) to assess the level of transparency in the 8 regions and 100 largest municipalities of Slovakia by giving a grade (from A+ to F) and creating rankings, which can also be customized by users. In particular, the two most recent rankings assess the several policy areas using a number of different sources.

Box 5.10. **Local Transparency Indexes for Regions and Municipalities in Slovakia** *(cont.)*

	REGIONS [Open Self Government: Regions 2015]	CITIES [Open Local Government 2014]
POLICY AREAS	Access to Information	Access to Information Policy
	Finance and Public Procurement	Public Participation Policy
	Professional Ethics and Conflict of Interests	Public Procurement Policy
	Public Property Sales and Lease	Public Property Sales and Leasing Policy
	Human Resources	Budgeting
	Municipal Businesses, Organisations and Investments	Grants Policy
	Public Participation	Housing and Social Services
	Media	Human Resources
	Grants	Professional Ethics and Conflict of Interests
	Social Services	Land Use Planning and Construction Policy
	Transport Policy	Municipal Businesses and Investments
SOURCE OF DATA SURVEYS	Quality of Information on the region's website	Quality of information on the municipal website
	Replies to Freedom of Information Act (211/2000) requests filled by Transparency	Replies to Freedom of Information Act (211/2000) requests solicited by TIS
	Replies to Freedom of Information Act (211/2000) requests filled by Transparency's co-workers ("mystery shopping")	Replies to Freedom of Information Act (211/2000) requests solicited unofficially by TIS – through third person
	Data from portal tender.sme.sk	Data from Public Procurement Office website and tender.sme.sk
	Information from regions' print media	
	Information from regions' Facebook profiles	
	Response of Chief Comptroller	
	Response of Chairman of the Region	

Sources: http://samosprava.transparency.sk/.

Proposals for Action

The advanced transparency framework built over the last years has created the premises for an open public sector in Coahuila. In order to leverage such efforts towards effective accountability, the OECD recommends that Coahuila considers taking the following actions in the realm of transparency and stakeholder participation:

Leveraging information and data for more accountable institutions

- Given that Coahuila is currently developing policies on open government, it could better exploit the data and information currently produced by public entities by improving data socialisation and developing online visualisation tools.
- In order to avoid gaps or overlaps and allow citizens and civil society to have comprehensive access to all the information and data provided by public institutions, Coahuila may wish to identify a single portal to consult and request information.

Improving stakeholders' engagement to promote transparency and the public interest

- Although the legal framework of Coahuila offers tools for stakeholder participation and oversight, they have not been regularly used in the past. In order to improve their effectiveness, mechanisms could be introduced to improve awareness and enable active engagement in innovative and interactive ways.
- Coahuila could make its transparency framework more responsive to society by introducing mechanisms to improve stakeholder engagement through a demand-drive approach based on dialogue, consultation, and on data collaboration and interoperability.

- Coahuila could improve oversight over the transparency commitments of its institutions by developing an easily accessible index measuring compliance and implementation of state- and municipal-level institutions.

References

G20 (2015), G20 Anti-Corruption Open Data Principles, *www.bmjv.de/SharedDocs/Downloads/EN/G20/G20-Anti-Corruption%20Open%20Data%20Principles.pdf;jsessionid=6AF3453E46D22ADABE482CC578BAB798.1_cid334?__blob=publicationFile&v=1*.

G8 (2013), G8 Open Data Charter and Technical Annex, *www.gov.uk/government/publications/open-data-charter/g8-open-data-charter-and-technical-annex*.

HATVP (2016), "Open Data & Intégrité Publique. Les Technologies Numériques au Service d'une Démocratie Exemplaire", *www.hatvp.fr/wordpress/wp-content/uploads/2016/12/Open-data-integrite-publique.pdf*.

Montemayor (2016), *La Política de Transparencia y Gobierno Abierto para impulsar la Participación Ciudadana y desarrollar la Gobernanza en el estado de Coahuila de Zaragoza*, Master Thesis, University of Vigo.

OECD (2009), *Focus on Citizens: Public Engagement for Better Policy and Services*, OECD Publishing, Paris. *http://dx.doi.org/10.1787/9789264048874-en*.

OECD (2013), *Colombia: Implementing Good Governance*, OECD Publishing, Paris. *http://dx.doi.org/10.1787/9789264202177-en*. *www.oecd.org/gov/colombia-urna-cristal.pdf*.

OECD (2015), *Government at a Glance 2015*, OECD Publishing, Paris. *http://dx.doi.org/10.1787/gov_glance-2015-en*.

OECD (2016), *Open Government Data Review of Mexico: Data Reuse for Public Sector Impact and Innovation*, OECD Digital Government Studies, OECD Publishing, Paris. *http://dx.doi.org/10.1787/9789264259270-en*.

OECD (2017a), *Recommendation of the Council on Public Integrity*, Paris, *http://www.oecd.org/gov/ethics/Recommendation-Public-Integrity.pdf*

OECD (2017b), *OECD Integrity Scan of Kazakhstan: Preventing Corruption for a Competitive Economy*, OECD Publishing, Paris. *http://dx.doi.org/10.1787/9789264272880-en*.

OECD (2014), *The Governance of Regulators*, OECD Publishing, Paris, *http://dx.doi.org/10.1787/9789264209015-en*.

Open Data Charter (2016), Anticorruption Open Data Package (Public Draft Open for Comments Version), *http://opendatacharter.net/resource/anticorruption-open-data-package/*.

STGA (2016), *Plan de acción de Gobierno Abierto para el Estado de Coahuila de Zaragoza 2016-2017*, *www.resi.org.mx/icainew_f/images/MICROSITIO%20GA/2016/docs/PAL.pdf*.

Ubaldi (2013), "Open Government Data: Towards Empirical Analysis of Open Government Data Initiatives", *OECD Working Papers on Public Governance*, No. 22, OECD Publishing, Paris. *http://dx.doi.org/10.1787/5k46bj4f03s7-en*.

OECD Integrity Review of Coahuila, Mexico
Restoring trust through an integrity system

Chapter 6

Public procurement in Coahuila: ensuring integrity and value for money

In line with the OECD Recommendation of the Council on Public Procurement, the present chapter assesses whether Coahuila has developed and implemented effective general standards for public procurement procedures and procurement-specific risk management tools in order to preserve integrity in this activity. Specifically, the chapter looks at newly-developed initiatives such as the Code of Conduct and the Conflict-of-Interest Manifest for suppliers. It then describes the actions undertaken so far to promote a culture of integrity among public procurement officials, potential suppliers, and civil society. It also evaluates how external stakeholders are involved in the public procurement system with a view to increase its transparency and integrity. Lastly, the chapter analyses levels of transparency of public procurement processes and the application of e-procurement solutions.

Introduction: Corruption risks in public procurement

Not all positions and activities in the public sector are the same in terms of potential integrity risks. Some sectors or officials, such as those in justice, tax and customs administrations, audit, inspection, and public procurement, may operate with higher potential risk of conflict of interest and corruption. Public procurement is particularly vulnerable to integrity violations due to the high complexity of activities, the close interaction between the public and private sectors, and the large volume of transactions. Indeed, every year governments spend large sums of public money on procurement contracts. In 2013 alone, for instance, it is estimated that OECD countries spent about 12% of their GDP and 29% of government expenditures on public procurement, which is estimated to be around EUR 4.2 trillion (OECD, 2015d). Unethical practices can occur in all phases of the public procurement cycle however, each phase may be prone to specific finds of integrity risks (see Table 6.1).

The OECD *Recommendation on Public Procurement* (2015) which comprises 12 integrated principles (see Figure 6.1 and Box 6.1) aims to address such risks and outlines some essential measures to be implemented in order to ensure integrity in the public procurement system and to fight corruption related to procurement processes. This chapter assesses the strengths and weaknesses of the public procurement framework of the state of Coahuila de Zaragoza against the OECD *Recommendation on Public Procurement*, and the extent to which the framework identifies and mitigates inherent corruption risks. Consequently, this chapter is organised into three sections covering several principles of the OECD Recommendation, including integrity, transparency, and participation (for more information, please refer to Annex 1): (1) Preserving public integrity through general standards of conduct and procurement-specific risk management tools; (2) Promoting a culture of integrity among public procurement officials, potential suppliers and civil society; and (3) Enhancing transparency and the disclosure of information around public procurement processes.

Table 6.1. **Corruption risks associated with the different phases of the public procurement cycle**

Pre-tendering phase	Needs assessment and market analysys	• Lack of adequate needs assessment • Influence of externalactors on official decisions • Informal agreement on contract
	Planning and budgeting	• Poor procurement planning • Procurence not aligned with overall investment decision-making process • Failure to budget realistically or deficiency in the budget
	Development of specifications/requirements	• Technical specifications are tailored for a specific company • Selection criteria is not objectively defined and not established in advance • Requesting unnecessary samples of goods and services • Buying information on the project specifications
	Choice of procurement procedure	• Lack of proper justification for the use of non-competitive procedures • Abuse of non-competitive procedures on the basis of legal exceptions: contract splitting, abuse of extreme urgency, non-supported modifications
Tendering phase	Request for proposal/bid	• Absence of public notice for the invitation to bid • Evaluation and award criteria are not announced • Procurement information is not disclosed and is not made public
	Bid submission	• Lack of competition or cases of collusive bidding (cover bidding, bid suppression, bid rotation, market allocation)

	Bid evaluation	• Conflict of interest and corruption in the evaluation proces through
		  • Familiarity with bidders overtime
		  • Personal interests such as gifts or future/additional employment
		  • No effective implementation of the "four eyes principle"

	Contract award	• Vendors fail to disclose accurate cost or pricing data in their price proposals, resulting in an increased contract price (i.e. invoice mark-ups, channel stuffing) • Conflict of interest and corruption in the approval process (i.e. no effective separation of financial, contractual and project authorities) • Lack of access to records on the procedure

Post-award phase	Contract management/performance	• Abuses of the supplier in performing the contract, in particular relation to its quality, price, and timing:
		  • Substantial change in contract conditions to allow more time and/or higher prices for the bidder
		  • Product substitution or sub-standard work or service not meeting contract specifications
		  • Thef of new assets before delivery to end-user or before being recorded
		  • Deficient supervision from public officials and/or collusion between contractors and supervising officials
		  • Subcontractors ant partners chosen in an on-transparent way or not kept accountable

	Planning and budgeting	• Deficient separation of financial duties and/or lack of supervision of public officials leading to:
		  • False accounting and cost misallocation or cost migrations between contracts
		  • Late payments of invoices
		• False or duplicate invoicing for good and services not supplied and for interim payment in advance entitlement

Source: OECD (2016a), *Preventing Corruption in Public Procurement*, OECD, Paris, *http://www.oecd.org/gov/ethics/Corruption-in-Public-Procurement-Brochure.pdf.*

Figure 6.1. **The 12 integrated principles of the OECD Recommendation on Public Procurement**

Source: OECD (2015), *OECD Recommendation on Public Procurement*. OECD, Paris, *www.oecd.org/gov/public-procurement/recommendation/*, accessed 24 August 2017.

Box 6.1. **The contribution of the 12 principles of the OECD Recommendation to the fight against corruption**

Transparency: The public disclosure of information around public procurement processes contributes to identifying and decreasing cases of mismanagement, fraud, and corruption.

Integrity: Effective managing of conflicts of interest in the public service and in post-public employment, which can lead to undue influence and «capture», are necessary to prevent fraud and theft.

Access: Access to procurement opportunities for potential competitors of all sizes, including the limited use of exceptions to competitive tendering (direct awards, accelerated procedures, etc.), increases competition and decreases corruption risks.

Balance: Public procurement can be used to achieve secondary policy objectives, such as the development of small- and medium-sized enterprises and standards for responsible business conduct, which have the potential to strengthen integrity to fight corruption in the framework of public procurement processes and beyond.

Participation: Participation, including the provision of opportunities for direct involvement of relevant external stakeholders in the procurement system, increases transparency and integrity and reduces the risks of corruption in public procurement processes.

Efficiency: Efficiency, by reducing waste, reduces the vulnerability to corruption since funds are better accounted for and used for the intended purposes.

E-procurement: E-procurement tools facilitate the access to public tenders and improve transparency of public procurement processes as well as accountability of procurement officials, which contributes to mitigate risks of corruption.

Box 6.1. **The contribution of the 12 principles of the OECD Recommendation to the fight against corruption** *(cont.)*

Capacity: More capable procurement officers are better able to comply with procedures and ensure that they are applied fairly and effectively to avoid corruption.

Evaluation: The collection of consistent, up-to-date, and reliable information and the use of data on prior procurement can facilitate the identification of corruption cases as well as collusion.

Risk management: Risk management systems contribute to identify and address threats to the proper functioning of the public procurement system, including risks of fraud, misuse of public funds, or corruption.

Accountability: Oversight and control mechanisms help to reinforce accountability throughout the procurement process. An effective complaint system contributes to identifying and sanctioning cases of corruption related to public procurement operations. If appropriately used, complaint systems may also reinforce risk management strategies and contribute to build a culture of integrity among procurement officials.

Integration: The visibility of the flow of public funds, from the beginning of the budgeting process to the end of the public procurement cycle, contributes to the transparency of the public procurement system and can reduce the risk of corruption.

Source: OECD (2015), OECD Recommendation on Public Procurement. OECD, Paris, *www.oecd.org/gov/public-procurement/recommendation/*.

Preserving public integrity through general standards of conduct and procurement-specific risk management tools

Coahuila's public procurement system is based primarily on the Law on Acquisitions, Leasing and Services for the State of Coahuila de Zaragoza (*Ley de Adquisiciones, Arrendamientos y Contratación de Servicios para el Estado de Coahuila*, LAACSEC) and the Law on Public Works and Related Services for the State of Coahuila de Zaragoza (*Ley de Obra Pública y servicios relacionados con las mismas para el Estado de Coahuila de Zaragoza*, LOPSEC). Both of these laws were revised in March 2016 and include new legal provisions aiming at strengthening transparency and integrity of public procurement processes: (1) a Conflict-of-Interest Declaration (*Manifiesto de no conflicto de intereses*) – Annex 11 of LAACSEC and Annex 32 of LOPSPEC - and (2) a Code of Conduct (*Código de Conducta*). Both initiatives target suppliers of the state of Coahuila.

The administrative sanctioning of public servants who take part in corrupt practices is mainly covered by the Law of Responsibilities of Public Servants at state and municipal level of the State of Coahuila de Zaragoza (*Ley de Responsabilidades de los Servidores Públicos Estatales y Municipales del Estado de Coahuila*, LRSPEMEC), enacted in 1984. With the approval of the new General Law on Administrative Responsibilities (*Ley General de Responsabilidades Administrativas*, LGRA), which came into effect in July 2017, the LRSPEMEC was replaced. A key feature of the new LGRA is indeed that it holds the character of general law, and will therefore apply beyond the federal level to public procurement officials across the country.

In addition, Coahuila introduced, in 2012, a Law to Prevent and Punish Corrupt Practices in Public Procurement Processes in the State of Coahuila de Zaragoza and its Municipalities (*Ley para Prevenir y Sancionar las Prácticas de Corrupción en los Procedimientos de Contratación Pública del Estado de Coahuila de Zaragoza y sus Municipios*). The latter is similar to the Federal

Anti-corruption Law on Public Procurement (*Ley Federal Anticorrupción en Contrataciones Públicas, LFACP*), which was adopted in June 2012 and directly addresses corruption and fraud in public procurement. The LFACP, however, is applicable only until 19 July 2017, after which it will also be supplanted by the LGRA. In 2014, Coahuila also adopted the Law on Access to Public Information and Protection of Personal Data (*Ley de Accesso a la Información Pública y Protección de Datos Personales, LAIP*), or Transparency Law. The second section of this Act governs the information that must be proactively made public and the government agencies need to provide upon request, including in the area of public procurement. It also introduces the supplier registry (*padrón de proveedores y contratistas*).

Using participative techniques, Coahuila should develop a specific Code of Ethics or Conduct and specific guidance for procurement officials, and ensure that specific provisions to public procurement are included in the codes developed by ministries and municipalities.

According to the Recommendation, adherents should preserve the integrity of the public procurement system through general standards and procurement specific safeguards and require high standards of integrity for all stakeholders in the procurement cycle. The Recommendation also recommends tailoring general integrity tools to the specific risks of the procurement cycle as necessary, e.g. the heightened risks involved in public-private interaction and fiduciary responsibility in public procurement (OECD, 2015a). According to the 2014 OECD *Survey on Management of Conflict of Interest*, specific conflict-of-interest policies and rules have for example been developed (see Figure 6.2) for procurement officials in 47% of OECD countries, right after senior public officials (50%) and ministers (59%).

Figure 6.2. **Development of specific conflict-of-interest policy/rules for particular categories of public officials in the OECD countries**

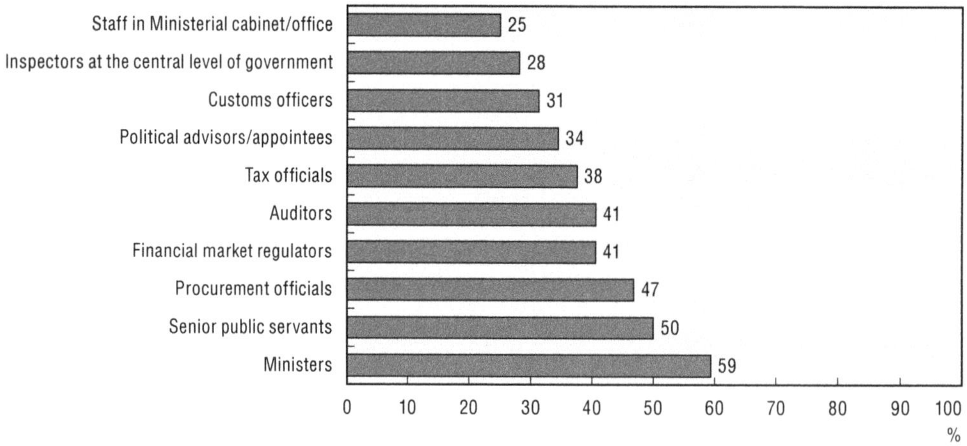

Source: 2014 OECD Survey on Management of Conflict of Interest, OECD, Paris, *http://www.oecd.org/governance/ethics/2014-survey-managing-conflict-of-interest.pdf*.

As described in Chapter 2 on Public Ethics, the Constitution of the State of Coahuila de Zaragoza lays out the institutional commitments (public trust, public participation, combatting corruption and impunity, etc.) as well as the constitutional principles and values (efficiency, effectiveness, honesty, fairness, impartiality, integrity, loyalty, legality, leadership, accountability, respect, and transparency) of the public service. Based on these commitments, principles, and values, the state of Coahuila has introduced a Code of Ethics and Conduct for Public Servants in the Executive Branch of the State of Coahuila de Zaragoza

(*Código de Ética y Conducta para los Servidores Públicos del Poder Ejecutivo del Estado de Coahuila de Zaragoza*). In 2015, it was complemented by a separate Code of Conduct for the Public Servants of the Ministry for Audit and Accountability (*Secretaría de Fiscalización y Rendición de Cuentas*, SEFIR). However, little attention has been paid in these codes to how they specifically target procurement personnel (or other high-risk positions in their organisations) and no specific Code of Ethics or Conduct has been developed for procurement officials – unlike at the federal level. At the federal level, Mexico recently passed an Ethics Code and Rules of Integrity (*Código de Ética y Reglas de Integridad*), which includes 17 specific provisions for officials working in the domain of public procurement (paragraph 3), out of 12 domains. These provisions include specific rules for public officials involved in public procurement processes, requiring that they must act in a transparent, impartial, and legal manner, making decisions based on the needs and interest of civil society and providing the best procurement conditions for the state (see Box 6.2).

Box 6.2. **Mexico's Ethics Code and Rules of Integrity: Provisions related to public procurement**

Public Contracts, Licenses, Permits, Authorisations, and Concessions

The public servant who participates in public contracting or in the granting and providing extensions to licenses, permits, authorisations and concessions, on the grounds of their employment, position, commission or function or through subordinates, should behave with transparency, impartiality, and legality, should orient their decisions towards the needs and interests of society, and should guarantee the best conditions for the state.

The following non-exhaustive list of behaviours threaten these values. It is therefore problematic to:

1. Omit to declare, in accordance with the applicable provisions, possible conflicts-of-interest as well as particular business and commercial links with persons or organisations registered in the Single Registry of Contractors for the Federal Public Administration.
2. Fail to apply the principle of equal competition that should prevail among participants in public procurement processes.
3. Formulate requirements differently from those strictly necessary for the fulfilment of the public service, causing excessive and unnecessary expenses.
4. Establish conditions in the invitations or calls for tenders which confer advantages or provide a differential treatment to certain bidders.
5. Favour certain bidders by considering that they meet the requirements or rules foreseen in the invitations or calls for tender when they do not; simulating the fulfilment of them or contributing to their temporary fulfilment.
6. Help suppliers to fulfil the requirements foreseen in the requests for quotes.
7. Provide undue information about individuals involved in public procurement processes.
8. Be partial in the selection, designation, contracting, and, as the case may be, removal or termination of the contract, in the framework of public procurement processes.
9. Influence decisions of other public servants in order for one participant to benefit from the public procurement processes or from the granting of licenses, permits, authorisations, and concessions.

Box 6.2. **Mexico's Ethics Code and Rules of Integrity: Provisions related to public procurement** *(cont.)*

10. Avoid imposing sanctions on bidders, suppliers, and contractors who violate applicable legal provisions.
11. Sending e-mails to bidders, suppliers, contractors or concessionaires through personal e-mail accounts or accounts which are distinct from institutional e-mail accounts.
12. Meet with bidders, suppliers, contractors, and concessionaires outside the official buildings, except for the proceedings related to on-site visits.
13. Request unsubstantiated requirements for the granting and providing extensions to licenses, permits, authorisations, and concessions.
14. Give inequitable or preferential treatment to any person or organisation in the framework of granting and extending licenses, permits, authorisations, and concessions.
15. Receive or request any type of compensation, offering, treat or gift in the framework of granting and providing extensions to licenses, permits, authorisations, and concessions.
16. Fail to observe the protocol of action in matters of public contracting and providing extensions to licenses, permits, authorisations, concessions, and their extensions.
17. To be a direct beneficiary or through relatives up to the fourth degree of government contracts related to the agency or entity that directs or to which are directed the services.

Source: Ethics Codes and Rules of Integrity, DOF-20-08-2015, *www.dof.gob.mx/nota_detalle.php?codigo=5404568&fecha=20/08/2015.*

As mentioned in Chapter 2, Coahuila should develop specific Codes of Ethics or Conduct for high-risk activities, including public procurement. A specific Code of Conduct for procurement officials would have the advantage of being tailored to the specific risks of the procurement cycle. Coahuila should also ensure that specific provisions to public procurement are included in the codes developed by individual line ministries, such as SEFIR and the municipalities. This recommendation is particularly relevant in the context of the implementation of the new Integrity Rules set out in the LGRA, which invites individual line ministries to revamp their specific Codes of Conduct. In line with the recommendation of Chapter 2, new ministerial (or municipal) codes would need to involve public procurement officials in order to strengthen the sense of ownership and its values throughout the individual line ministries (and municipalities). Experience has shown that governments in Mexico have not consulted targeted audiences while developing such codes in the past, hindering ownership by public officials as well as implementation of those codes.

This specific Code of Conduct for procurement officials should be complementary to the new Protocol of Conduct for Public Servants in Public Procurement, and on the granting and extension of licenses, permits, authorisations, and concessions (*Acuerdo por el que se expide el protocolo de actuación en materia de contrataciones públicas, otorgamiento y prórroga de licencias, permisos, autorizaciones y concesiones*), included in the LGRA, which seeks to specifically target conflict-of-interest situations for public procurement dealings.

The codes should be complemented with specific guidance on how public procurement officials can and are expected to react when faced with common ethical dilemmas and conflict-of-interest situations that could arise in public procurement processes. Such guidance could consider the current rules-based LAACSEC (Article 73.II for instance) and the Protocol and Codes of Conduct of Coahuila, which provide a foundation for guidance based on principles, values, and ethical reasoning. This guidance should, for instance, list situations which would constitute a material conflict-of-interest for a staff member working with a company submitting a tender. For the development of such guidance, Coahuila may want to consider the example of Australia (see Box 6.3) as well as the Guide developed at federal level to identify and prevent conducts that could constitute a conflict-of-interest for public officials (*Guía para identificar y prevenir conductas que puedan constituir conflicto de interés de los servidores públicos*). International good practice could also be a source of guidance on these matters. The guide developed at federal level provides a list of high-risk processes, including those related to public procurement and public works (out of nine processes), as well as a table to analyse the risks according to those areas. The codes and the guidance would add to the asset declaration and conflict-of-interest declaration system introduced by the new LGRA.

Box 6.3. **Conflict-of-interest management during tender evaluation in Australia**

The government of South Australia's Department of Planning, Transport, and Infrastructure (DPTI) applies ways to address potential and material conflict-of-interest situations during the procurement process through the Procurement Management Framework. It states that the DPTI staff member should notify the evaluation Panel Chairperson as soon as they notice signs of a conflict-of-interest situation. Even though a potential conflict of interest will not necessarily preclude a person from being involved in the evaluation process, it is declared and can be independently assessed.

It also lists situations which would be considered as a material conflict of interest of a staff in relation to a company submitting a tender including: 1) a significant shareholding in a small private company which is submitting a tender; 2) having an immediate relative (e.g. son, daughter, partner, sibling) employed by a company which is tendering, even though that person is not involved in the preparation of the tender and winning the tender would have a material impact on the company; 3) having a relative who is involved in the preparation of the tender to be submitted by a company; 4) exhibiting a bias or partiality for or against a tender (e.g. because of events that occurred during a previous contract); 5) a person, engaged under a contract to assist DPTI with the assessment, assessing a direct competitor who is submitting a tender; 6) regularly socialising with an employee of tenderer who is involved with the preparation of the tender; 7) having received gifts, hospitality or similar benefits from a tenderer in the period leading up to the call of tenders; 8) having recently left the employment of a tenderer; or 9) considering an offer of future employment or some other inducement from a tenderer.

Source: Procurement Management Framework. Confidentiality and Conflict of Interest, PR115, *http://dpti.sa.gov.au/__data/assets/word_doc/0016/162322/PR115_Confidentiality_and_Conflict_of_Interest_-_Procurement_Procedure.docx*, accessed 1 June 2016.

While the Code of Conduct and the Conflict-of-Interest Manifest are positive first steps in preventing corruption among suppliers, Coahuila should now leverage those tools in order to better identify integrity risks in public procurement processes.

In order to advance the integrity of the public procurement system, it is also critical to work with external actors, in particular the private sector. The public procurement cycle involves multiple actors and therefore integrity should not be a requirement for public officials alone. This is the reason why the Recommendation (OECD, 2015a) suggests that standards embodied in integrity frameworks or codes of conduct applicable to public-sector employees (such as managing conflict of interest, disclosure of information, or other standards of professional behaviour) be further expanded (e.g. through integrity pacts). For example, integrity standards applicable to public sector employees may be expanded to private sector stakeholders through integrity pacts (OECD, 2016). Integrity pacts are discussed in the second part of this chapter (*Promoting a culture of integrity among public procurement officials, potential suppliers and civil society*).

In Coahuila, both public procurement laws, the LAACSEC and the LOPSEC, were revised in March 2016 in order to include new legal provisions aiming at strengthening transparency and integrity of suppliers in the framework of public procurement processes.

- Indeed, the laws introduced a Conflict-of-Interest Declaration (*Manifiesto de no conflicto de intereses*), in Annex 11 of LAACSEC and Annex 32 of LOPSEC, as well as (2) a Code of Conduct (*Código de Conducta*) for suppliers of the state of Coahuila. According to these laws, the suppliers who would like to participate in any public procurement process need to present and comply with the Code of Conduct (Article 42 of the LAACSEC). The law specifies which information should be provided in the framework of the conflict-of-interest declarations, included in the application for the supplier's registry (*padrón de proveedores*), which needs to be completed each year (Article 42A of LAACSEC).
- The LAACSEC also specifies information to include in the Code of Conduct for suppliers (Article 42B): the purpose and scope of the application, the basic requirements related to the responsibilities of suppliers, and sanctions in the case of non-compliance. A Code of Conduct for suppliers was issued following the revision of the laws in March 2016. According to this provision, SEFIR is supposed to issue such a Code of Conduct. It remains unclear if the latter has been developed in a participative manner. As highlighted above, the consultation of targeted audiences, in this case the suppliers, in the framework of the development of the code would have strengthened the sense of ownership and its values throughout the supplier community. A few municipalities, such as Acuña, developed a specific Code of Conduct in addition to the Code developed by SEFIR.

While the Code of Conduct and the Conflict-of-Interest Manifest are positive first steps toward preventing corruption among suppliers, there are several aspects that weaken their potential to achieve the desired impact. The new Code of Conduct could, for instance, benefit from a more balanced approach. Indeed, there is a limit to the benefits of prohibitions, control, and sanctions, and balancing rules-based and values-based approaches is considered to be crucial (OECD, 2009). For the time being, the Code is based almost exclusively on a rules-based approach, neglecting values-based behaviours. The Code of Conduct seems to the supplier community to suggest that they are inherently corrupt. This situation is very similar in the case of the LAACSEC and the Law to Prevent and Punish Corrupt Practices in Public Procurement Processes in the State of Coahuila de Zaragoza and its Municipalities (*Ley para Prevenir y Sancionar las Prácticas de Corrupción en los Procedimientos de Contratación Pública del Estado de Coahuila de Zaragoza y sus Municipios*), which are both strongly focused on prohibitions, control, and sanctions. The OECD *Recommendation on Public Procurement* emphasises the importance of not creating undue fear of consequences or risk-aversion in the procurement workforce or supplier community (OECD, 2015a). Against that background, Coahuila may want to adopt a more values-based approach rather than emphasising prohibitions.

In addition, Coahuila should also better leverage the Conflict-of-Interest Declaration and the Code of Conduct to raise awareness on corruption risk in the framework of public procurement processes and to identify integrity risks in public procurement processes. SEFIR and the Ministry of Finance (*Secretaría de Finanzas*, SEFIN) should, for instance, make sure to inform the supplier's community about the new Code of Conduct in an appropriate way. At the time of preparation of the review, the Code of Conduct is not visible on the SEFIR or SEFIN websites, and it is not included in the documents provided by SEFIR in the framework of application for registration in the supplier's registry. This may be one reason why very few suppliers know about the new Code. Coahuila may also want to make sure that the objectives and content of both tools are included in integrity training for the supplier community. Once Coahuila has developed its Code of Ethics or Conduct for procurement officials (see recommendation above), SEFIR will need to make sure to explain the differences between both codes in order to avoid confusion among public officials and suppliers, as mentioned in Chapter 2 of this review.

In order for the information to be helpful to fight against corruption and decrease conflict-of-interest cases, the information contained in the Conflict-of-Interest Manifests provided by suppliers needs to be cross-checked with the asset declarations (*declaración de situación patrimonial*) and interests declaration (*declaración de intereses*) of public procurement officials (see Chapter 2 for more information). The verification of the information would be in line with Article 23 of the LAACSEC, which foresees the possibility of undertaking consultations in order to cross-check the information provided in the framework of application for registration in the supplier's registry. Cross-checking such information would help ensure that the information provided by suppliers and public procurement officials are coherent. This could be one of the roles of the recommended Specialised Unit for Ethics and Prevention of Conflicts of Interest of SEFIR, in case it is introduced (see Chapter 2 for more information). It is unclear if public procurement officials and contracting authorities have access to the information provided in those Manifests. In case they do not have access to this information, it may be difficult for public procurement officials to verify any relevant information and to follow up on any apparent conflict of interest.

Also, while the initiative of creating such a Manifest is an important step towards identifying conflict-of-interest situations, it would be more efficient to request suppliers and bidders to fill in the Manifest only in the case of potential, real and apparent conflict. In order to do so, the Manifest should provide a clear definition of conflict of interest (potential, real and apparent conflict); in line with relevant laws (see Chapter 2). Coahuila should also provide the possibility of updating the Manifest throughout the year (and incite suppliers to do so) and not only while applying to the supplier's registry once a year (according to Article 25 of the LAACSEC, the Certificate of Competence [*Certificado de Aptitud*] is only valid for one year). Also, the Manifest should be complemented by a specific guide for public procurement officials, internal control bodies, suppliers, and bidders on how to use those Manifests, by the creation of a FAQ section, as well as by the identification of a focal point in charge of advising public servants and external actors.

Coahuila would also need to evaluate the impact of the adoption of the new LGRA, which introduces the Procurement Protocol and a Manifest (*Manifiesto que podrán formular los particulares en los procedimientos de contrataciones públicas, de otorgamiento y prórroga de licencias, permisos, autorizaciones y concesiones*). The Manifest is for individual natural persons to declare or deny any businesses, work, personal, or family links or relationships of consanguinity or affinity to the fourth degree with public servants specified in the Protocol each time they are involved in public procurement processes, grants and extensions of licenses, permits, and authorisations. The Manifest can be filled in online (*www.manifiesto.gob.mx*) and can be updated anytime.

In order to preserve public integrity, Coahuila should develop risk assessment tools to identify and address the threats to the proper functioning of the public procurement system and make sure that contracting authorities are implementing them.

Risk management tools can map, detect, and mitigate corruption risks and preserve public integrity throughout the public procurement cycle. According to the OECD Recommendation, adherents should develop specific risk assessment tools to identify and address threats to the proper functioning of the public procurement system. Where possible, tools should be developed to identify risks of all sorts – including potential mistakes in the performance of administrative tasks and deliberate transgressions – and bring them to the attention of relevant personnel, providing an intervention point where prevention or mitigation is possible. Adherents should also publicise risk management strategies, for instance, systems of red flags or whistleblower programmes, and raise awareness and knowledge of the procurement workforce and other stakeholders about the risk management strategies, their implementation plans and measures set up to deal with the identified risks (OECD, 2015a). Public authorities, including contracting authorities, should minimise the opportunity for fraud and corruption as much as possible through developing a sound control environment and putting in place the proper control activities to mitigate the relevant risks.

Coahuila has progressively introduced an internal control system, since the 2013 adoption of the Internal Control General Standard (*Norma General de Control Interno*). In 2016, Coahuila also adopted Manuals on Internal Control (*Manual administrativo de aplicación general en materia de control interno* and the *Manual operativo del Sistema de evaluación del control interno*). The manuals are complemented with a matrix of risk management (*Matriz de Administración de* Riesgos). Interviews carried out during the fact-finding mission nevertheless showed that public entities have not yet implemented these recently-developed internal control and risk management tools. They also lack specific Working Programmes of Risk Management (*Programa de Trabajo de Administración de Riesgos*). Unlike at the federal level, public procurement is not recognised as a process particularly vulnerable to corruption, and on which public entities should focus in the framework of their risk management systems. Interviews also suggest that there are no awareness raising or capacity-building programmes around risk management, including corruption risks.

As such, Coahuila should make sure that contracting authorities are implementing the internal control and risk management system, strategy and tools that it has developed. Coahuila needs to publicise the manuals and tools on internal control and risk management and raise awareness and knowledge of the public officials, including the procurement workforce and other stakeholders, on those strategies, including through trainings. Coahuila also may want to consider the introduction of risk management tools that identify and address specific public procurement risks. Coahuila could, for instance, develop a specific checklist listing the risks linked to the public procurement activity, in particular the corruption risks. SEFIR could also develop specific guidance on how the five internal control components (control environment, risk assessment, control activities, information and communication and monitoring) can link with the public procurement process. It could also provide a checklist for contracting authorities to verify that the five components are being taken into account in their daily activities and that the risks are evaluated and mitigated (see Table 6.2).

Table 6.2. **Leveraging internal control over the procurement cycle**

Internal Control components	Tailor made linkages with the procurement process
Control Environment	Are there clearly defined ethics requirements and professional certifications for those employed in the procurement units?
Risk Assessment	Has the entity assessed areas of vulnerabilities in the procurement procedures?
Control Activities	Are there effective controls to mitigate the identified procurement risks?
Information & Communication	Are deficiencies in the procurement process communicated and remediation activities shared?
Monitoring	Is the procurement process linked with indicators and monitoring system to document its efficiency and effectiveness as well as implementation of corrective actions?

Source: Developed by the OECD Secretariat.

Finally, SEFIR may want to consider the development of specific guidance for the establishment of a red flags system for corruption in procurement. Red flags are warning signals or hints of something that needs extra attention to exclude or confirm potential fraud and corruption. Red flags may be individual- or organisation-related (see Box 6.4). Those tools should be accompanied by specific templates to facilitate their implementation in the daily business of the public procurement entities and use digital solutions and technologies to the greatest extent possible.

Box 6.4. **Examples of red flags for corruption in procurement**

World Bank red flags of fraud and corruption in procurement:

1. Complaint from bidders or other parties
2. Multiple contracts below procurement threshold
3. Unusual bid patterns
4. Seemingly inflated agent fees
5. Suspicious bidder
6. Lowest bidder not selected
7. Repeated awards to the same contractor
8. Changes in contract terms and value
9. Multiple contract change orders
10. Poor quality works and/or services

Chartered Institute of Public Finance and Accountancy red flags:

1. Physical losses
2. Unusual relationship with suppliers
3. Manipulation of data
4. Photocopied documents
5. Incomplete management/audit trail
6. IT-controls of audit logs disabled
7. Budget overspends
8. IT-login outside working hours
9. Unusual invoices (e.g. format, numbers, address, phone, VAT number)
10. Vague description of goods/services to be supplied
11. Duplicate/photocopy invoice

Box 6.4. **Examples of red flags for corruption in procurement** *(cont.)*

12. High number of failed IT logins
13. Round sum amounts invoiced
14. Favoured customer treatment
15. Sequential invoice numbers over an extended period of time
16. Interest/ownership in external organisation
17. Non-declaration of interest/gifts/hospitality
18. Lack of supporiting records
19. No process identifying risks (e.g. risk register)
20. Unusual increases/decreases

Source: OECD (2015), *Effective Delivery of Large Infrastructure Projects: The Case of the New International Airport of Mexico City*, OECD Publishing, Paris.

Promoting a culture of integrity among public procurement officials, potential suppliers, and civil society

Coahuila should support the implementation of new integrity standards by streamlining and updating the legislation and by developing and implementing adequate communications strategies.

A law, a protocol, or code alone cannot guarantee ethical behaviour. It can offer written guidance on expected behaviour by outlining the values and standards to which public procurement officials should aspire. But to be effectively implemented, adequate communication strategies, including awareness-raising activities, should be developed. A clear communication strategy to raise awareness with regard to integrity policies and available tools and guidance, ideally, makes use of different existing and innovative channels of communication. Also, it should target internal stakeholders (public procurement officials) as well as external stakeholders (the private sector, civil society organisations, and individuals), in particular when it comes to public procurement. External communication of the relevant laws and codes of conduct can support key stakeholders in their commitment to integrity. The role of external actors, in particular users of public services and the private sector, is indeed critical to maintaining the integrity of government operations.

The 2012 adoption of a Law to Prevent and Punish Corrupt Practices in Public Procurement Processes in the State of Coahuila de Zaragoza and its Municipalities (*Ley para Prevenir y Sancionar las Prácticas de Corrupción en los Procedimientos de Contratación Pública del Estado de Coahuila de Zaragoza y sus Municipios*) illustrates the commitment of Coahuila to fight corruption in the area of public procurement. This law is complemented with integrity and anti-corruption provisions included in the public procurement laws, as well as provisions included in Coahuila's Transparency Law. For now, the legislation related to fighting corruption in public procurement is fragmented and does not facilitate implementation by public procurement officials, suppliers, and citizens. In addition, Coahuila will need to implement the new LGRA, which includes a new Protocol of Conduct for Public Servants in Public Procurement, including a Manifest for suppliers. Those two initiatives which Coahuila's will have to implement as of July 2017 may duplicate some of the existing efforts developed by the state government. The legislative fragmentation and potential duplication of initiatives and tools creates confusion and does not facilitate their proper implementation. As such, Coahuila may want to consider streamlining the current legislation related to the fight of corruption in public procurement.

In addition, Coahuila should develop and implement targeted communication strategies, in particular in regards to the recent tools (Coahuila's Conflict-of-Interest Declaration and Code of Conduct for suppliers) as well as the new tools developed at federal level (the Procurement Protocol and the Manifest). The interviews carried out during the fact-finding mission showed that the recent tools were not very well-known among public officials and suppliers and that the latter were, in some cases, critical of them. The objectives, content, usage, and benefits of the Conflict-of-Interest Declaration and the Code of Conduct for suppliers should be communicated to the public procurement workforce, and manuals and guidelines could also be created to help public procurement officials and suppliers to understand and apply the new provisions. SEFIR should also start raising awareness among public procurement officials, suppliers, and other relevant external actors about the new tools developed at federal level. In the communication strategies, emphasis should be placed on both their rights and their duties to abide by the rules. The recent and new integrity standards and codes should be included in the trainings (see further for more details) and could be attached to requests for proposals and calls for applications or generally mailed to all vendors. The inclusion of the Conflict-of-Interest Declaration in the application for the supplier's registry can be considered a good practice. Raising awareness externally about public officials' integrity commitments is also crucial as a pre-requisite to encourage the participation of citizens in public procurement processes and in strengthening accountability and increasing institutional trust.

Coahuila should strengthen the culture of integrity among the procurement workforce by developing a clear integrity capacity strategy and implementing tailored training for procurement officials.

According to the Recommendation, integrity training programmes need to be developed for the procurement workforce, both public and private, to raise awareness about integrity risks, such as corruption, fraud, collusion and discrimination, develop knowledge on ways to counter these risks and favour a culture of integrity to prevent corruption (principle of integrity). The Recommendation also underlines the need to ensure that procurement officials meet high professional standards for knowledge, practical implementation and integrity by providing a dedicated and regularly updated set of tools, for example, sufficient staff in terms of numbers or skills, recognition of public procurement as a specific profession, certification and regular trainings, integrity standards for public procurement officials (OECD, 2015a). Human Resource Management (HRM) is indeed particularly relevant in promoting and ensuring integrity. Public ethics and the management of conflicts of interest are about directly or indirectly changing the behaviour of an organisation's human resources. As a result, HRM policies are both part of the problem and part of the solution in promoting integrity in the public administration, including among public procurement officials.

As specified in Chapter 2 of the review, SEFIR is responsible for the overall framework of training on integrity issues and co-ordination among state ministries and agencies, including SEFIN. It co-ordinates a one-day training on management of conflicts-of-interest. According to the information provided by Coahuila, SEFIR has not developed capacity-building programmes specific to integrity issues or corruption prevention in public procurement. It remains unclear which trainings are being provided to procurement officials and if those trainings include specific modules on managing integrity and corruption risks. Specific training videos on integrity for public officials, including public procurement officials, do not exist either. There seems to be no comprehensive integrity capacity building strategy for public officials, including public procurement officials. The State Programme of administrative modernisation, audit, and accountability for the period 2011-2017 (*Programa Estatal de Modernización Administrativa, Fiscalización y Rendición de Cuentas*) mentions the development of the State Capacity Programme (*Programa Estatal de Capacitación*), but it has not been defined so far, according to the latest Government Report of Coahuila 2011-2017 (*Cuarto Informe de Gobierno 2011-2017*) published in November 2015. Only a survey aiming at detecting the needs in terms of capacity building (*Encuesta de Detección de Necesidades de Capacitación*, DNC) has been undertaken in 2014. The results of the survey are not available online.

As such, Coahuila could consider developing a clear integrity capacity-building strategy for the public administration, including public procurement officials, along with a certification system. This strategy could be part of the State Capacity Programme and should take into account the diagnostic resulting from the DNC. It should also take into account the specificities of high-risk areas such as public procurement. Coahuila could also envisage the development of a public procurement capacity strategy, which would include specific initiatives to strengthen the culture of integrity among the procurement workforce. In the framework of those capacity strategies, Coahuila could consider developing and implementing tailored training programmes for public procurement officials. Those specific trainings should be included in the framework of the induction trainings developed for new employees for instance and specific courses should be developed to present the recent and new provisions and tools (the latter could be implemented through e-learning solutions). The specific trainings should ideally lead to certification. Such strategy would not only strengthen the integrity of public officials, but would also contribute to professionalising the workforce and to improving its performance. In Germany, specific integrity training has been developed for public procurement officials (see Box 6.5).

One pre-requisite for the implementation of such a public procurement capacity strategy is the identification of the public procurement workforce, in particular the number of officials working in the area of public procurement. It seems that Coahuila has not introduced a specific tool to identify those public procurement officials, unlike at the federal level. Following a series of Executive Orders by the President of Mexico, Mexico has indeed created a Registry of Public Servants of the Federal Public Administration who are involved in public procurement processes and other high-risk processes in terms of corruption (*Registro de servidores públicos de la Administración Publica Federal que intervienen en procedimientos de contrataciones públicas*). Public officials listed in the registry are obliged to obtain adequate certifications in order to ensure their integrity and performance. Coahuila may want to consider introducing such a tool in order to have a better overview of public procurement officials, to manage certifications, to target integrity and public procurement trainings and to cross-check information (included in conflict-of-interest declarations for instance).

As stressed in the OECD Recommendation, the preservation of integrity of the public procurement system also requires integrity training requirements for supplier personnel (OECD, 2015a). Therefore, Coahuila may also include the supplier's needs in its future integrity capacity building strategy and public procurement capacity strategy, by developing and proposing specific trainings for suppliers on issues related to integrity and the fight against corruption in the framework of public procurement processes. Those trainings and information actions could be developed and undertaken jointly with the business chambers and suppliers associations.

Box 6.5. **Integrity training in Germany**

The Federal Procurement Agency is a government agency which manages purchasing for 26 different federal authorities, foundations, and research institutions that fall under the responsibility of the Federal Ministry of the Interior. It is the second largest federal procurement agency after the Federal Office for Defence Technology and Procurement.

The Procurement Agency has taken several measures to promote integrity among its personnel, including support and advice by a corruption prevention officer ("Contact Person for the Prevention of Corruption"), the organisation of workshops and training on corruption, and the rotation of its employees.

Since 2001, it is mandatory for new staff members to participate in a corruption-prevention workshop. They learn about the risks of getting involved in bribery and the briber's possible strategies. They also learn how to behave when these situations occur; for example, they are encouraged to report it (or to "blow the whistle"). Workshops highlight the central role of employees whose ethical behaviour is an essential part of corruption prevention. About ten workshops took place with 190 persons who provided positive feedback concerning the content and the usefulness of the training. The involvement of the Agency's "Contact Person for the Prevention of Corruption" and the Head of the Department for Central Services in the workshops demonstrated to participants that corruption prevention is one of the priorities for the agency. In 2005 the target group of the workshops was enlarged to include not only induction training but also ongoing training for the entire personnel. Since then, six to seven workshops are being held per year at regular intervals, training approximately 70 new and existing employees per year.

Another key corruption prevention measure is the staff rotation after a period of five to eight years in order to avoid prolonged contact with suppliers, as well as improve motivation and make the job more attractive. However, the rotation of members of staff still meets with difficulty in the Agency. Due to a high level of specialisation, many officials cannot change their organisational unit, their knowledge being indispensable for the work of the unit. In these cases alternative measures such as intensified (supervisory) control are being taken.

Source: OECD (2016). *Towards Efficient Public Procurement in Colombia: Making the Difference*, OECD Public Governance Reviews, OECD Publishing, Paris. *http://dx.doi.org/10.1787/9789264252103-en*.

Coahuila should further engage with the private sector, developing co-operation agreements and integrity pacts in an effort to minimise corruption risks.

In order to preserve the integrity of the public procurement system, it is critical to work with external actors, in particular the private sector. The public procurement cycle involves multiple actors and therefore integrity is not a requirement for public officials alone. Just as the public sector has the responsibility to take measures on its end, so does the private sector. Private companies often have their own integrity system in place, and many countries engage with private sector actors to instil integrity in public procurement. For example, integrity standards applicable to public sector employees may be expanded to private sector stakeholders through integrity pacts (OECD, 2016). The OECD Recommendation on Public Procurement underlines the need to develop requirements for internal controls, compliance measures, and anti-corruption programmes for suppliers, including appropriate monitoring. It stresses the need for procurement contracts to contain "no corruption" warranties and measures to verify the truthfulness of supplier's warranties that they have not and will not engage in corruption in connection with the contract. According to the OECD Recommendation, such programmes should also require appropriate supply-chain transparency to fight corruption in subcontracts and integrity training for supplier personnel (OECD, 2015a).

Coahuila's Law to Prevent and Punish Corrupt Practices in Public Procurement Processes in the State of Coahuila de Zaragoza and its Municipalities (*Ley para Prevenir y Sancionar las Prácticas de Corrupción en los Procedimientos de Contratación Pública del Estado de Coahuila de Zaragoza y sus Municipios*) takes into account the role of the private sector in the fight against corruption. For example, it foresees the development of co-operation agreements with chambers of commerce or other industrial organisations in order to guide them in the development of internal control tools and integrity programmes to ensure the development of an ethical culture (Article 12). The law even invites contracting authorities to consider international best practices related to anti-corruption in business transactions (Article 12). These provisions are in line with the President's 2015 Executive Orders which mandated the Federal Ministry of Public Administration (*Secretaría de Función Pública*, SFP) to increase collaboration with the private sector in relation with transparency and the fight against corruption as well as the active participation of citizens in the identification of vulnerable processes and procedures through the development of co-operation agreements with chambers of commerce and civil society organisations. However, there is no evidence on the number of co-operation agreements that have been signed in Coahuila. Coahuila should therefore support the development of such agreements and ensure the implementation of joint actions. At the federal level these joint actions include sharing diagnostics, statistics, and other relevant information, identifying and communicating on good practices in terms of transparency and the fight against corruption, promoting sector-specific initiatives such as the initiative to strengthen the monitoring of public works, and facilitating dialogue fora on issues related to integrity and public ethics, as well as the prevention of conflicts of interest.

In Coahuila, public procurement contracts do not contain "no corruption" warranties and measures to verify the truthfulness of suppliers' warranties that they have not engaged and will not engage in corruption in connection with the contract either (also known as "integrity pacts"). Integrity Pacts are agreements between the government agency offering a contract and the companies bidding for it that they will abstain from bribery, collusion, and other corrupt practices for the extent of the contract. Coahuila's Public Procurement Law, unlike the Federal Public Procurement Law, does not foresee such integrity pacts (*pactos de integridad*). This instrument is considered a good practice and it is recommended by the OECD Recommendation on Public Procurement and the OECD Guidelines on Fighting Bid Rigging because it makes the legal representatives of firms aware of and directly accountable for the unlawful behaviour (OECD, 2015b). In case Coahuila envisages the introduction of such integrity pacts, the signed declarations of bidders could be published on the federal e-procurement system CompraNet, for tenders involving federal funds, or any other website aiming at strengthening transparency and fighting against corruption. Coahuila could consider developing requirements for internal controls, compliance measures, and anti-corruption programmes for suppliers.

Coahuila should create opportunities for direct involvement of civil society in the public procurement processes by implementing the social witness programme and other monitoring tools.

Creating a culture of integrity and openness in the public sector is also achieved through the involvement of citizens, experts, and civil society in the policy making process through forms of "direct social control". The OECD Recommendation echoes this statement and recommends the provision of direct opportunities for involvement of relevant external stakeholders in the procurement system with a view to increase transparency and integrity while assuring adequate scrutiny, provided that confidentiality, equal treatment, and other legal obligations in the procurement process are maintained (OECD, 2015a). Those opportunities can be, for instance, provided through social witnesses, usually members of a non-governmental organisation (NGO), who are invited to observe one or several parts of the procurement process. Social witnesses have the opportunity to raise concerns about corrupt behaviour and to provide recommendations for increasing the integrity of the process. Social witnesses are third parties deemed to have no conflict-of-interest in procurement procedures, and whose task is to observe the tender process in order to enhance its accountability, legality, and transparency (OECD, 2015b).

As presented in Chapter 5 of this review, Coahuila adopted a specific Law on Civic Participation in 2001 (*Ley de Participación Ciudadana para el Estado de Coahuila de Zaragoza*), which aims to support Coahuila citizens' right to participate in public life as well as to promote policies for community development. Coahuila's Law to Prevent and Punish Corrupt Practices in Public Procurement Processes in the State of Coahuila de Zaragoza and its Municipalities (*Ley para Prevenir y Sancionar las Prácticas de Corrupción en los Procedimientos de Contratación Pública del Estado de Coahuila de Zaragoza y sus Municipios*) takes into account the role of civil society in the monitoring of public procurement processes. It requires contracting authorities to inform citizens on the use of goods and the expenses and investments of the resources of each administration (Article 14). The Transparency and Access to Information Law (*Ley de Acceso a Información Pública y Protección de Datos Personales para el Estado de Coahuila de Zaragoza*), referred to in Chapter 5 of this review, specifies that the public administration needs to create and use systematic and advanced technology systems and adopt new tools in order for citizens to consult information in a direct, simple and quick manner (Article 8). The Transparency Law also invites public authorities to establish communication channels with citizens through social networks and digital platforms that would allow them to participate in the decision-making process (Article 53). In line with these provisions, Coahuila developed the SITODEM website (more information in the next section) in order to strengthen the transparency and the oversight related to public works.

Even if the legal framework acknowledges the role of civil society in the monitoring of public procurement processes, there currently exist only a few opportunities for direct involvement of relevant external stakeholders in the procurement system with a view to increase transparency and integrity.

As introduced in Chapter 5, a few initiatives have been developed in the framework of SEFIR's Institutional Programme on Social Monitoring/Control. One initiative, developed by SEFIR in co-operation with the *Universidad Autónoma de Coahuila*, UAdeC, focuses on the supervision of public works, in particular by students. In October 2016, over a two-week period, students were tasked with measuring the quality of 83 public works projects and writing audit reports. The information included in the latter served to update the SITODEM website. This initiative contributed to strengthening the transparency, integrity, and accountability of public procurement processes, but is still implemented on an *ad hoc* basis. Coahuila should create and institutionalise more opportunities, by accelerating the introduction of social witnesses (*testigos sociales*) for public procurement processes and using the experience of Mexico at federal level as a model (see Box 6.6). Indeed, the LAACSEC and the LOPSEC were amended on April 2017 to introduce the figure of the social witness.

As mentioned in the OECD Public Procurement Review of the Mexican Institute of Social Security: Enhancing Efficiency and Integrity for Better Health Care, SFP notes that "the monitoring of the most relevant procurement processes of the federal government through social witnesses has had an impact in improving procurement procedures by virtue of their contributions and experience, to the point that they have become a strategic element for ensuring the transparency and credibility of the procurement system". An OECD-World Bank Institute study (2006) indicates that the participation of social witnesses in procurement processes of the Federal Electricity Commission (*Comisión Federal de Electricidad*, CFE) created savings of approximately USD 26 million in 2006 and increased the number of bidders by over 50% (OECD, 2013). Coahuila should nevertheless take into account the risk of corruption within this programme. The bribing of social witnesses is also a risk to be considered. In order for social witness programmes to be effective, social witnesses need to have access to specific training courses, because they must have the necessary background and experience to enable them to provide expert procurement advice to public procurement officials (OECD, 2015b). Trainings could be complemented by specific guides such as at the federal level (*Guía anual de acciones de participación ciudadana*) and good practices.

Box 6.6. **Implementation of social witnesses at federal level (in Mexico)**

At federal level, social witnesses are required to participate in all stages of public tendering procedures above certain thresholds, since 2009. These thresholds are MXN 350 million (approximately USD 17 million) for goods and services and MXN 710 million (approximately USD 34 million) for public works in 2015. Social witnesses may also participate in public tendering procedures below the legal threshold, direct award procedures and restricted tendering if it is considered appropriate by SFP. Social witnesses are selected by the Ministry of Public Administration (*Secretaría de la Función Pública*, SFP) through public tendering (*Convocatoria pública para la selección de personas físicas y morales a registrar en el padrón público de testigos sociales*) and selected witnesses enter a pool (*Padrón Público de Testigos Sociales*) for a period of three years. Their names are being published online: As of October 2016, SFP had registered 25 social witnesses for public procurement projects, six Civil Society Organisations and 19 individuals. The social witnesses are certified and their performance is evaluated by the ministry (unsatisfactory performance potentially results in their removal from the registry). They also get certified and compensated for their services. When a federal entity requires the involvement of a social witness, SFP designates one from the preselected pool. Following their participation in procurement procedures, social witnesses issue a final report providing comments and recommendations on the process. These reports are made available to the public through the Mexican federal e-procurement platform, CompraNet.

Source: OECD (2013), Public Procurement Review of the Mexican Institute of Social Security: Enhancing Efficiency and Integrity for Better Health Care, OECD Publishing, Paris. *http://dx.doi.org/10.1787/9789264197480-en*.

Enhancing transparency and the disclosure of information around public procurement processes

Coahuila should consolidate the information related to public procurement through a unique online portal and ensure the visibility of the flow of public funds, from the beginning of the budgeting process through the public procurement cycle, in order to facilitate an adequate level scrutiny of public procurement processes.

Integrity and transparency of public procurement systems are closely linked. Transparency and the disclosure of information around public procurement processes contribute to identifying and decreasing cases of mismanagement, fraud and corruption and is therefore a key accountability mechanism for integrity. The OECD Recommendation therefore encourages adherents to ensure an adequate degree of transparency of the public procurement system in all stages of the procurement cycle and 1) promote fair and equitable treatment for potential suppliers by providing an adequate and timely degree of transparency at each phase of the public procurement cycle; 2) allow free access, through an online portal, for all stakeholders, including potential domestic and foreign suppliers, civil society and the general public, to public procurement information; and 3) ensure visibility of the flow of public funds, from the beginning of the budgeting process throughout the public procurement cycle (OECD, 2015a). It also should be noted that excessive transparency may facilitate anticompetitive agreements (OECD, 2015b).

As explained in Chapter 5 of this review, issues related to transparency and access to information are covered by Coahuila's Transparency and Access to Information Law (*Ley de Acceso a Información Pública y Protección de Datos Personales para el Estado de Coahuila de Zaragoza*), which was most recently reformed in March 2016. It provides an extensive list of information which each administration, including contracting authorities, must provide proactively. In terms of public procurement, the Law foresees the publication of the supplier's registry (*padrón de proveedores y contratistas*), the results of direct awards, restricted tenders and any other procurement processes (Article 21). In terms of public works, the Law foresees the publication of the construction companies having won a public works contract, the name of the person monitoring the public works, and the dates and the resources related to each public work (Article 41). The documents related to public procurement that need to be accessible to the public are also listed in Article 42 of the LAACSEC. The latter underlines the need to publish, through e-procurement tools, the following information: tender notifications, the terms of the tenders, the Conflict-of-Interest Declaration, documents related to clarification meetings and field visits, and other relevant information.

In line with the Transparency Law, Coahuila has introduced the SITODEM portal (*Sistema de Información y Transparencia de Obras para el Desarrollo Metropolitano*) to geo-reference expenditures (*http://sitodem.sefircoahuila.gob.mx/*). It presents information linked to the Integral System of Public Investment, including the names of approved public works, their cost, the responsible departments, beneficiaries, auditors, the pictures of the finished work, and the report of social comptrollership (*contraloría social*). However, it does not include information about the contractor or the suppliers. As mentioned in Chapter 5, SITODEM does not provide information on the progress of the public work(s), in real time. SITODEM is listed as one of Coahuila's transparency initiatives on the *Transparencia Focalizada* website, along with the live transmission of tenders (see further) as well as the supplier's registry (*www.transparenciafocalizada.cdmx.gob.mx/*). SITODEM is similar to the federal *Transparencia Presupuestaria* website (*www.transparenciapresupuestaria.gob.mx/*), which includes a module on public works (*Obra Pública Abierta*). The latter also does not provide information on the suppliers and contractors. The SITODEM portal is managed by four auditors of SEFIR's Verification Directorate (*Dirección de Verificación*), who undertake field visits in order to monitor the implementation of public works.

In order to strengthen the transparency and the oversight of public procurement processes, Coahuila has also introduced the live transmission of tenders as of 2011. According to representatives of Coahuila, the live transmission of tenders has reduced the number of disagreements and complaints. The live transmission goes beyond the Public Procurement Protocol included in the new LGRA, which foresees the taping of phone calls and the videotaping of meetings. It remains unclear if the live transmission of tenders is compulsory for all public procurement processes, given that it is included neither in the LAACSEC nor in the Transparency Law of Coahuila. Introducing live transmission indeed only makes sense if all processes are being transmitted in order to ensure full transparency.

The third initiative related to public procurement listed on the *Transparencia Focalizada* website is the supplier's registry (*Padrón de Proveedores y Contratistas de la Administratación Pública Estatal*), introduced by the Transparency Law (Article 21) as well as in the LAACSEC (Article 22) in 2012. The supplier's registry, managed by SEFIR, includes 936 suppliers and 322 contractors (as of January 2017) as well as the following information: the name and address of the supplier/contractor, the expertise, the registry number, the date of entry, and the validity of the registration. It does not provide information on the number of contracts that have been awarded to each of the suppliers registered. In order to be included in the registry, suppliers have to fill in a registration form, which includes a Conflict-of-Interest Declaration (*Manifiesto de no conflicto de intereses*) and other information (listed in Article 23 of the LAACSEC). On the basis of the information provided, SEFIR issues a Certificate of Competence (*Certificado de Aptitud*), valid for one year. For the time being, the registration cannot be completed online, though online registry is currently foreseen by Article 23 of the LAACSEC. The purpose of the supplier registry is for the state government to make sure that the potential suppliers are formal and legal companies with the capacity to deliver what they offer. This is a legitimate interest of the state of Coahuila, and would be undermined if unregistered companies were given contracts. Therefore, Coahuila should ensure unlisted companies are not contracted and, when they are, that the public officials responsible are sanctioned.

Coahuila has strengthened the transparency of its procurement system by introducing the initiatives mentioned above, but information is sometimes incomplete (see above) and scattered. In order to strengthen the clarity of information, Coahuila should consolidate the information related to public procurement through a unique online portal or by introducing a specific public procurement page on the Transparency website of Coahuila (*Coahuila Transparente*: *www.coahuilatransparente.gob.mx/*). This recommendation is in line with the analysis made in Chapter 5 of this review. The consolidated page could contain the information on the public procurement system (e.g. institutional frameworks, laws and regulations), which is currently on SEFIR's page; the specific procurement (e.g. procurement forecasts, calls for tender, award announcements), which are currently unavailable either on the websites of SEFIR or SEFIN (according to Article 51 of LAAACSEC, calls for tender need to be published only once in a major newspaper); and the performance of the public procurement system (e.g. benchmarks, monitoring results), which are currently available on SEFIN's page. Coahuila should in particular ensure that tender notifications are published in a transparent way and are accessible to all potential competitors. It remains indeed unclear where the tender notifications not involving federal funds are being published. According to SEFIR, the tender notification involving federal funds are indeed published on the federal e-procurement system CompraNet. In addition, Coahuila needs to make sure that tender documents can be accessed for free. According to the public procurement law (Article 51 of the LAACSEC) tender documents are not always free of charge. This hinders the access to procurement opportunities for potential competitors of all sizes and weakens the transparency and integrity of public procurement processes.

Coahuila should also ensure the visibility of the flow of public funds, from the beginning of the budgeting process to the end of the public procurement cycle in order to allow stakeholders to understand government priorities and spending, and to allow policy makers to organise procurement strategically. Even though SITODEM is linked to the Integral

System of Public Investment of Coahuila, it does not allow stakeholders to visualise the implementation of the budget through public procurement processes and the progress of public works. Coahuila could therefore upgrade the SITODEM tool in order to strengthen this link. Representatives of SEFIR and SEFIN also mentioned the development of a tool that allows linking the implementation of the budget with public procurement processes. By doing so, both SEFIR and SEFIN should make sure to link it to relevant SEFIN and SEFIR websites in order to avoid duplication and to help users to find the relevant information. In case SEFIR would like to make information available in real time on its SITODEM portal and provide more information on the evolution of the project and related contracts, it would need to allocate more staff to the SITODEM project.

The publication of information related to the number of contracts per supplier or the amount of the awarded contracts per supplier could also help to identify potential corruption issues. A complaint box (*buzón de quejas*) could also be foreseen in order to facilitate complaint processes with regard to public procurement processes. These are aspects that Coahuila should take into account while developing the new supplier registry (*Registro Estatal de Proveedores y Contratistas*, REPROCO), which aims at not only serving as a registration platform for suppliers, but will also be used to archive all digital records.

Coahuila should continue maximising transparency in competitive tendering and take precautionary measures to enhance integrity, in particular for exceptions to competitive tendering.

By providing an adequate and timely degree of transparency in each phase of the public procurement cycle, in particular during the tendering processes, contracting authorities can reduce the corruption risks. As specified in Table 6.1 on corruption risks associated with the different phases of the public procurement cycle, the choice of the procurement procedure is an important corruption risk. Competitive procedures should be the standard method for conducting procurement as a means of driving efficiencies, fighting corruption, obtaining fair and reasonable pricing, and ensuring competitive outcomes. If exceptional circumstances justify limitations to competitive tendering and the use of single-source procurement, such exceptions should be limited, pre-defined, and should require appropriate justification when employed, subject to adequate oversight taking into account the increased risk of corruption, including by foreign suppliers (OECD, 2015a). Unfortunately, corruption often arises in relation with the choice of the procurement procedure. Examples include a lack of proper justification of the use of non-competitive procedures or an abuse of non-competitive procedures on the basis of legal exceptions, through contract splitting, abuse of extreme urgency, or non-supported modifications.

The LAACSEC distinguishes three processes by which contracting authorities may acquire goods: public tenders, restricted invitation to at least three providers, and direct awards (with or without three quotes). The public procurement law specifies the maximum amounts permitted for direct awards and restricted invitations (Article 65). In 2012, the maximum amounts permitted for direct awards were reduced, which led to a significant increase of public tenders (from 3 tenders in 2010 to 309 tenders in 2016). In order to avoid a high number of exceptions (through contract splitting for instance), and potential corruption cases, the public procurement law also specifies that the amount of exemptions cannot exceed 30% of the authorised budget. In 2016, the amount of exemptions (direct awards and restricted invitations) to tenders has gone below the 30% limit, given that the value of exemptions as a percentage of non-tender proceedings represented 28% (45% in 2014).

As specified above, Coahuila's Transparency Law foresees the publication of the results of direct awards, restricted tenders, and any other procurement processes (Article 21), which are carried out by SEFIN. The law also lists the information that needs to be published in the case of public tenders and restricted tenders (the same information) and direct awards.

The reduction of the amounts allowed for a direct award in the framework of the 2012 law represents an important step forward for the fight against corruption in Coahuila. The state government should nevertheless continue maximising transparency in competitive tendering and should take precautionary measures to enhance integrity, in particular for exceptions to competitive tendering. SEFIR should make sure that all the contracting authorities publish the information requested by the Transparency Law (Article 21) and SEFIN should make sure that the list of exceptions it publishes on its website contains all the direct awards and restricted invitations. Coahuila should also continuously monitor the use of exceptions by verifying that the exceptions do not exceed 30% of the authorised budget of the contracting authorities and that contracting authorities prepare proper justifications for direct awards at state and municipal levels. The Superior Audit Office of Coahuila (*Auditoría Superior del Estado de Coahuila*, ASEC) has indeed indicated that decisions to use direct award processes are sometimes questionable at municipal level. SEFIR and SEFIN should also assess relevant data to identify possible corruption cases. The introduction of an e-procurement system and the collection of digital records through the new supplier's registry REPROCO will certainly contribute to monitor the use of exceptions and to maximise transparency in competitive tendering.

Coahuila should consider the development of e-procurement solutions that cover the entire public procurement cycle in order to cut direct contact between public officials and suppliers and, therefore, decrease the risks of corrupt behaviour.

Transparency and integrity of public procurement systems can also be strengthened through e-procurement systems. The adoption of digital processes serves to enhance integrity of the public procurement system as face-to-face interactions between officials and potential suppliers and other opportunities for corruption are reduced through the centralised and automatic transfer of data between systems. E-procurement systems and tools can also strengthen transparency by making information available on public procurement processes. The OECD Recommendation also recommends that adherents improve public procurement systems by harnessing the use of digital technologies to support appropriate e-procurement innovation throughout the procurement cycle. Those technologies are powerful tools to ensure transparency and integrity, but also access to public tenders. According to the Recommendation, adherents should pursue state-of-the-art e-procurement tools that are modular, flexible, scalable, and secure in order to assure business continuity, privacy and integrity, provide fair treatment and protect sensitive data, while supplying the core capabilities and functions that allow business innovation. E-procurement tools should be simple to use, appropriate to their purpose, and consistent across procurement agencies, to the extent possible; excessively complicated systems could create implementation risks and challenges for new entrants or small and medium enterprises (OECD, 2015a).

Coahuila does not yet have an e-procurement system in place, but contracting authorities use the federal e-procurement system, CompraNet, in existence since 1997 (see Box 6.7). Even though all the public procurement processes involving federal budget must indeed use CompraNet, the physical presence of suppliers during purchasing processes is still required. According to the public procurement law (Article 43 of the LAACSEC), proposals can be delivered physically in a sealed envelope or, if permitted by the contracting authority (*la convocante*), proposals can be sent by mail, e-mail, or through e-procurement tools (provision introduced in the framework of the reform of 2012). According to the same law, the tender documents can be accessed online (Article 51). In practice, however, e-procurement systems (or electronic publication and submission) do not happen. Interviews during the fact-finding mission made clear that most of the public procurement processes are conducted face-to-face. In addition, bidders may be present when bids are opened (Article 57 of the LAACSEC). The way public procurement processes are conducted in Coahuila provides many opportunities for direct contact between public officials and suppliers and, as such, increases risks of corruption.

Box 6.7. **The Federal e-procurement system CompraNet**

At the federal level, Mexico has implemented several good practices suggested by the 2015 OECD Recommendation on Public Procurement. Since 1997, Mexico (SFP) has been developing its e-procurement information system, CompraNet. Since June 2011, the registration of procedures and procurement documents on CompraNet has been mandatory for every governmental agency, at federal or state level, that uses the federal budget for its procurement procedures and that exceeds a value threshold of 300 days of minimum wage. CompraNet contains information from June 2010 about procurement procedures and leases and services. According to Article 2 of the Law on Acquisitions, Leasing and Services of the Public Sector (*Ley de Adquisiciones, Arrendamientos y Servicios del Sector Público*, LAASSP), CompraNet provides the following information: the annual procurement programme, a supplier registry, a social witness registry, a list of sanctioned suppliers, the calls for tenders (and restricted invitations) and their modifications, records of clarification meetings, records of submissions and proposal openings, the social witness testimonials, data related to the contracts and addenda, direct awards, and resolutions and challenge instances. Its access is free. CompraNet also includes an online form that allows the general public to inform SFP of irregularities (*Portal de quejas y denuncias*).

Source: OECD (2013), Public Procurement Review of the Mexican Institute of Social Security: Enhancing Efficiency and Integrity for Better Health Care, OECD Publishing, Paris. *http://dx.doi.org/10.1787/9789264197480-en*.

In order avoid the physical presence of suppliers during the procurement process and to decrease corruption risks, Coahuila should consider developing an e-procurement system to cover all the procurement processes financed with state funds. While developing this state e-procurement system (*Sistema electrónico de contrataciones públicas*), SEFIN and SEFIR may want to build on the experience gained at federal level with CompraNet (see Box 6.7 for more details on the information provided by CompraNet). In order to strengthen integrity, the e-procurement systems should preferably be used at all the procurement stages and should include real-time disclosure of tender notices, bidding details and results, and awarding and contracting information. According to SEFIR, Coahuila is planning to publish he following information through the e-procurement system: pre-information notice, tender notifications, call for tenders in process, notifications on each step of the public procurement process, award decisions, and contracts.

Coahuila also needs to ensure that both systems are integrated in order to easily manage projects that involve federal and state-level funds. The design of the new e-procurement system should also be integrated with (or include) the SINTAD (*Sistema Integral de Adquisiciones*) system that is currently used for internal finance and administrative issues, as well as the new digital platform (*Plataforma Digital Estatal*) scheduled to be introduced by the Anti-corruption State System (*Sistema Estatal Anticorrupción de Coahuila*). Furthermore, the new system should facilitate organising electronic reverse auctions when appropriate. The data on public procurement processes generated through the new e-procurement system at state level and REPROCO (see above) should be used by Coahuila to measure the performance of the public procurement system (OECD, 2015c). Collecting, assessing, and publishing information on public procurement processes can indeed contribute to the transparency of public procurement information, encourage stakeholder participation, and strengthen accountability and integrity.

In order to ensure the implementation of the new e-procurement system, Coahuila should organise a consultation process in the framework of the development of the system and provide specific trainings. Those trainings should not only target public procurement officials, but also potential suppliers as well as civil society representatives in order to ensure access to public tenders and the monitoring of public procurement processes by external stakeholders. Trainings can be complemented with a user-friendly guide, following the example of the guide developed at federal level (*Guía de apoyo para consultar información en CompraNet*) and a specific webpage dedicated to bidders.

Proposals for action

In order to ensure the implementation of the new public procurement law, the following actions could be undertaken by Coahuila:

Preserving public integrity through general standards of conduct and procurement specific risk management tools

- Using participative techniques, Coahuila should develop a specific Code of Ethics or Conduct and specific guidance for procurement officials, and ensure that specific provisions to public procurement are included in the codes developed by ministries and municipalities.
- While the Code of Conduct and the Conflict-of-Interest Manifest are positive first steps in preventing corruption among suppliers, Coahuila should now leverage those tools to better identify integrity risks in public procurement processes.
- In order to preserve public integrity, Coahuila should develop risk assessment tools to identify and address the threats to the proper functioning of the public procurement system and make sure that contracting authorities implement them.

Promoting a culture of integrity among public procurement officials, potential suppliers, and civil society

- Coahuila should support the implementation of the new integrity standards by streamlining and updating the legislation and by developing and implementing adequate communications strategies.
- Coahuila should strengthen the culture of integrity among the procurement workforce by developing a clear integrity capacity strategy and implementing tailored training for procurement officials.
- Coahuila should further engage with the private sector, developing co-operation agreements and integrity pacts in an effort to minimise corruption risks.
- Coahuila should create opportunities for direct involvement of civil society in the public procurement processes by implementing the social witness programme and other monitoring tools.

Enhancing transparency and the disclosure of information around the public procurement processes

- Coahuila should consolidate the information related to public procurement through a unique online portal and ensure the visibility of the flow of public funds, from the beginning of the budgeting process through the public procurement cycle, in order to facilitate an adequate level scrutiny of public procurement processes.
- Coahuila should continue maximising transparency in competitive tendering and take precautionary measures to enhance integrity, in particular for exceptions to competitive tendering.
- Coahuila should consider the development of e-procurement solutions that cover the entire public procurement cycle in order to cut direct contact between public officials and suppliers and, therefore, decrease the risks of corrupt behaviour.

References

OECD (2013), *Public Procurement Review of the Mexican Institute of Social Security: Enhancing Efficiency and Integrity for Better Health Care*, OECD Publishing, Paris. *http://dx.doi.org/10.1787/9789264197480-en*

OECD (2015a), *Recommendation of the Council on Public Procurement*, OECD, Paris. *www.oecd.org/gov/ethics/OECD-Recommendation-on-Public-Procurement.pdf*

OECD (2015b), *Fighting Bid Rigging in Public Procurement in Mexico – A Secretariat Analytical Report on Compliance with OECD Standards of Procurement Legislation, regulations and Practices in CFE*, OECD Publishing, Paris. *www.oecd.org/daf/competition/FightingBidRigging-Mexico-CFE-Report-2015.pdf*

OECD (2015c), *Strengthening Regulation and Economic Competition in Public Procurement in Mexico - A Report of Best Practices in Local Public Procurement in Five Mexican States* (draft not published).

OECD (2015d), *Government at a Glance 2015*, OECD Publishing, Paris. *http://dx.doi.org/10.1787/gov_glance-2015-en*

OECD (2016), *Preventing Corruption in Public Procurement*, *http://www.oecd.org/gov/ethics/Corruption-in-Public-Procurement-Brochure.pdf*

General Law of Administrative Responsibilities (*Ley General de Responsabilidades Administrativas*), *www.diputados.gob.mx/LeyesBiblio/pdf/LGRA.pdf*, accessed 30 January 2017.

Ethics Code and Integrity Rules (*Acuerdo que tiene por objeto emitir el Código de Ética de los servidores públicos del Gobierno Federal y las Reglas de Integridad para el ejercicio de la función pública*), *www.dof.gob.mx/nota_detalle.php?codigo=5404568&fecha=20/08/2015*, accessed 30 January 2017.

Guide to identify and prevent conducts that could constitute a conflict of interest for public officials (*Guía para identificar y prevenir conductas que puedan constituir conflicto de interés de los servidores públicos*), *www.normateca.sedesol.gob.mx/work/models/NORMATECA/Normateca/3_Carrousel/5_CE/GUIA_PARA_IDENTIFICAR_Y_PREVENIR_CONDUCTAS_QUE_PUEDAN_CONSTITUIR_CONFLICTO_DE_INTERES.pdf*, accessed 30 January 2017.

Protocol of Conduct for Public Servants in Public Procurement, the granting and extension of licenses, permits, authorizations and concessions (*Acuerdo por el que se expide el protocolo de actuación en materia de contrataciones públicas, otorgamiento y prórroga de licencias, permisos, autorizaciones y concesiones*), *www.dof.gob.mx/nota_detalle.php?codigo=5404567&fecha=20/08/2015*, accessed 30 January 2017.

Ministry of Oversight and Accountability (*Secretaría de Fiscalización y Rendición de Cuentas*, SEFIR), *www.sefircoahuila.gob.mx/*, accessed 30 January 2017.

Ministry of Finance (*Secretaría de Finanzas*, SEFIN), *www.sefincoahuila.gob.mx/contenido/index.php*, accessed 20 January 2017.

Law on Acquisitions, Leasing and Services for the State of Coahuila de Zaragoza (*Ley de Adquisiciones, Arrendamientos y Contratación de Servicios para el Estado de Coahuila*, LAACSEC), *http://congresocoahuila.gob.mx/portal/?page_id=538*, accessed 30 January 2017.

Law on Public Works and Related Services for the State of Coahuila de Zaragoza (*Ley de Obra Pública y servicios relacionados con las mismas para el estado de Coahuila de Zaragoza*), *http://congresocoahuila.gob.mx/portal/?page_id=538*, accessed 30 January 2017.

Law to Prevent and Punish Corrupt Practices in Public Procurement Processes in the State of Coahuila de Zaragoza and its Municipalities (*Ley para Prevenir y Sancionar las Prácticas de Corrupción en los Procedimientos de Contratación Pública del Estado de Coahuila de Zaragoza y sus Municipios*), *http://congresocoahuila.gob.mx/portal/?page_id=538*, accessed 30 January 2017.

Law of Responsibilities of Public Servants at state and municipal level of the State of Coahuila de Zaragoza (*Ley de Responsabilidades de los Servidores Públicos Estatales y Municipales del Estado de Coahuila*), *http://congresocoahuila.gob.mx/portal/?page_id=538*, accessed 30 January 2017.

Organic Law of the Public Administration of the State of Coahuila de Zaragoza (*Ley Orgánica de la Administración Pública del Estado de Coahuila de Zaragoza*), *http://congresocoahuila.gob.mx/portal/?page_id=538*, accessed 30 January 2017.

Internal Control General Standard (*Norma General de Control Interno*), *www.gob.mx/sfp/documentos/coahuila-normas-generales-de-control-interno*, accessed 1 March 2017.

Code of Ethics and Conduct for public servants in the executive branch of the State of Coahuila de Zaragoza (*Código de Ética y Conducta para los Servidores Públicos del Poder Ejecutivo del Estado de Coahuila de Zaragoza*), *www.ordenjuridico.gob.mx/Documentos/Estatal/Coahuila/wo82802.pdf*, accessed 16 January 2017.

State Programme of Administrative modernisation, audit and accountability (*Programa Estatal de Modernización Administrativa, Fiscalización y Rendición de Cuentas*), *www.sefincoahuila.gob.mx/contenido/docs/ITDIF-2014/03-MARCO%20PROGRAMATICO%20PRESUPUESTAL/III.2%20Programas/Sectoriales/1%20PS_MODERNIZACION%20ADMINISTRATIVA%20Y%20RENDICION%20DE%20CUENTAS.pdf*, accessed 31 January 2017.

Fourth Government Report of Coahuila 2011-2017 (*Cuarto Informe de Gobierno 2011-2017*), November 2015. *http://coahuila.gob.mx/archivos/pdf/Publicaciones/Libro-4oInformeGobierno-web.pdf*, accessed 31 January 2017.

Administrative Manual for the General Application of Internal Control (*Manual administrativo de aplicación general en materia de control interno*), November 2016.

Operative Manual for the Internal Control Evaluation System (Manual operativo del Sistema de evaluación del control interno), November 2016.

SITODEM Portal (*Sistema de Información y Transparencia de Obras para el Desarrollo Metropolitano*), *http://sitodem.sefircoahuila.gob.mx/*, accessed 19 January 2017.

Transparencia Focalizada Website, *www.transparenciafocalizada.cdmx.gob.mx/*, accessed 19 January 2017.

Transparencia Presupuestaria Website, *www.transparenciapresupuestaria.gob.mx/*, accessed 19 January 2017.

Coahuila Transparente Website, *www.coahuilatransparente.gob.mx/*, accessed 19 January 2017.

ANNEX 1

The integrity, transparency, and participation principles of the OECD recommendation of the council on public procurement (2015)

The integrity principle

RECOMMENDS that Adherents preserve the integrity of the public procurement system through general standards and procurement-specific safeguards.

To this end, Adherents should:

i) Require high standards of integrity for all stakeholders in the procurement cycle. Standards embodied in integrity frameworks or codes of conduct applicable to public-sector employees (such as on managing conflict of interest, disclosure of information, or other standards of professional behaviour) could be expanded (e.g. through integrity pacts).

ii) Implement general public sector integrity tools and tailor them to the specific risks of the procurement cycle as necessary (e.g. the heightened risks involved in public-private interaction and fiduciary responsibility in public procurement).

iii) Develop integrity training programmes for the procurement workforce, both public and private, to raise awareness about integrity risks, such as corruption, fraud, collusion, and discrimination, develop knowledge on ways to counter these risks and foster a culture of integrity to prevent corruption.

iv) Develop requirements for internal controls, compliance measures, and anti-corruption programmes for suppliers, including appropriate monitoring. Public procurement contracts should contain "no corruption" warranties and measures should be implemented to verify the truthfulness of suppliers' warranties that they have not and will not engage in corruption in connection with the contract. Such programmes should also require appropriate supply-chain transparency to fight corruption in subcontracts, and integrity training requirements for supplier personnel.

The transparency principle

RECOMMENDS that Adherents ensure an adequate degree of transparency of the public procurement system in all stages of the procurement cycle.

To this end, Adherents should:

i) **Promote fair and equitable treatment for potential suppliers by providing an adequate and timely degree of transparency in each phase of the public procurement cycle** while taking into account the legitimate needs for protection of trade secrets and proprietary information and other privacy concerns, as well as the need to avoid information that can be used by interested suppliers to distort competition in the procurement process. Additionally, suppliers should be required to provide appropriate transparency in subcontracting relationships.

ii) **Allow free access, through an online portal, for all stakeholders, including potential domestic and foreign suppliers, civil society and the general public, to public procurement information** notably related to the public procurement system (e.g. institutional frameworks, laws, and regulations), the specific procurements (e.g. procurement forecasts, calls for tender, award announcements), and the performance of the public procurement system (e.g. benchmarks, monitoring results). Published data should be meaningful for stakeholder uses.

iii) **Ensure visibility of the flow of public funds, from the beginning of the budgeting process throughout the public procurement cycle** to allow (i) stakeholders to understand government priorities and spending, and (ii) policy makers to organise procurement strategically.

The participation principle

RECOMMENDS that Adherents foster transparent and effective stakeholder participation.

To this end, Adherents should:

i) **Develop and follow a standard process when formulating changes to the public procurement system.** Such standard process should promote public consultations, invite the comments of the private sector and civil society, ensure the publication of the results of the consultation phase, and explain the options chosen, all in a transparent manner.

ii) **Engage in transparent and regular dialogues with suppliers and business associations to present public procurement objectives and to assure a correct understanding of markets.** Effective communication should be conducted to provide potential vendors with a better understanding of the country's needs, and government buyers with information to develop more realistic and effective tender specifications by better understanding market capabilities. Such interactions should be subject to due fairness, transparency, and integrity safeguards, which vary depending on whether an active procurement process is ongoing. Such interactions should also be adapted to ensure that foreign companies participating in tenders receive transparent and effective information.

iii) **Provide opportunities for direct involvement of relevant external stakeholders** in the procurement system with a view to increase transparency and integrity while assuring an adequate level of scrutiny, provided that confidentiality, equal treatment, and other legal obligations in the procurement process are maintained.

Source: OECD (2017a), *Recommendation of the Council on Public Integrity*, OECD, Paris, *http://www.oecd.org/gov/ethics/Recommendation-Public-Integrity.pdf*.

Chapter 7

Plan of action for the implementation of the OECD recommendations

This chapter presents a plan of actions for an adequate implementation of the OECD recommendations in the areas covered by this report, namely institutional set-up, culture of integrity, whistleblower protection, internal control and risk management, transparency, and integrity in public procurement. It provides a chart for the state administration 2017-23 to define the timeline and the units responsible for implementing the plan.

The chart below provides an indication of actionable steps to follow in order to facilitate the implementation of the recommendations covered in this review. Given the current transition time for the state government of Coahuila, where a new administration will take over on 1 December 2017, OECD suggests to analyse together with the incoming officials the timeline for implementation and the units which will be responsible for each of the recommendations and their actionable items. This could be done during the first trimester of 2018.

Toward a coherent and comprehensive integrity system

Proposal for action: The CLACS should ensure that integrity policies are mainstreamed through the whole-of-government and that they are linked with state-wide strategies.

Actionable items	Responsible unit	Timeline
1. Set up mechanisms to allow continuous consultation and co-ordination between the CLACS and all relevant actors of Coahuila's public sector not formally part of the Co-ordination Committee.		
2. Establish specific cross-government/sectoral working groups for the design of the State Anti-corruption Action Plan as well as the implementation of corresponding initiatives.		
3. Link the State Anti-corruption Action Plan with key state strategic documents (including Coahuila's State Development Plan, Coahuila's Programme for Administrative Modernisation, Audit and Accountability, Coahuila's Special Programme for Transparency, and Coahuila's Open Government Action Plan).		

Proposal for action: Nominate a contact point within each of the CLACS constituent institutions to strengthen the co-ordination with its governing bodies and favour the implementation of its activities throughout the government.

Actionable items	Responsible unit	Timeline
1. Establish rules and procedures on the responsibilities of CLACS constituent institutions, including on their participation in the system and the implementation of its decisions.		
2. Request that each CLACS constituent institution nominate a person or unit responsible for co-ordinating work with the bodies of the system and for ensuring follow-up and implementation of activities and decisions.		

Proposal for action: The CLACS could create an ad-hoc working group in charge of elaborating co-ordination mechanisms with municipalities and providing continuous support to build coherent municipal anti-corruption systems.

Actionable items	Responsible unit	Timeline
1. Ensure active involvement and participation of municipalities when discussing relevant pending legislation to be reformed or adopted within the NACS reform process.		
2. Establish a working group within the CLACS Executive Secretariat to design tools and instruments of co-operation between the state and municipalities, but also to encourage communication and information exchange among municipalities.		
3. Carry out a preliminary assessment of existing anti-corruption policies and structures in municipalities in order to map gaps, duplication of rules, and overlapping and low-quality regulations.		
4. Assess the status of existing integrity and anti-corruption-related co-ordination agreements with municipalities, and provide technical support to monitor their implementation and improve their effectiveness.		

Proposal for action: Ensure adequate planning and allocation of resources for CLACS implementation.

Actionable items	Responsible unit	Timeline
1. Carry out an assessment within CLACS constituent institutions and bodies to identify synergies and capacity needs in relation to new responsibilities, activities, and co-ordination mechanisms.		
2. Identify specific expertise criteria needed to fulfil the technical positions of staff within the CLACS Executive Secretariat.		
3. Discuss and plan the short- and long-term budget implications of the CLACS with all relevant institutions.		

Proposal for action: The political leadership in Coahuila should show visible commitment to facing the technical challenges involved, addressing political resistance, and favouring an inclusive transition into the new system.

Actionable items	Responsible unit	Timeline
1. Elaborate a roadmap establishing clear objectives and responsibilities for the adoption of the pending CLACS-related legislation and regulations.		
2. Adopt pending CLACS-related legislation and regulations through the full engagement and commitment of all relevant ministries, municipalities, and stakeholders.		
3. Put into motion the creation of the CLACS and, in particular, launch the member selection process for the Citizen Participation Committee.		

Proposal for action: Mechanisms should be introduced to define clear responsibilities of senior and middle managers in implementing the CLACS, and to hold them accountable throughout the reform process.

Actionable items	Responsible unit	Timeline
1. Carry out an awareness campaign among senior managers concerning the effects and changes needed to implement the CLACS-related reforms at the organisational level.		
2. Define specific responsibilities in the implementation of the reform for each management level.		
3. Set up tools to monitor and assess senior and middle managers' responsibilities in implementing CLACS-related reforms.		

Proposal for action: The appointment and renewal procedures for members of the Citizen Committee should be carried out in an open and transparent way.

Actionable items	Responsible unit	Timeline
1. The appointment procedure of the Citizen Committee should enable the participation of independent and reputable experts representing various components of civil society.		
2. All steps of the appointment process should comply with highest standards of transparency and guarantee fairness and inclusiveness.		
3. Make publicly available additional data on selected members of the Citizen Committee, including their relevant experience and knowledge as well as a signed declaration disclosing any conflict of interest.		

Proposal for action: Ensure broader participation of stakeholders into the local anti-corruption system of Coahuila in order to build a more inclusive and responsive public sector integrity system.

Actionable items	Responsible unit	Timeline
1. Establish specific working group(s) within the CLACS bodies such as the Co-ordination Committee and the Citizen Participation Committee. This will ensure wide multi-stakeholder participation in the CLACS (private sector, trade unions and media).		
2. Ensure continuous co-operation and commitment between the CLACS and external stakeholder organisations through agreements to be monitored by the Co-ordination Committee.		
3. Involve and consult external stakeholders when discussing remaining legislation to be reformed or adopted in relation to the NACS reform process.		

Building a culture of integrity in the public sector

Proposal for action: Following the model of the federal government, Coahuila could establish an ethics unit within SEFIR to harmonise existing policies across the administration. The ethics unit should have a counselling and guidance role.

Actionable items	Responsible unit	Timeline
1. Create the Specialised Unit for Ethics and Prevention of Conflicts of Interest (UEECPI) within SEFIR with the role of counselling and guiding public officials, but not sanctioning.		

Proposal for action: To ensure an effective implementation of integrity policies throughout the public administration, Coahuila could consider establishing Integrity Contact Points (or persons) within each public entity. The Integrity Contact Points should be responsible for public ethics and not for investigating breaches of integrity.

Actionable items	Responsible unit	Timeline
1. Determine size and budget of Integrity Contact Points/Person in each ministry.		
2. Create Integrity Contact Points and assign them a purely preventive role.		
3. UEEPCI could establish a network among the Integrity Contact Points in each ministry		

Proposal for action: The co-ordination agreement on collaboration on transparency and the fight against corruption between Coahuila and the federal Ministry of Public Function (SFP) could benefit from expertise on the federal level and could harmonise policies.

Actionable items	Responsible unit	Timeline
1. Leverage the co-ordination agreement on collaboration and transparency and the fight against corruption to support the implementation of the public ethics policies		

Proposal for action: The public integrity management framework could benefit from a more streamlined, duplication-free Code of Ethics and Conduct. Under the guidance of the Ethics Unit, Coahuila could consider the elaboration of manuals or guidance on practical examples and procedures for conflict-of-interest situations and ethical dilemmas.

Actionable items	Responsible unit	Timeline
1. Streamline the values included in the Code of Ethics and Conduct and ensure that links with sanctions are clear.		
2. Adapt the Code of Ethics and Conduct to introduce a provision on the management of conflict-of-interest situations.		
3. Develop guidance material that explains the Code's values through practical examples.		
4. Distribute guidance material throughout the entire administration, including municipalities, regulatory bodies, and state-owned enterprises.		

Proposal for action: A common overarching integrity management framework opens the opportunity to elaborate codes of ethics and conduct on the organisational level in a participative way, and implementing them more effectively.

Actionable items	Responsible unit	Timeline
1. Provide clear methodological guidance to assist the entities in developing their own specific Codes of Ethics and Conduct.		
2. Develop specific Codes of Ethics and Conduct in line ministries and public sector organisations respecting entity-specific risk according to a consensus-based approach.		
3. Develop relevant and concrete examples of values in the organisation's day-to-day business to which employees can easily relate.		

Proposal for action: SEFIR could develop specific guidelines for at-risk categories of public officials such as senior civil servants, auditors, tax officials, political advisors, and procurement officials.

Actionable items	Responsible unit	Timeline
1. Develop a manual on conflict-of-interest situations specific to public procurement and explain how public officials can identify conflict-of-interest situations.		
2. Establish specific conflict-of-interest policies and guidance for other remaining at-risk areas such as senior civil servants, auditors, tax officials, and political advisors.		

Proposal for action: A cross-departmental public ethics awareness campaign could be implemented as a shared and co-ordinated activity between the ethics unit, the Integrity Contact Points (or persons) and the human resources departments, including reaching out to the private sector, civil society, and citizens.

Actionable items	Responsible unit	Timeline
1. Identify key messages, communication channels, and expected outputs.		
2. Develop awareness-raising campaigns based on previous identification of messages, channels, and outputs.		
3. Implement awareness-raising campaign in entities.		
4. Periodically evaluate awareness-raising campaigns.		

Proposal for action: Under the lead of the SEFIR Ethics Unit, a public integrity training programme could be developed based on the results of the survey on training needs (Encuesta de Detección de Necesidades de Capacitación) applied in 2014. A public ethics and conflict-of-interest training when joining the public service could be made mandatory for all public officials, while specific tailored trainings could be provided on an annual basis.

Actionable items	Responsible unit	Timeline
1. Identify key messages, training format, and expected outputs for induction training and specific trainings for at-risk positions.		
2. Develop trainings based on previous identification of messages, channels, and outputs.		
3. Implement training activities.		
4. Periodically evaluate training efforts.		

Proposal for action: The impact of the existing Network of Trainers (Red Estatal de Instructores) could be amplified by formalising the network and building a pool of trainers in each ministry. As a form of recognition for their efforts, trainers could receive a formal qualification and/or remuneration.

Actionable items	Responsible unit	Timeline
1. Identify training needs to determine necessary number of trainers.		
2. Determine necessary skills and qualities for trainers.		
3. Develop formal public integrity trainer certification courses.		
4. Raise awareness with managers and public officials about opportunities to become a trainer.		

Proposal for action: The future Ethics Unit in SEFIR and Integrity Contact Points (or persons) in the entities could also consider to raise awareness of the conceptual overlap of managing a conflict-of-interest situation on an ad-hoc basis and the annual asset declaration.

Actionable items	Responsible unit	Timeline
1. Update guidelines for preventing and managing conflict of interest and distinguish conflict-of-interest policies from policies concerning submission of asset declarations.		
2. Identify existing awareness campaigns (internal and external) in which to embed a campaign on the disclosure system.		

Proposal for action: Adapting state regulations to the General Law on Administrative Responsibilities will entail modifications of the current asset disclosure system and will require all public officials to submit an asset declaration. Narrowing down the circle of public officials required to submit an asset declaration to those in senior positions and those representing a high corruption risk would ensure that no culture of distrust is created and would improve the system's cost-effectiveness.

Actionable items	Responsible unit	Timeline
1. Develop a clear and specific set of criteria to determine which public officials are required to submit an asset declaration.		
2. Ensure that size of potential filers is aligned with the resources and capacity of the disclosure agency.		
3. Mandate an entity to be responsible for interpretation of criteria.		
4. Build a list of filers and make sure it is frequently updated.		

Proposal for action: To detect illicit enrichment effectively, a systematic verification and audit process should be established. The electronic submission system could be leveraged by integrating the automatic verification of submission and automatic detection of "red flags".

Actionable items	Responsible unit	Timeline
1. Develop a clear and specific set of criteria to determine which declarations are verified. 2. Establish which methods are used in the verification process, and in which order. 3. Determine which actions are taken when irregularities are found during the verification process.		

Proposal for action: Coahuila could co-ordinate with other State Comptrollers' Offices through the National Permanent Commission of State-Federation Comptrollers (Comisión Permanente de Contralores Estados-Federación, CPCE-F) and the National Conference of Governors (Conferencia Nacional de Gobernadores, CONAGO) to establish agreements with other agencies to cross-check databases.

Actionable items	Responsible unit	Timeline
1. Map sources of information needed for effective verification. 2. Establish agreements with other agencies to cross-check databases through the National Permanent Commission of State-Federation Comptrollers (*Comisión Permanente de Contralores Estado-Federación*, CPCE-F) and the National Conference of Governors (*Conferencia Nacional de Gobernadores*, CONAGO).		

Proposal for action: To enable the monitoring and evaluation of the implementation of the Code of Conduct and Ethics and the Law of Responsibilities and to publish annual progress reports, tools and processes and clear and transparent indicators need to be developed.

Actionable items	Responsible unit	Timeline
1. Define objectives at the output level for public ethics-related integrity policies. 2. Consult entities and experts to identify relevant indicators for each objective. 3. Develop clear, measurable, and realistic indicators. 4. Examine existing databases for the applicability of these indicators and, if needed, create new methods to collect data. 5. Create a monitoring report according to a pre-determined timeframe. 6. Develop recommendations according to this monitoring report.		

Proposal for action: To monitor and evaluate the effectiveness of the asset declaration system, SEFIR could conduct a survey among the declarants and Internal Control Units to ensure user-friendliness and relevance of the requested information. Annual reports could be published to reassure the public of the effectiveness of the system.

Actionable items	Responsible unit	Timeline
1. Conduct a survey among the declarants and Internal Control Units to ensure user-friendliness and relevance of the requested information. 2. Collect data on human and financial resources in relation to the asset declaration system's effectiveness. 3. Collect data on sanctions related to the asset declaration system. 4. Centralise information and develop monitoring reports accordingly. 5. Develop recommendations according to monitoring reports.		

Guaranteeing effective whistleblower protection

Proposal for action: To avoid fragmentation and ensure the effectiveness of the whistleblower protection provisions spread throughout different laws, Coahuila could enact a dedicated whistleblower protection law that avoids duplication and ensures clarity.

Actionable items	Responsible unit	Timeline
1. Collect current legislative duplication and identify gaps in whistleblower protection.		
2. Develop dedicated whistleblower protection law.		
3. Meet with stakeholders to ensure comprehensiveness and clarity of law proposal.		

Proposal for action: To mitigate the risk of having whistleblowers come forward with information that may not constitute protected disclosures, and to avoid potentially exposing them to unnecessary risks and overburdening the intake system with non-applicable cases, Coahuila could clarify the nature of a protected disclosure.

Actionable items	Responsible unit	Timeline
1. Develop clear criteria for a protected disclosure.		
2. Consult with stakeholders on comprehensiveness and clarity of criteria.		
3. Communicate criteria internally and externally through different communication channels.		

Proposal for action: Given the low trust in institutional safeguards, the possibility of reporting anonymously should be made available to facilitate the reporting of misconduct.

Actionable items	Responsible unit	Timeline
1. Include a provision in the law that makes anonymous disclosures possible.		
2. Communicate the possibility of anonymous disclosure internally and externally through different communication channels.		

Proposal for action: Coahuila could consider clarifying the overlap between witness and whistleblower protection and ensuring that disclosures that do not lead to a full investigation or to prosecution are still eligible for legal protection.

Actionable items	Responsible unit	Timeline
1. Establish protection for those disclosing information pertaining to an act of corruption that might not be recognised as a crime, but could be subject to administrative investigations.		

Proposal for action: Coahuila could provide more comprehensive protection to whistleblowers by specifically prohibiting dismissal of whistleblowers without a cause, or any other kind of formal or informal work-related sanction that has been exercised in response to the disclosure, if the information reported can reasonably be believed to be true at the time of the disclosure.

Actionable items	Responsible unit	Timeline
1. Design dedicated Whistleblower Protection Law to prohibit dismissal of whistleblowers without a cause and to prohibit any other kind of formal or informal work-related sanction that has been exercised in response to the disclosure.		
2. Communicate the scope of protective measures internally and externally through different communication channels.		

Proposal for action: Expanding the scope of the criminal prohibition to exercise reprisals on whistleblowers to a broader range of reprisals and to disclosures that are related to any breach of state laws could reinforce Coahuila's commitment to effective whistleblower protection and could reassure potential whistleblowers.

Actionable items	Responsible unit	Timeline
1. Establish in the Criminal Code the prohibition to exercise reprisals against whistleblowers in line with international standards.		
2. Expand the criminal prohibition of reprisals so that it does not only apply to alleged criminal acts.		
3. Establish in the Criminal Code the prohibition to disclose, or to threaten to disclose,the identity of a whistleblower.		

Proposal for action: Coahuila could introduce sanctions on individuals who exercise reprisals against whistleblowers who have disclosed misconduct in accordance with applicable rules.

Actionable items	Responsible unit	Timeline
1. Expand the scope of criminal prohibition to the threat to exercise reprisals against whistleblowers.		

Proposal for action: Coahuila could consider shifting the burden of proof to the employer to provide evidence that any sanction exercised on a whistleblower following a disclosure of misconduct is not related to that disclosure.

Actionable items	Responsible unit	Timeline
1. Reverse the burden of proof to the employer to provide evidence that a sanction is not related to a disclosure of misconduct.		
2. Adapt the criteria the disclosure needs to meet in order to shift the burden of proof to the employer.		

Proposal for action: Providing express civil remedies for civil servants who experience reprisals after disclosing misconduct as defined by the Law would add a further layer of protection to the whistleblower protection framework.

Actionable items	Responsible unit	Timeline
1. Include a comprehensive list of remedies in the Whistleblower Protection Law.		
2. Allow whistleblowers to introduce their own recourse before courts.		

Proposal for action: Coahuila could consider defining and formalising the communication channels for reporting misconduct to ensure public officials are fully aware of who they can contact if they decide to disclose misconduct, of how their anonymity or confidentiality will be protected, and of the remedies available to them if they experience reprisal.

Actionable items	Responsible unit	Timeline
1. Formalise a channel for disclosure of misconduct to senior public officials.		
2. Ensure that a choice of disclosure channels (internal, external to designated body, external to media/public) is available.		
3. Explain the steps to follow and the processes to abide by for each available channel.		
4. Design and conduct information campaigns that make public officials and the public aware of the different disclosure channels, how anonymity or confidentiality is protected, and which remedies would be available in the case of reprisals.		

Proposal for action: Establishing clear follow-up mechanisms and communication procedures between the whistleblower and the receiving agency would ensure the effective management of reports. This should include information about the receipt of the report, regular updates on the status of investigation, and the final outcome or explanation of reasons why an investigation has not been undertaken.

Actionable items	Responsible unit	Timeline
1. Utilising the future electronic platform, define a follow-up mechanism through which whistleblowers are kept informed of the proceedings.		
2. Regularly evaluate the procedural burden of the follow-up mechanism.		

Proposal for action: To strengthen trust in the procedures and guarantees of the whistleblower protection framework, Coahuila could create an independent agency mandated to receive and investigate reports on misconduct and provide remedies as necessary.

Actionable items	Responsible unit	Timeline
1. Review international good practices of independent whistleblower agencies.		
2. Create an independent body with the capacity to receive, investigate, and provide remedies for complaints related to retaliation. Alternatively, if adequate financial resources cannot be guaranteed due to budget constraints, create the position of an anti-corruption commissioner or trust attorney.		
3. Ensure that the agency is independent, that it has sufficient budgetary resources to enable it to operate effectively, and that it meets the objectives of the law.		
4. Obligate the agency to report to congress annually.		
5. Independently evaluate the agency on a regular basis.		

Proposal for action: To implement the law effectively, Coahuila could consider promoting a broad communication strategy and undertaking increased awareness efforts through various channels.

Actionable items	Responsible unit	Timeline
1. Identify key messages, communication channels, and expected outputs.		
2. Develop awareness-raising campaigns based on previous identification of messages, channels, and outputs.		
3. Implement awareness-raising campaigns in entities and externally.		

Proposal for action: Coahuila could consider including a mandate to review periodically its whistleblower protection scheme in the corresponding legislative bill so that the state government could evaluate the relevance of its objectives, implementation, and effectiveness. Coahuila could consider systematically collecting data and establishing robust indicators.

Actionable items	Responsible unit	Timeline
1. Define objectives at the output level for the goals of the whistleblower policies.		
2. Consult entities and experts to identify relevant indicators for each objective.		
3. Develop clear, measurable, and realistic indicators.		
4. Examine existing databases for the applicability of these indicators and, if needed, create new methods to collect data.		
5. Create a monitoring report according to a pre-determined timeframe.		
6. Develop recommendations according to this monitoring report.		

Strengthening the internal control and risk management framework

Proposal for action: Coahuila could strengthen its internal control standards and policies in order to place greater emphasis on corruption and fraud.

Actionable items	Responsible unit	Timeline
1. Integrate the existing internal control and risk management framework with additional guidance and information on how to deal with corruption risks. 2. Align Coahuila's General Standard for Internal Control to the Standard Model of Internal Control adopted by the federal Ministry of Public Administration in 2016, introducing a principle dedicated to managing corruption risks as well as specific methodologies, risk factors, and mitigation strategies to address them. 3. Adopt a set of dedicated procedures, standards, and tools to effectively prevent, detect, and respond to risks of fraud and corruption.		

Proposal for action: Coahuila could strengthen its "tone at the top" and its leadership's commitment to integrity and an effective control environment.

Actionable items	Responsible unit	Timeline
1. Revise Coahuila's General Standard for Internal Control in line with the federal Standard Model of Internal Control, which codifies the principle that "the organisation demonstrates a commitment to integrity and ethical values". 2. Create a control environment non-conducive to corruption. 3. Emphasise the value of role models through initiatives such as ethical screening of managers, seminars and awareness campaigns, communicating concrete compliance actions, self-assessment tools, and 360° evaluations for managers.		

Proposal for action: Management ownership and awareness of the internal control system and risk management should be improved.

Actionable items	Responsible unit	Timeline
1. Clarify the roles and responsibilities of managers in relation to internal control and risk management processes and activities through official channels or directives. 2. Take measures to integrate internal control processes into the four phases of the management cycle (planning, execution, analysis, reaction). 3. Complement the general guidelines provided through the Manual for General Application on Internal Control with ad-hoc guidance on risk-management arrangements, tools, and methodology.		

Proposal for action: Make better use of data to identify and address integrity risks, and thereby improve the quality of institutional risk maps and mitigation strategies.

Actionable items	Responsible unit	Timeline
1. Develop a concrete action plan to promote data quality and the use of data analytics tools for effective risk management. 2. Use the Local Digital Platform to be created within the CLACS as a tool to test data analytics tools and strategies to improve internal control and risk assessment. 3. Develop a strategy to move towards a more advanced use of data analytics for anti-corruption purposes such as to verify and validate transactions or to uncover potential and actual corruption.		

Proposal for action: Ensure that all ministries have an internal control unit in order to strengthen the internal audit function and improve the effectiveness of governance, risk management, and internal controls.

Actionable items	Responsible unit	Timeline
1. Gradually appoint internal control units in all ministries after elaborating a priority list based on a corruption risk-assessment.		

Proposal for action: Improve the internal audit function with regards to fraud and corruption investigations by scaling up professionalism and resources.

Actionable items	Responsible unit	Timeline
1. Improve SEFIR's internal audit function with regards to fraud and corruption investigations by scaling up training and capacity building efforts, especially in relation to the increased competence to conducting administrative proceedings for non-serious offences.		
2. Ensure, within SEFIR, adequate financial and human resources to improve effectiveness in its investigations and to be able to conduct administrative proceedings in relation to non-serious administrative offences.		

Enhance transparency and participation for effective accountability

Proposal for action: Coahuila could better exploit the data and information currently produced by public entities by improving data socialisation and developing on-line visualisation tools.

Actionable items	Responsible unit	Timeline
1. Elaborate and make public data more intelligible by presenting them in a plain, aggregated, and simplified format, also by means of online visualisation tools.		
2. Promote awareness-raising and capacity-building initiatives to narrow the digital divide and promote the use of public data among citizens.		

Proposal for action: Coahuila could identify a single transparency portal used to consult and request information in order to avoid gaps and overlaps created by existing tools.

Actionable items	Responsible unit	Timeline
1. Identify a single transparency portal providing comprehensive access to all the information and data provided by public institutions.		
2. Ensure that this single transparency portal is user-friendly and possesses a high level of usability and reusability of data and information.		

Proposal for action: Coahuila could improve awareness of existing tools for stakeholder participation and oversight, and could enable active engagement in innovative and interactive ways.

Actionable items	Responsible unit	Timeline
1. Improve the understanding of available stakeholder participation and oversight tools by devoting a specific section of its future single transparency portal to explaining, describing, and promoting them.		
2. Use ICTs to further enable the engagement of society in public life, for instance through a multi-channel platform.		

Proposal for action: Improve stakeholder engagement through a demand-drive approach based on dialogue, consultation, and data collaboration and inter-operability.

Actionable items	Responsible unit	Timeline
1. Organise periodic meetings among relevant institutions and social actors to identify additional typologies of information which could potentially enhance transparency and accountability of public institutions.		
2. Create a simple and user-friendly platform for citizens to submit ideas on how to improve transparency.		
3. Allow users to take full advantage of the existing open data platform by allowing them to enrich it with new datasets.		

Proposal for action: Coahuila could improve oversight over the transparency commitments of its institutions.

Actionable items	Responsible unit	Timeline
1. Create a transparency index measuring compliance of Coahuila's public entities with transparency obligations, and make the corresponding results public and easily accessible.		
2. Present the transparency index through visualisation tools and customisation options, and elaborate indicators not only related to compliance with the legal framework but also to the implementation and effectiveness of corresponding efforts.		

Integrity in public procurement

Proposal for action: Using participative techniques, Coahuila should develop a specific Code of Ethics or Conduct and specific guidance for procurement officials, and ensure that specific provisions to public procurement are included in the codes developed by ministries and municipalities.

Actionable items	Responsible unit	Timeline
1. Develop a plan to consult procurement officials and other stakeholders (internal and external) on what a Code of Conduct or Ethics for procurement officials should prescribe.		
2. Consult with procurement officials and stakeholders.		
3. Review the national (SFP) and international (OECD) experiences on integrity standards for procurement officials.		
4. Draft the Code of Conduct or Ethics for procurement officials, focusing on the risks implied by this activity.		
5. Draft guidance documents, tutorials, and training materials to illustrate how procurement officials should apply the values and principles included in the Code (comprising practical situations).		
6. Set up a team to support other entities and municipalities in the development of their own codes and integrity rules for procurement officials.		

Proposal for action: While the Code of Conduct and the Conflict-of-Interest Manifest are positive first steps in preventing corruption among suppliers, Coahuila should now leverage those tools to better identify integrity risks in public procurement processes.

Actionable items	Responsible unit	Timeline
1. Review the Code of Conduct for suppliers in an effort to balance values-based behaviours with the current rules-based approach.		
2. Organise a consultation, awareness-raising, and communication plan for the new Code of Conduct for suppliers and the Conflict-of-Interest Manifest (websites, during the application for the supplier registry, etc.).		
3. Organise a programme of integrity training for the supplier community, with possible leverage on business chambers to widen the outreach.		
4. Design a system to scrutinise Conflict-of-Interest Manifests provided by suppliers and cross-check them against procurement officials' declarations. Such scrutiny should be risk-based.		
5. Publish guidance for suppliers defining potential, real, and apparent conflict of interest (may want to use SFP and OECD materials and publications) and explaining to different audiences how to use the Conflict-of-Interest Manifests.		
6. Amend the conflict-of-interest declaration system to allow suppliers to update their manifests as required.		
7. Appoint contact points in the tendering institutions to provide advice to suppliers on how to fill out the Conflict-of-Interest Manifests.		
8. Evaluate periodically the effectiveness of the conflict-of-interest policy as applied to procurement operations.		

Proposal for action: In order to preserve public integrity, Coahuila should develop risk assessment tools to identify and address the threats to the proper functioning of the public procurement system and make sure that contracting authorities implement them.

Actionable items	Responsible unit	Timeline
1. Publicise and communicate more widely the manuals on internal control and risk management and raise awareness on the internal control strategy, including through training.		
2. Develop a risk mapping and a red flag system for procurement activities, including corruption and fraud risks, and anticipating mitigation measures. Specific templates should be used.		
3. Develop guidance and training on how to apply internal control in procurement activities.		
4. Evaluate and periodically update risk mapping, reviewing the criticality of each risk and the effectiveness of the mitigation measures.		

Proposal for action: Coahuila should support the implementation of the new integrity standards by streamlining and updating the legislation and by developing and implementing adequate communications strategies.

Actionable items	Responsible unit	Timeline
1. Review the regulatory framework governing integrity in public procurement to avoid dispersion and duplication.		
2. Develop a comprehensive communications programme on the integrity strategy for procurement operations, emphasising recent tools developed by the state and the federal governments, and targeting different audiences.		

Proposal for action: Coahuila should strengthen the culture of integrity among the procurement workforce by developing a clear integrity capacity strategy and implementing tailored training for procurement officials.

Actionable items	Responsible unit	Timeline
1. Identify the universe of public officials with procurement-related tasks		
2. Develop integrity training programmes for procurement officials to raise awareness about integrity risks and develop knowledge on ways to mitigate such risks. Trainings could take place as part of induction mechanisms and on an ongoing basis.		
3. Establish e-learning courses on integrity in public procurement.		
4. Design a certification/evaluation mechanism to assess the effectiveness of the training programmes and e-learning courses.		

Proposal for action: Coahuila should further engage with the private sector, developing co-operation agreements and integrity pacts in an effort to minimise corruption risks.

Actionable items	Responsible unit	Timeline
1. Promote and facilitate the development of integrity standards by supplier companies and/or the adoption of those standards upheld by the government of Coahuila.		
2. Develop a Business Integrity Programme, including codes of conduct, internal controls, compliance measures and monitoring, mirroring the efforts undertaken by SFP at the federal level.		
3. Include "no corruption" commitments in contracts to supply goods, services, or works to the state government.		
4. Amend the LAACSEC and the LOPSEC to include the figure of "integrity pacts".		
5. Establish co-operation agreements and integrity pacts with business associations to carry out joint actions in favour of integrity in public procurement.		

Proposal for action: Coahuila should create opportunities for direct involvement of civil society in the public procurement processes by implementing the social witness programme and other monitoring tools.

Actionable items	Responsible unit	Timeline
1. Accelerate the implementation of social witnesses, particularly in high risk tender procedures. This will require a process of selection and training of the individuals or organisations acting as social witnesses.		
2. Systematise the implementation of social comptrollership programmes and widen their application.		
3. Periodically evaluate the effectiveness of social witnesses and social comptrollership programmes and communicate the results widely.		

Proposal for action: Coahuila should consolidate the information related to public procurement through a unique online portal and ensure the visibility of the flow of public funds, from the beginning of the budgeting process through the public procurement cycle, in order to facilitate an adequate level scrutiny of public procurement processes.

Actionable items	Responsible unit	Timeline
1. Create a specific public procurement page on the *Coahuila Transparente* website to consolidate procurement-related information and avoid dispersion. This page could be called "Coahuila Compra" and could include information from the pre-tender, tendering, and post-tender stages.		
2. Upgrade SITODEM to provide information about procurement operations, spending, and physical and budget exercise of public works.		
3. Include complaints boxes in *Coahuila Transparente* and SITODEM to report corrupt behaviours in public procurement.		
4. Run focus groups with different audiences (i.e., business chambers, civil society, academics, etc.) to identify useful procurement information that is not being published, and organise access to information websites in a more user-friendly manner.		

Proposal for action: Coahuila should continue maximising transparency in competitive tendering and take precautionary measures to enhance integrity, in particular for exceptions to competitive tendering.

Actionable items	Responsible unit	Timeline
1. Continuously monitor the choice for non-competitive procurement processes (i.e. direct awards) and restricted invitations to ensure proper justification is provided.		
2. Ensure that all the documentation pertaining to direct awards, including market analyses and justifications, are published, unless an exception applies under the Transparency and Access to Information Law.		

Proposal for action: Coahuila should consider the development of e-procurement solutions that cover the entire public procurement cycle in order to cut direct contact between public officials and suppliers and, therefore, decrease the risks of corrupt behaviour.

Actionable items	Responsible unit	Timeline
1. Finalise the implementation of the system for online supplier registration (REPROCO)		
2. Develop an e-procurement solution for purchases financed with state funds. This solution should encompass the full public procurement cycle (i.e. from procurement planning to contract management and payment to suppliers) and should include a module for reverse auctions.		

ORGANISATION FOR ECONOMIC CO-OPERATION AND DEVELOPMENT

The OECD is a unique forum where governments work together to address the economic, social and environmental challenges of globalisation. The OECD is also at the forefront of efforts to understand and to help governments respond to new developments and concerns, such as corporate governance, the information economy and the challenges of an ageing population. The Organisation provides a setting where governments can compare policy experiences, seek answers to common problems, identify good practice and work to co-ordinate domestic and international policies.

The OECD member countries are: Australia, Austria, Belgium, Canada, Chile, the Czech Republic, Denmark, Estonia, Finland, France, Germany, Greece, Hungary, Iceland, Ireland, Israel, Italy, Japan, Korea, Latvia, Luxembourg, Mexico, the Netherlands, New Zealand, Norway, Poland, Portugal, the Slovak Republic, Slovenia, Spain, Sweden, Switzerland, Turkey, the United Kingdom and the United States. The European Union takes part in the work of the OECD.

OECD Publishing disseminates widely the results of the Organisation's statistics gathering and research on economic, social and environmental issues, as well as the conventions, guidelines and standards agreed by its members.

OECD PUBLISHING, 2, rue André-Pascal, 75775 PARIS CEDEX16
(04 2017 11 1 P1) ISBN 978-92-64-28308-4 – 2017

www.ingramcontent.com/pod-product-compliance
Ingram Content Group UK Ltd.
Pitfield, Milton Keynes, MK11 3LW, UK
UKHW051501290926
15471UKWH00008B/1346

9 789264 283084